HOW TO PASS THE
GMAT®

D1429671

GMAT® questions are difficult to answer and they are even more difficult to write! If you do find an error then the author should be grateful if you would notify him so that they can be removed at a future reprint. During your program of revision and review, if you hit a problem not covered here or if you would like suggestions of further sources of practice material then do please contact the author care of Kogan Page.

I dedicate this book to Anne Waters

HOW TO PASS THE
GMAT®

Unbeatable preparation for success in the Graduate Management Admission Test®

CALVIN T. RYAN LIBRARY
U. OF NEBRASKA AT KEARNEY

Mike Bryon

KOGAN
PAGE

London and Philadelphia

Publisher's note

Every possible effort has been made to ensure that the information contained in this book is accurate at the time of going to press, and the publishers and author cannot accept responsibility for any errors or omissions, however caused. No responsibility for loss or damage occasioned to any person acting, or refraining from action, as a result of the material in this publication can be accepted by the editor, the publisher or the author.

First published in Great Britain and the United States in 2007 by Kogan Page Limited

Apart from any fair dealing for the purposes of research or private study, or criticism or review, as permitted under the Copyright, Designs and Patents Act 1988, this publication may only be reproduced, stored or transmitted, in any form or by any means, with the prior permission in writing of the publishers, or in the case of reprographic reproduction in accordance with the terms and licenses issued by the CLA. Enquiries concerning reproduction outside these terms should be sent to the publishers at the undermentioned addresses:

120 Pentonville Road
London N1 9JN
United Kingdom
www.kogan-page.co.uk

525 South 4th Street, #241
Philadelphia PA 19147
USA

© Mike Bryon, 2007

The right of Mike Bryon to be identified as the author of this work has been asserted by him in accordance with the Copyright, Designs and Patents Act 1988.

GMAC®, GMAT®, GMAT CAT®, and Graduate Management Admission Test® are registered trademarks of the Graduate Management Admission Council® (GMAC®). This publication does not contain any real GMAT® test material. The Graduate Management Admission Council® does not endorse this product.

ISBN-10   0 7494 4459 2
ISBN-13   978 0 7494 4459 4

British Library Cataloguing-in-Publication Data

A CIP record for this book is available from the British Library.

Library of Congress Cataloging-in-Publication Data

Bryon, Mike.
  How to pass the GMAT: unbeatable preparation for success in the Graduate Management Admission Test / Mike Bryon.
    p. cm.
  ISBN-13: 978–0–7494–4459–4
  ISBN-10: 0–7494–4459–2
  1. Graduate Management Admission Test--Study guides. 2. Management--Examinations, questions, etc. I. Title.
  HF1118.B79 2007
  658.0076--dc22

                              2007001100

Typeset by Saxon Graphics Ltd, Derby
Printed and bound in Great Britain by Cambridge University Press

Contents

Preface

Choose this book for GMAT® success

This volume deserves a place among your GMAT® preparation material for the following reasons:

- It is value for money when compared with many other GMAT® practice titles some of which cost more than $30.

- There are 20, 10-minute practice mini-tests so that you can practice little and often and get off to a flying start in the real GMAT® sub-tests.

- Over 600 realistic practice questions, answers and explanations will allow you to get down to some serious score-improving practice, especially if you find the algebra, geometry, English grammar and critical reasoning the most challenging parts of the GMAT®.

This book is intended for people who need to realize a well-balanced, above-average GMAT® score. It will be of greatest value to the GMAT® candidate who may not have experienced in their academic career to date, all the verbal and quantitative skills tested in the GMAT®. It will also help the candidate facing the GMAT® after some years since leaving university, the mathematically challenged or the candidate who does not speak English as a first language.

If you are such a candidate then you have most to gain. Become familiar with the test's demands, and practice, and review, lots of relevant questions. You are then most likely to see a significant and worthwhile improvement in your score. This revision or review may help secure you a place in the business school of your choice, an outcome that you may not otherwise have achieved. To succeed, be prepared to undertake an extensive program of revision over many weeks and, ideally, months.

No single book or author should be relied on to provide all the material needed to prepare for the GMAT®. Most candidates, to demonstrate their full potential, need to undertake a major program of revision that will require the use of quite a number of publications. In Chapter 2, I refer to sources of free material, and what I consider is published material that is worth purchasing.

Please note that this volume does not provide advice on the Analytical Writing Assessment (AWA). Such advice is available from some of the other publications listed in Chapter 2, and I feel I can add little to what others have already said on this subject. I have also not provided reviews of grammar and mathematics, as there are other books that cover these subjects perfectly well.

Also note that the explanations offered in Chapter 6 are only intended as an aide-memoire and to help readers realize where they may have gone wrong. A full explanation of all the operations and rules covered is beyond the scope of this book and if required are obtainable from academic and educational titles.

You may find this book a challenge but it is intended first and foremost as a source of help. May I wish you every success with your application to business school and especially with the GMAT®!

Acknowledgments

I owe thanks to Dr Jim Clayden for contributing the algebraic questions and many of the data sufficiency questions. His contribution makes this a far better book than it otherwise would be.

I am grateful to Steven Redman, who, for a number of years, directed a Spanish GMAT® prep school and provided useful insights into the challenge of the GMAT®, particularly to the non-US-educated candidate.

I am also indebted to Moz Gamble who undertook a careful reading of the verbal sub-test questions, and suggested a series of improvements and corrected a number of errors and ambiguities. Any remaining errors or omissions are entirely mine.

What is the GMAT CAT®?

GMAT® stands for the Graduate Management Admission Test and CAT stands for Computer Adaptive Test. Originally, the GMAT® was a paper and pen test, but since 1997, it has been taken in its current CAT format at a computer screen. The test is currently administered by ETS, Educational Testing Services, based in Princeton, New Jersey in the United States, but this could change, with a different administrating body taking over. You can find invaluable information about the GMAT® and register to take the test at http://www.gmat.org.

The stated purpose of the GMAT® is to predict how well you will do in the first year of business school. It attempts to do this by investigating your ability to answer multiple-choice questions in algebra, geometry and arithmetic, the conventions of written English, the comprehension of complex passages and analysis of complex argument. You are also expected to write two essays.

Over half of the institutions worldwide that offer graduate business programs are reported to require a GMAT® score from applicants, especially for a place on the full-time courses. The test will currently (2007) cost about $250. In addition to this, you will have to fund the cost of travel to a test center. There is no reduced fee or waiver for low-income candidates.

For many schools you need a good GMAT® score

Competition for places at the more prestigious business schools is fierce. These are the schools that tend to require you to take the GMAT®, and a high GMAT® score is essential if you are to secure a place in one of these institutions.

The score range for the GMAT® is 200–800, but ETS reports that scores above 750 and below 250 are rare. Two-thirds of all candidates score between 400 and 600. The students at a good school will have an average score of over 600. The students at

Harvard in 2004 had an average score of 707, around the top 10 percent of all scores. To gain a place at the majority of popular schools you need to be able to score better than two-thirds of all candidates. Then you can be sure that your GMAT® score will support your application.

These averages are based on a very broad range. Some people will get into the school of their choice with lower scores than others. There will not be a minimum GMAT® score that you will have to achieve. The GMAT® is only one of the assessments used to decide if an applicant is to be offered a place.

You may need a well-balanced score

While many schools concentrate on your overall score, others also look for a well-balanced score. By this they mean a score that is consistently good across the sub-tests and essays. For this reason, the candidate who, for example, is strong verbally, but numerically challenged, may not get the place they hoped for, despite a good overall GMAT® score. Equally, the mathematics genius who cannot write a good essay or is totally mystified by the conventions of English usage may also find they are denied a place in the school of their choice.

Doing really well, for example, in the mathematics part of the GMAT® will compensate for a weaker performance in the verbal parts of the test. But this compensation needs to be within certain limits. The need for a balanced GMAT® score makes it important that candidates identify and work to address areas of personal weakness. If you have always found mathematics difficult but until now have succeeded despite this, then it is time to correct that situation. Equally, if you have happily applied the rule of English usage implicitly but found the rules of grammar baffling, then it is better to review them now and come to know the rules explicitly. You will then be more confident, will recognize what is behind a question and be better able to recognize the significance of the subtle differences in the suggested answers.

Many, probably most, GMAT® candidates are stronger in one part of the test. But if you believe that in your case this imbalance risks being judged as too great, then make sure you start work early to address it. Everyone can become proficient in the numeracy and syntactics required by the GMAT®. It is simply a matter of practice and sufficient time to complete it. It takes some candidates longer to reach the required standard in any area of personal challenge but given hard work and determination, everyone can achieve it. It can be boring, painful even, but if you have decided to do an MBA and your business school requires you to obtain a good balanced score in the GMAT® then you have little alternative but to get down to some serious hard work.

The types of questions and assessments

Become entirely familiar with each aspect of the GMAT®. Whatever your background, or personal challenges, begin your program of revision or review by becoming completely familiar with each part of the GMAT®: the kinds of questions or assessments, the amount of time allowed and the number of tasks or questions. These are all essential pieces of information and acquiring them must be the first step in your campaign.

Read carefully the information provided at www.gmat.org and www.mba.com. You will realize that the GMAT® is made up of three principal parts and you are allowed an optional five-minute pause between each of these parts:

1. The Analytical Writing Assessment (AWA) comprises two essays, to be completed in one hour (30 minutes each). One involves the analysis of an issue; the other, the analysis of an argument.
2. The quantitative sub-test comprises 37 questions to be completed in 75 minutes. It is made up of two styles of questions, entitled problem-solving and data sufficiency. The order in which these questions occur is randomly determined by the computer.
3. The verbal sub-test comprises 41 questions to be completed in 75 minutes. This sub-test has three styles of questions, entitled reading comprehension, sentence correction and critical reasoning, and once again, the order in which these questions occur is determined by the computer.

Some of the questions in the quantitative and verbal tests are non-scoring, as they are being trialed for inclusion as scoring items in future tests. You are not given any indication as to which are scoring, so treat them all with the same determination.

Things to remember on the day of the test

The most important thing to take with you when you attend the test center is suitable ID. For reasons of test security, the test administrator will want to be able to confirm that no one is impersonating you and completing the test on your behalf. It is essential therefore that the name on your ID exactly matches the name on your test appointment.

The most usual forms of ID are a passport, national ID card or a driver's license. Note that acceptable ID must not have expired and must contain your name (spelled exactly the same as on your test appointment), a recognizable photograph and your signature. Read carefully and follow the instructions regarding ID on the mba.com website, and contact the MBA if you have any doubts as to the suitability of your ID.

You are also required to sign a confidentiality statement and must follow the test center's regulations. Beforehand, be sure to read through the pages on the mba.com website on the test center conditions, procedures and regulations.

You are not allowed to take very much into the test room. They provide you with everything you need or are allowed, including scrap, or scratch paper, for doing rough work. You are not allowed to bring a calculator or any other sort of aid or cell phone in the testing room. A stopwatch is provided on the computer screen.

It would be a big mistake to arrive late for your appointment. So locate the center and make sure you can find it with time to spare. Aim to arrive at least 30 minutes before your appointment time.

If English is not your first language

The business school of your choice may require you to pass the TOEFL (Test of English as a Foreign Language) or IELTS (International English Language Testing System) tests as well as the GMAT®. The school to which you apply will inform you of its policy.

Some parts of the GMAT® are likely to present a greater challenge, so you need to adjust your program of revision and review accordingly. For a speaker of English as a second language, the reading comprehension and critical reasoning questions are likely to prove the most challenging. You might find yourself at an advantage in the sentence correction part of the test: many native speakers of English have forgotten or never formally learned the rules of English grammar, while you will have. The mathematics sections, however, are not likely to prove a greater challenge or offer you any advantage over a native speaker.

To meet the challenge of reading comprehension and critical reasoning, at an early stage and, if possible, daily, spend time reading quality newspapers and journals. This will help build your vocabulary and improve your proficiency at assimilating the meanings of the complex sentences and sentence structures that occur in the GMAT® passages. Look up unfamiliar words. Practice writing 70-word reviews of articles found in these publications.

Be prepared to undertake a considerable amount of GMAT® practice before the real test. Practice will help you achieve a considerably better score, so start early and make a significant commitment in terms of the time spent practicing on realistic material. For many non-native speakers of English, practice will mean the difference between success and disappointment. When practicing, become disciplined at looking up words you are unfamiliar with, in particular the terms that relate to the GMAT® test itself. Be sure that when you undertake practice tests, if you come across any term you are unfamiliar with then look it up.

If you are planning to take the GMAT® many years since college

If it is some or many years since you studied and, in particular, since you studied or even thought about geometry, algebra and English grammar, or took a multiple-choice exam, then the GMAT® may well present a number of specific hurdles.

The first thing to do is to review examples of each type of question and assessment that make up the GMAT® and make an honest appraisal of which of these components represent the greatest challenge for you. To demonstrate your full potential, and well before taking the test, you will need to begin a program of revision or review. Start with the aspects of the test that you feel you are least good at. Practice on a computer the free mock tests available from mba.com. You only need minimal computer skills to undertake the GMAT® CAT, but a little practice will help ensure that you become proficient in taking a test at a computer screen. If need be, refresh your command of mental arithmetic

You may need to set aside a fairly considerable amount of time for revising the demands of the verbal and numerical sub-tests. Ideally, over a number of months, aim for 10 hours a week practice. Without undertaking such a program you could risk not achieving a good, well-balanced GMAT® score.

Making the necessary commitment will demand discipline and determination. The time spent practicing will at times seem tedious and frustrating. For many people, revising geometry or reliving the possibly bad memories of the algebra or grammar classes at school is not what they dream of doing in their spare time. But if you want to go to a graduate business school and it insists on a good GMAT® score, you have no real alternative.

Work to redevelop a good exam technique. This demands a balance between speed and accuracy. Some very good candidates will need to unlearn a thoughtful, considered approach to issues. You can actually think too deeply or take too few risks in a test like the GMAT®. Practice under the pressure of time at realistic questions. Where appropriate, look to the suggested answers for clues and practice at informed guessing (where you can eliminate some of the suggested answers and then guess from those that remain).

On a positive note, practice should afford you a marked improvement in your performance. Your work history may have prepared you well for the reading comprehension and critical reasoning questions and you may also discover that you are able to shine in the Analytical Writing Assessments.

If you have not taken a CAT-type test before

If you have not previously taken a test administered on a computer then be sure to take the time to become entirely familiar with the way in which the GMAT® is administered at a keyboard and screen. In most parts of the world, the GMAT® is taken at a computer terminal, and it takes a bit of getting used to. Practice with the free GMAT® download at mba.com.

Beware that diagrams on the computer screen may be misleading, especially in the case of geometric shapes, tables and graphs, as the screen can distort the image or the scale or both! The test author is aware of this and will have provided sufficient information to arrive at the answer. So, wherever possible, take what is said and avoid drawing unnecessary assumptions about the appearance of a diagram, table or graph on the screen. For example, if a shape is described as a cube, but on the screen the sides do not all seem equal, ignore it and treat the shape as a cube. Equally, if a table or graph says that x is the largest but on the screen it looks like y is the same or, in fact, bigger, take no notice and treat x as the largest.

If you suffer a disability

If your ability to undertake the GMAT® could be adversely affected by a disability, then speak to the business school you are applying to and seek its advice on how your requirements can best be accommodated. Provide full details of your condition and be clear on the special arrangements you require when you register online for the test. You may be allowed: (1) extra time; or (2) a test reader; or (3) someone to record your answers. Braille or large-text versions of the test may be made available.

It is reasonable to expect that your requirements are given proper consideration and, wherever possible, are accommodated. Evidence of your condition may be required. Be sure to mention your needs at an early stage so that the organizers have time to accommodate them and you have sufficient time to obtain any formal proof of your condition that they may require.

2

Practice makes a big difference in GMAT® scores

This book gives advice on how to prepare for the GMAT®, offers a succinct account of the purpose and format of the test, identifies other sources of good practice material, and, most importantly, contains many hundreds of practice questions with answers and explanations so that you get down to some serious practice and improve on your likely score.

It is important that you realize that most people who score well in the GMAT® have worked hard preparing for the test. This, above all else, requires time and especially commitment. Without the latter, it is unlikely that you will do very well in the GMAT®.

Many candidates will take the test a second time. ETS reports an average 30-point improvement in score between first- and second-timers. Both scores are reported to business schools and many schools will take an average of your two most recent GMAT® scores, so halving the benefit of any improvement you may have achieved. For this reason, it is far better to set out to improve your score by taking practice tests rather than real ones, then only one score is reported to your graduate school, and you will benefit from the full extent of any improvement as the school will not be able to take an average of scores.

Some prep courses claim an average 70-point improvement between the first and second test score for their candidates. From my experience of test coaching, this level of improvement is very possible and not dependent on attending a prep course, however. What matters is that you set about a major program of revision or review and practice over many weeks and hours. Be sure to realize and take advantage of all the score-improving strategies discussed in this and other books. And don't stop concentrating on any personal areas of weakness until they become strengths.

As I have said, making a significant improvement in your test score demands a considerable level of self-discipline and determination. It can be lonely, boring, painful even. Enrolling on a prep course can help counter some of these challenges, in that you will learn within a small group and may find it easier to commit the time. It comes down to a question of preference and money.

Important GMAT® strategies

In the CAT there is no going back

Be sure of your answer before submitting it because you cannot go back and review your answers. This feature of the GMAT CAT® requires that you develop a certain mindset of being determined to make every question count before you move on to the next question. Do not hit the submit button without a final, brief review of your choice.

Expect sub-tests to include a mixture of questions

When you practice on POWERPREP® and GMATPrep® (the free downloads from www.mba.com) or in some parts of this and other publications, you are given questions of the same type. By this, I mean you practice on, for example, data sufficiency questions and, in another sub-test, problem-solving. However, in the CAT version of the GMAT®, expect the computer program to mix the types of quantitative and verbal questions up together. This means that you may well start the quantitative test with, for example, a data sufficiency question and then find that the next question is a problem-solving question. Equally, in the verbal test, expect the question types to be mixed up and perhaps start with a sentence correction question followed by a critical reasoning question.

Learn to manage your time expertly

Because there is no going back in the GMAT®, if you make the mistake of rushing through questions and not double-checking an answer before submitting it, then you can find yourself at the end of the test with time to spare.

You need to allow an average around two minutes per question if you are to complete them in the 75 minutes allowed for each sub-test. You need to develop this pace through practice. Full-length practice sub-tests can really help you learn to manage your time to perfection. You will find six full-length practice sub-tests in Chapter 5.

Aim to make a really good start

In the GMAT CAT®, every question counts, but try especially hard to get the first question right, then the first five questions and then all the rest! The opening questions are especially significant as they are used to determine the level of the next few questions that follow. This adaptive process continues through the test. Get as many questions right as possible and you will be awarded a winning score.

In Chapter 4 you will find 100 questions dedicated to practicing making a really good start. These are also really useful mini-tests that take only 10 minutes so can be fitted into even the really busy schedule.

Whatever you do, avoid a bad start

A bad start is something you should work hard to avoid in any test, but especially in the GMAT CAT®. The problem created by a bad start is that the adaptive nature of the test forces you to play catch-up before you get to questions of a level expected by many institutions. Consider the following illustration. In the GMAT CAT®, all the questions are graded in terms of their difficulty (you cannot see these grades) and in your real GMAT® the first question is very likely to be one that a candidate who scores 500 can be expected to get right. But if you are unfortunate enough to get it wrong, then the program presents you with the next question that a candidate who scores say 400 should answer correctly. Get that right and you are presented with a question appropriate to a candidate who scores 470. Get that one right and you can expect a question of the level of a score of 520. You should not read too much into this illustration, but it demonstrates how in the GMAT, if you make a bad start you may find yourself struggling to get onto sufficiently high-scoring questions to win you a place at the institute of your choice.

Guessing can pay

In the CAT you cannot go forward to the next question without answering the current one. If you do not know the answer you have little alternative but to guess. Straight guessing offers a 20 percent chance of guessing correctly. Always look to the suggested answers to see if you can rule any out as definitely wrong. If you can, then you will improve your chances of guessing right. Guessing plays an important part in many GMAT® candidates' test-taking strategies, especially in the last part of each sub-test when time may be running out.

Key stages in preparing for the GMAT®

We each have our preferred method of revising for exams and your study to date will have ensured that you already realize how you can best meet the challenge of the GMAT®. However, if it is some years since you last took an exam, then consider these common features of many successful GMAT® campaigns.

Adopt a winning mindset

Doing well in the GMAT® is not simply a matter of intelligence. It is critical that you realize that to do well you have to try very hard. Weeks before the test you will need to undertake extensive revision and review. During the exam you will need to really 'go for it'. After the exam you should feel mentally fatigued. If you don't, then you probably failed to apply yourself sufficiently and may not have fully done yourself justice.

It is common to experience feelings of irritation or resentment about having to do the test. It is crucial that you put these feeling aside. They can be very counterproductive. Try not to wonder about the validity of the test. What you or I think of the GMAT® and its predictive value is entirely irrelevant. You need to do well in this test if you are to achieve your goal of winning a place in business school. Do well and an important opportunity will become possible. Focus on only that goal and put all else aside for a few weeks. You really need to let your determination to do well in the GMAT® take over your life for a while.

Practice a successful exam technique

Some very clever and highly educated people do not do well in the GMAT®. In some cases, their training and inclination does not best serve them well under the rather artificial conditions of a timed test. This happens when, for example, the candidate thinks too deeply about the question or reads the passages and questions too carefully. Some place too high an emphasis on accuracy at the expense of speed. The outcome is that their test result does not reflect their true ability or their achievements to date. If you may be such a person, then realize that reading too careful or thinking deeply may put you at a considerable disadvantage. You may need to develop an approach that involves a slightly greater risk of getting a question wrong for the sake of speed or you may need to accept the assertions and statements at face value and focus on the immediate task of answering the questions. Work hard on your exam technique and do not rest until you can demonstrate the necessary balance between speed and accuracy. Practice is key to achieving this. Make sure you allow yourself lots of time to develop a winning approach.

Devise and implement an unbeatable study plan

The high-scoring candidate in every exam is confident of their abilities. They know what to expect and find the exam contains few if any surprises. They turn up at the test center looking forward to the opportunity to demonstrate how good they have become, and are able to demonstrate a highly effective exam technique. To make sure you are such a candidate, begin by preparing a study plan well in advance of the test date.

Step 1   Get each stage of the challenge clear in your mind

The first thing to do is to make sure that you know exactly what to expect at each stage of the GMAT®. This should include the exact nature of each task and how long you are allowed.

It is important that you are familiar with the screen icons and format of the computer adaptive version of the GMAT®. You want to be able to concentrate on the questions and not worry about which screen icon you should use.

GMAT® comprises:

- Two Analytical Writing Assessments, entitled Analysis of an Issue and Analysis of an Argument. You are allowed 30 minutes for each assessment.

- A verbal test involving 41 questions made up of sentence correction, critical reasoning and reading comprehension questions. You are allowed 75 minutes.

- A quantitative test comprising 37 questions made up of data sufficiency and problem-solving questions, for which you are also allowed 75 minutes.

Make sure that you are entirely familiar with the demands of each of these assessment and question types.

Step 2 Make an honest assessment of your strengths and weaknesses

To prepare thoroughly for any test you should obviously concentrate your efforts to improve in the areas in which you are weakest. You probably already know which part of the GMAT® you will do least well in were you to take the test tomorrow. But you really need to try to go a step further than this and as objectively as possible assess the extent to which your area(s) of personal challenge will let you down. Only then can you ensure that you spend sufficient time addressing the challenge. You should repeat such an assessment at a number of points through your program of revision. Then you can observe your progress and focus on the area(s) that continue to represent a risk of failure.

To obtain a good indication of the extent of the challenge you face, select three or four examples of each style of question and one assessment, making sure that they are broadly representative of the level of difficulty found in the real GMAT®. You could use POWERPREP® and GMATPrep® or questions from this or any other GMAT® practice book. Attempt these questions under exam-type conditions and score them. It is then a simple matter of concentrating on the parts of the test in which you did least well. Remember to repeat this exercise throughout your program of revision.

Step 3 Plan a program of practice

Now you need to decide how much time you should find to spend preparing for the challenge. The GMAT® is very much a US test and one that examines key features covered in a good US formal education. If it is some years since you left formal education, if you were not educated in the United States, or never really mastered geometry, algebra or English grammar, then you may need to set aside a quite considerable amount of time to practice for the GMAT®. The sooner you start the better, and a little and often is better than occasional long sessions. Other candidates, most likely those who have left formal education more recently, and who have benefited from a good US education, may only need to spend a number of weeks practicing what they have already previously mastered.

The self-appraisal that you undertook in Step 2 should allow you to decide how much of a challenge the GMAT® represents. Take it seriously and avoid the trap of promising yourself that you will start tomorrow. For some candidates, tomorrow never comes or comes far too late.

A winning plan is likely to involve work over a minimum of two months, twice and preferably three times a week. If English is not your first language, if to date you have accomplished much despite never mastering mathematics, or, if you find the rules of English usage a complete enigma, then be prepared to set aside more time than this and over a longer period.

Step 4   Obtain every bit of free material and then borrow or buy more

Many candidates facing psychometric tests cannot find sufficient relevant material to practice on. In the case of the GMAT®, fortunately there is a good amount of practice material available, and you should be prepared to use most of it. Some of it is available free of charge and you should begin your practice on this free material. Much more is sold either through subscription websites or books, and you will almost certainly need to use this material in addition to that freely available. If you were to buy it all, it would constitute a quite significant investment, but remember, career services and libraries will lend you copies of books free of charge. So start with the free material such as POWERPREP® and GMATPrep®, then borrow books such as this from your careers services or library. These sources of material will be sufficient for the majority of candidates. If you need more, than consider enrolling on one of the subscription websites or prep courses.

Some prep books claim that they are the only book you will ever need! But there are very good reasons for not relying on one author or book to prepare for the GMAT®. For a start, to get a good score, many candidates will need to practice on more questions than are contained in any one volume. Every author offers some insight, but at the level of the GMAT® you will not find everything that you need in any one title. Appreciate that candidates approach the GMAT® from a very wide range of backgrounds and abilities and most books will try to provide something for all of them. An explanation that helps one candidate can be insufficient for another. It is likely therefore, that some parts of this and other publications are less useful than others. Or, you may find that one publication suits your position more than another.

You can download POWERPREP® and GMATPrep® from www.mba.com (you will need to register with the site first) and good practice material available from career services and libraries may include, for example:

- *Advanced Numeracy Test Workbook* (2003), Kogan Page, an earlier title of mine, which contains over 400 practice questions that will also help you prepare for the quantitative sub-test;

- *Barron's GMAT*® 2007–08, Barron's Educational Series;
- *GMAT CAT*® *Success* (2004), Thomson Peterson;
- *The GMAT*® *for Dummies* (2006), Wiley;
- *The Official Guide for GMAT*® *Review,* Graduate Management Admission Council.

An internet search will identify many subscription practice websites for the GMAT® and also a number of GMAT® prep courses.

Step 5   Undertake two sorts of practice

First, to get the most from your practice, begin working in a relaxed situation, without constraint of time, reviewing examples of questions, working out the answers in order to become familiar with the demands of typical questions. Feel free to review answers and explanations. Refer to text books, dictionaries or a calculator as much as you wish. Chapter 3 of this book is dedicated to undertaking this sort of warm up practice.

Then, once you are familiar with the challenge of each question type, you should start to practice under realistic test conditions. This involves putting aside the dictionary or calculator and working against the clock without help or interruption. The purpose is to develop a good exam technique and to improve your stamina and endurance. Learn not to spend too long on any one question and practice at educated guessing.

Especially practice your strategy for the first few questions. Then practice your strategy for the remaining questions. Chapter 4 of this book is dedicated to practicing a really good GMAT® start and allows you to take frequent 10-minute practice sessions. To get the most out of this sort of practice set yourself the personal challenge of trying to beat your last score each time you take a test. You will need to try very hard and take the challenge seriously if you are to really succeed in beating your previous best score. When you finish a test you should be mentally tired but satisfied that you are creating a realistic test feel.

When you have completed Chapter 4, then start practicing on full-length sub-tests. You will find a series of realistic verbal and quantitative sub-tests in Chapter 5. Answers and explanation to the total of over 600 practice questions are found in Chapter 6.

Warm up questions for the quantitative and verbal sub-tests

This chapter provides 266 practice questions. Work through it before you tackle Chapters 4 and 5. The idea is that you can ease yourself into the style and format of GMAT® questions and build up your familiarity, accuracy and confidence.

There are important differences between the questions in this chapter and those in the GMAT®. The first is that some (but not all) of these questions are easier than real GMAT® questions. The easier questions will allow many candidates to learn or review the relevant competencies and become familiar with the language and format of the questions. With time, this practice will build confidence, comprehension and skills, to the point where candidates are able to tackle questions at the level of the real thing. If you are lucky enough not to need to start your program of revision and review with easier material, then just practice on the examples of the style of question that you find the most challenging.

Another difference between the questions in this chapter and the real GMAT®, and, for that matter, the questions in later chapters, is that some are not multiple-choice questions. You simply have to work out the answers and write them in the box provided.

A third difference is that, in this chapter, types of questions are not mixed up. In the GMAT® sub-tests, the various types of question are, so, for example, in the quantitative sub-test, a problem-solving question may follow a data sufficiency one, and that in turn may be followed by another problem-solving question. In this chapter, the practice questions are arranged together so that, for example, all the problem-solving questions follow each other. As a result, you can concentrate on one question type at a time or conveniently select only the question types that you find the greatest challenge.

In the quantitative section I have provided extra practice algebraic questions. This is because a great many GMAT® candidates find this part the most challenging. These are also questions in which practice can bring quite significant improvements in performance. So, if you are one of the many candidates who find these questions the most difficult, then set aside sufficient time and get down to some serious practice. It will result in a significant improvement in your real GMAT® score.

Some answers and explanations are printed below the question. This is to help with the smooth, convenient build up of confidence. Answers and explanations to the remaining questions are provided in Chapter 6.

Do not forget to use the free material at www.mba.com. You will find there, for example, a very good mathematic review, as well as practice questions and timed quantitative tests. Remember, it is recommended that you make use of a wide range of sources of practice material in preparation for the GMAT®. This book should feature as just one of a number of books and websites that you use.

Remember also to concentrate most of your practice on the parts of the GMAT® that you find most difficult. Only then will you be certain that you can take the real test and demonstrate your full potential.

Warm up questions for the quantitative sub-test

Speed is not of the essence when it comes to the GMAT®'s quantitative questions. In the GMAT® you are allowed 75 minutes in which to tackle the 37 quantitative questions. The sub-test comprises two sort of question: problem-solving and data sufficiency.

Obviously, you need to keep track of time but you have enough to think things through carefully. To get a good GMAT® score you must make every question count. The test authors set traps and ask questions in a deliberately misleading way, so read each question carefully and read each again before you confirm your answer. Once you confirm your answer there is no going back.

Many candidates find the quantitative questions harder than they in fact are. Some may seem impossible, which, of course, they are not. So, when you face a series of difficult questions, don't give up. Take a little bit more time. Test the question to see if some of the typical GMAT® themes apply. This is where your program of revision, review and practice will really count. In time and with practice you will better recognize the mathematics behind the question. Only guess as a last resort or when you have only a few questions to go and if time is running out. Do not use a calculator. No time limit is imposed.

Problem-solving questions

These are straightforward questions of mathematics, including pure arithmetic, algebra and geometry. I have concentrated on these subjects because you may not have studied them for some considerable time. There are also word problems and information presented in graphs that you must interpret. Your task is to identify from a list of five suggested answers which you believe is correct.

Below, you will find 90 warm up problem-solving questions. Many, but not all, are multiple-choice (in the real GMAT® they are all multiple-choice). Use them to refresh your command of the regular (if quite old-fashioned) mathematics that forms the basis of the GMAT® quantitative sub-test.

Example question

1. If $x + y = 4$, then $2x + 2y$ is:

    (A) 4

    (B) 2

    (C) 8   Answer   [C]

    (D) 16

    (E) Cannot be determined

    Explanation: It is not necessary to know the values of x and y, simply to multiply the sum of $x + y$ from the first equation by 2.

2. What are the first four multiples of 14?   Answer   [ ]

3. If $y/x = 4$ and $x + y = 5$, then x is:

    (A) 4

    (B) 1

    (C) 5   Answer ☐

    (D) 4/5

    (E) 5/4

4. What are the prime factors of 12?   Answer ☐

5. If $x + 3y = 2x - y$, then $x - 2y$ is:

    (A) 0

    (B) 1

    (C) $\frac{1}{2}$ Answer ☐

    (D) $\frac{2}{3}$

    (E) Cannot be determined

6. What are the divisors of 35?   Answer ☐

7. If $x + y = 2x + 2y$, then $4x + 4y$ is:

    (A) 1

    (B) 0

    (C) 2   Answer ☐ B

    (D) 4

    (E) Cannot be determined

8. What is the lowest common multiple of 6 and 8?   Answer ☐

9. If $x/y = 2$, what percentage of x is $x - y$?

    (A) 20

    (B) 100

    (C) 50   Answer ☐

    (D) 200

    (E) Cannot be determined

10. Is 49 a prime number? Can you prove it?   Answer ☐

11. If $x/y = 199$, what percentage of x is $x - y$?

    (A) 99

    (B) 100

    (C) 51   Answer ☐

    (D) 49

    (E) Cannot be determined

12. What number do you start with if you multiply it by 5,   Answer ☐
    then divide by 4 and then halve that to get 5?

13. How many divisors do the numbers 23, 41 and 79 have
    (do not count the same divisor more than once; for example,   Answer ☐
    all are divisible by 1 but only count 1 once in your answer)?

14. If $x/4 + y/4 = 10$, what percentage of x is $80 - 2y$?

    (A) 10

    (B) 200

    (C) 150   Answer ☐

    (D) 100

    (E) Cannot be determined

15. Which value is both a squared and a cubed number?

    (A) 4

    (B) 8

    (C) 36   Answer ☐

    (D) 64

    (E) 100

16. If $x > 1$ and $y > -1$, then:

    (A) $xy > -1$

    (B) $xy < -1$

    (C) $-x > y$ Answer ☐

    (D) $-x < y$

    (E) $x < y$

17. Which of the following is a squared number?
    15, 27, 43, 72, 125, 169   Answer ☐

18. If $x > 0$ and $y > 0$, then:

    (A) $x/y > 1$

    (B) $xy > x$

    (C) $x/y < y$ Answer ☐

    (D) $y - x < 0$

    (E) $xy > 0$

19. Which of the following are prime numbers?

    16, 17, 31, 53, 79   Answer ☐

20. If $x > 1$ and $y > 2$, then:

    (A) $x - y > -1$

    (B) $x/y > 1/2$

    (C) $x/y > 0$ Answer ☐

    (D) $x - y > 0$

    (E) $y - x > 1$

21. 135 is $1/5$ of 45% of what number?   Answer ☐

22. If $x > y$, then:

    (A) $x/y > 1$

    (B) $x/y > 0$

    (C) $x - y > 0$ Answer ☐

    (D) $xy > 0$

    (E) $y - x > 1$

23. 37.5 is $1/4$ of 25% of what number?   Answer ☐

24. Which of the following inequalities is the solution to the inequality $3x - 3 < x + 2$?

    (A) $x < 2.5$

    (B) $x > 2.5$

    (C) $x > 5/3$ Answer ☐

    (D) $x < 3/5$

    (E) $x < -1/2$

25. What is the average of the inclusive integers from 999   Answer ☐
    through to 1,245?

26. Which of the following inequalities is the solution to the inequality $3x + 2 > 9x + 6$?

(A) $x < -2/3$

(B) $x > -2/3$

(C) $x < -3/4$ Answer

(D) $x > -3/4$

(E) $x > 2/3$

27. How many numbers are there from 67 through to 99?   Answer

28. If $2x + 3y = 8$ and $2x - 2y = 2$, then x is:

(A) 2

(B) 2.75

(C) 2.2   Answer

(D) 2.25

(E) 2.5

29. What is the sum of all the numbers from 18 through to 40?   Answer

30. If $x/2 + y/3 = 2$, $2x + 3y = 13$, then y is:

(A) 13/3

(B) 8/3

(C) 5   Answer

(D) 3/5

(E) 3

31. Find three consecutive numbers that have the sum of 117.   Answer

32. If $x/y = 2$, $y/x = 1/2$, then y is:

(A) Cannot be determined

(B) 2

(C) 1   Answer

(D) 4

(E) 8

33. One number is 3 times another and their sum is 28.   Answer
     What are the two numbers?

34. The function *x returns the value of the highest integer smaller than x. What is *4 times *2.5?

    (A) 10

    (B) 8

    (C) 6   Answer ☐

    (D) 7.5

    (E) 4

35. If 8 is subtracted from 4 times a number the answer is 40.   Answer ☐
    What is the number?

36. The function *x returns the value of the highest integer smaller than x. What is *(13.5 − 0.51) divided by *(2.5 + 2.49)?

    (A) 13/5

    (B) 5

    (C) 13/4   Answer ☐

    (D) 3

    (E) 12/5

37. 10 is $\frac{1}{2}$ of 5% of what number?   Answer ☐

38. The function &(x) is a clock function; it gives values between 0 and 12. &(13) returns the value 1, for example. What, then, is the result of &(15) − &(16)?

    (A) 12

    (B) −1

    (C) 11   Answer ☐

    (D) 7

    (E) 1

39. If 99 is subtracted from 5 times a number (x) the answer is 1.   Answer ☐
    What is x?

40. The function &(x) is a clock function; it gives values between 0 and 12. &(13) returns the value 1, for example. What, then, is the result of &(36) divided by &(12)?

    (A) 2

    (B) 3

    (C) 12   Answer ☐

    (D) 6

    (E) 1

41. If it takes one person 5 hours to load a truck while another person can complete the task in 3 hours, how long should it take then to half fill the truck if they work together at the same rate?

    (A) 2 hours

    (B) 3 hours

    (C) 4 hours   Answer ☐

    (D) 5 hours

    (E) 6 hours

42. If $4x = 2y = z$ and $xyz = 64$, x is:

    (A) 16

    (B) 4

    (C) 8   Answer ☐

    (D) 6

    (E) 2

43. If 18% of the fuel is used, how many gallons did we   Answer ☐
    start with if 492 gallons remain?

44. If $x = 2y = 4z$ and $xyz = 64$, x is:

    (A) 16 $4.\frac{4}{2}$

    (B) 4

    (C) 8 $4.2.1$ Answer ☐

    (D) 6

    (E) 2

45. If the average return journey time over 10 days is 30 minutes but on the first outward journey a hold up added 30 minutes to that journey, by how much did the delay increase the daily average?

Answer ☐

46. If $x = y / z$, $y = 4x$ and $xyz = 64$, x is:

    (A) 2

    (B) 4

    (C) 8   Answer ☐

    (D) 1

    (E) 16

47. What is the ratio between the employed and unemployed economically active people in this community?

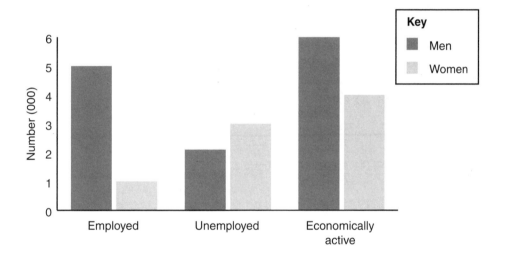

Employment by gender in a small community

    (A) 5:4

    (B) 5:3

    (C) 3:2   Answer ☐

    (D) 2:1

    (E) 1:1

48. If x = 5y, y = 4z and xy / z = 64, x is:

(A) 2

(B) 4

(C) 8   Answer

(D) 1

(E) 16

49. In 2002 what percentage of all corporate tax receipts were derived from corporations active in banking and finance?

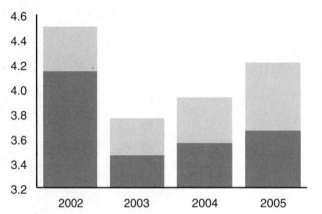

Key

☐ Corporations active in banking and finance

■ Corporations active in all other sectors

Increases in receipts of Corporation tax   Answer

50. If x = y², y = z² and (xyz)⁴ / 2 = 64, x is:

(A) 2

(B) 4

(C) 8   Answer

(D) 1

(E) 16

51. If knowledge workers born in India represent 3% of all workers at Pi Corporation, then what percentage does the total population of immigrant knowledge workers represent?

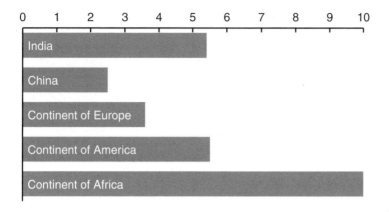

Immigrant knowledge workers in Pi Corporation   Answer ☐

52. If a + b = 6 and ab = 8 what is $4/a + 4/b$?

    (A) 6
    (B) 8
    (C) 4   Answer ☐
    (D) 2
    (E) 3

53. If the manufacturer was to sell 40 units at a discount of 15% of the recommended selling price (RSP) what would be the percentage profit or loss?

Direct materials	Not stated
Direct labour	Not stated
Production overheads	Not stated
Total factory cost of 40 units	$2,170.56
Recommended selling price to retailers (per unit)	$91.20

Manufacturing cost of 40 air conditioning units   Answer ☐

54. If $a/2 + b/3 = 3$ and $a - b = 3$, what is $a + b$?

    (A) 5/3

    (B) 2

    (C) 3   Answer

    (D) 2.5

    (E) 6.6

55. What was the share price/earnings ratio of Doing Well Inc at the time of going to press?

Group turnover	$3.3 bn
Pre-tax profit	$236 m
Earnings per share	$5.84
Share price	8 cents

Year results of Doing Well Inc – all figures correct at time of going to press

                                      Answer

56. If $6a + b = 12$ and $4a + 2b = 0$, what is b/a?

    (A) –4

    (B) 2

    (C) –2   Answer

    (D) $-\frac{1}{2}$

    (E) $-1\frac{1}{2}$

57.   GDP %

Spain	+3.2	+3.6
USA	+3.5	+4.0
	Q3	Q4

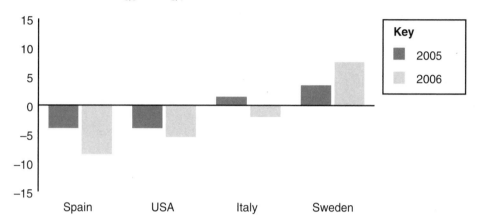

Current account balances as a % of GDP (Gross Domestic Product)

Which statement is true?

(A) Spain's current account surplus is bigger than America's

(B) Spain's current account deficit is bigger than America's

(C) Spain's current account surplus is relatively bigger   Answer ☐
    than America's

(D) Spain's current account deficit is relatively bigger than America's

58. If $a/b = 5$ and $ab = 5$, what is $a + b$?

(A) 6

(B) 5

(C) 4   Answer ☐

(D) –6

(E) 6 or –6

59. If you cycle 6 times faster than you walk and you take in
total 28 minutes to cycle to work and walk the same   Answer ☐
distance back, how long did you spend walking?

60. For which values of x is $x^2 - 4x + 3$ negative?

    (A) $1 < x < 3$

    (B) $x < -3$

    (C) $-4 < x < 3$ Answer ☐

    (D) $1 > x > 3$

    (E) $x > 1$

61. What is the probability of getting a number greater
    than 4 or an odd number when you throw a 6-sided dice?   Answer ☐

62. For which values of x is $x^2 - 2x + 2$ negative?

    (A) $0 > x > 1$

    (B) $0 < x < 1$

    (C) None   Answer ☐

    (D) $0 < x < 2$

    (E) $0 > x > 2$

63. What is the probability of throwing a 3, 5 or an even
    number with a 6-sided dice?   Answer ☐

64. For which values of x is $5x - x^2 - 3$ greater than x?

    (A) $1 > x > 3$

    (B) $0 > x > 2$

    (C) $-3 < x < 5$ Answer ☐

    (D) $0 < x < 2$

    (E) None

65. If two 6-sided dice are thrown, what is the probability
    that the sum of the faces is 7?   Answer ☐

66. If $4a = 3b$ and $6b = 0$, then:

    (A) $a = 3/4$

    (B) $a = b$

    (C) $a = 3$ and $b = 4$ Answer ☐

    (D) $a/b = 4/3$

    (E) $b/a = 3/4$

67. What is the area of this square?

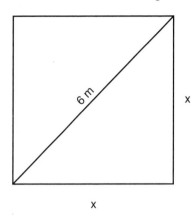

Answer ☐

68. If 5a = 2b and 6b = 12, then:

(A) a/b = 2/5

(B) a = b/4

(C) a = 5 and b = 2   Answer ☐

(D) a/b = 5/2

(E) b/a = 10/6

69. What is the length of x if the area of the square is 25 m²?

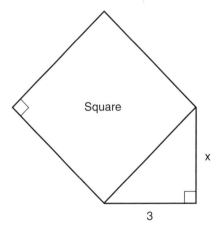

Answer ☐

70. If $3a + b = 6$ and $2a + 2b = 12$, then $2b - 2a$ is:

    (A) 8

    (B) 10

    (C) 6   Answer

    (D) 18

    (E) 12

71. What is the volume of this cube if each side is 3 ft long?

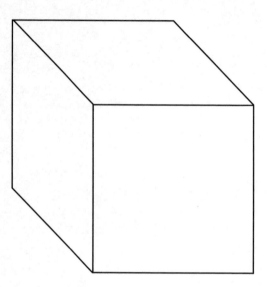

                                                 Answer

72. If $(1/a) + (1/b) = 2$ and $(2/a) + (3/b) = 5$, b is:

    (A) 3

    (B) 4

    (C) 2   Answer

    (D) 1

    (E) ½

73. What is the length of x if the area of the square is 169 m²?

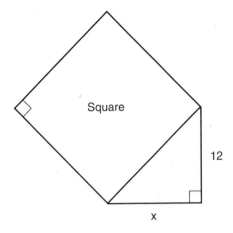

12

Answer ☐

74. If y/x < 1, then:

(A) Both x and y are negative

(B) Both x and y are positive

(C) x > y

(D) x < y

(E) None of the above

Answer ☐

75. What is the volume of a sphere with a radius of 3 cm (take π to be 3.14 and give your answer to the nearest full cm³)?

Answer ☐

76. If yx < 1, then:

(A) Both x and y are negative

(B) Both x and y are positive

(C) Only one of the two is negative

(D) x < y

(E) None of the above

Answer ☐

77. What is the length of x if the square has an area of 100 m²?

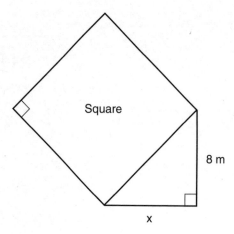

Answer ☐

78. If $10y + 5x < 30$:

(A) $y < 3 - x/3$

(B) $-2y > 6 + x/2$

(C) $y < 6 - x/2$ Answer ☐

(D) $x > 6 - 2y$

(E) None of the above

79. What is the volume of a cylinder with a radius of 3 cm
     and a height of 6 cm (take π as 3.14 and work to the   Answer ☐
     nearest full cm)?

80. If $2y + x < 0$ and $y + 2x > 0$:

(A) $-2x < y < -x/2$

(B) $-2x > y > -x/2$

(C) $2x > y > -x/2$ Answer ☐

(D) $-2x < y < x/2$

(E) None of the above

81. What is the length of x if the square has an area of 289 m²?

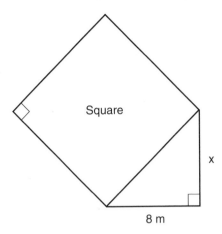

Square

x

8 m

Answer ☐

82. If $y = 1/x + x$ and $x = 4$ then y is:
    (A) 17/4
    (B) 4/5
    (C) 5/4   Answer ☐
    (D) 17/8
    (E) None of the above

83. What is the volume of a hemisphere with a radius
    of 4 ft (take π to be 3.14 and work to the nearest full ft³)?   Answer ☐

84. If $y = 2x + 2/x$ and $x = 3$ then y is:
    (A) 10/3
    (B) 18/3
    (C) 8²/₃   Answer ☐
    (D) 20/3
    (E) None of the above

85. What is the volume of a 4-sided pyramid if its base is 9 cm²
    and its perpendicular height is 5 cm (take π to be 3.14)?   Answer ☐

86. If $y = 2/3x + 5/6x$ and $x = 1$ then y is:

    (A) 2/3

    (B) 7/9

    (C) 7/3   Answer

    (D) 7/6

    (E) None of the above

87. What is the volume of a cone with a radius of 3 cm
and a height of 5 cm (take π to be 3.14 and work to   Answer
the nearest cm^3)?

88. If $y = 2x + x^2$ and $x = 2y$ then y is:

    (A) 8

    (B) 18

    (C) 12   Answer

    (D) 6

    (E) None of the above

89. What is the volume of a triangular prism with a base of
5 cm, a perpendicular height of 4 cm and a length of 15 cm?   Answer

90. A tin can 10 cm high contains 500 ml of water, how
much would a similar can hold if it were 20 cm high?   Answer

Data sufficiency questions

This second type of question in the quantitative sub-test is also based on the same regular mathematics as the problem-solving questions. But that is where the similarity between these two sorts of questions ends. Your task in these questions is quite different. Each question comprises a mathematics question and two statements that refer to the question. You must decide whether the question can be answered with the information given in the statements. There are five possible answers and you must indicate which is correct. You must decide whether the question can be answered using the first statement alone, the second statement alone, both statements together (but neither separately), either statement alone, or if the problem cannot be solved. If you are new to this style of question, then you will need to undertake some practice before you fully understand the challenge.

Below, you will find 57 practice data sufficiency questions. As with all the questions in this chapter, do not impose a time limit on yourself, but use them to become fully conversant with the task and continue building your speed, accuracy and confidence in the mathematics on which the questions are based.

Example question

1. Can you find the diameter of a circle?

    (1)   A straight line through the circle is twice its radius
    (2)   The circumference can be found with the formula π d

    A.   1 alone, not 2 alone
    B.   2 alone, not 1 alone
    C.   1 and 2 together (need both)   Answer | E |
    D.   1 alone or 2 alone
    E.   1 and 2 together are not sufficient

    Explanation: We cannot establish the length of the diameter of the circle with either statement so cannot calculate its circumference.

2. Is y negative?

    (1) $y^2 - y - 2 = 0$
    (2) $2y < 0$

    A.   1 alone, not 2 alone
    B.   2 alone, not 1 alone
    C.   1 and 2 together (need both)   Answer | |
    D.   1 alone or 2 alone
    E.   1 and 2 together are not sufficient

3.

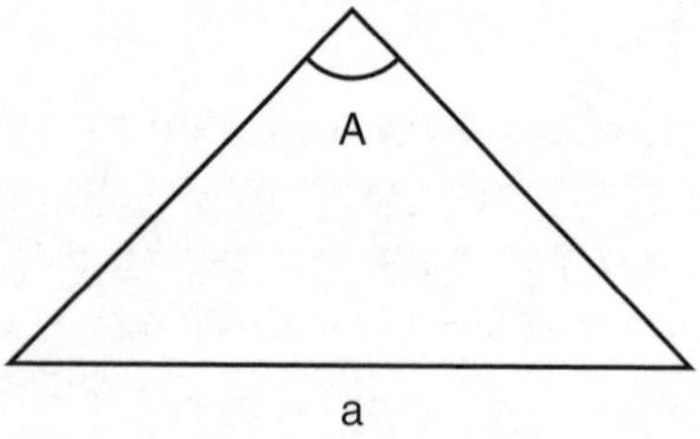

a

Is angle A the largest and side a the longest?

(1) The sum of the length of the other two sides is greater than the length of a
(2) A is the largest angle

A. 1 alone, not 2 alone
B. 2 alone, not 1 alone
C. 1 and 2 together (need both)   Answer
D. 1 alone or 2 alone
E. 1 and 2 together are not sufficient

4. Is x negative?

(1) $xy < 1$
(2) y is positive

A. 1 alone, not 2 alone
B. 2 alone, not 1 alone
C. 1 and 2 together (need both)   Answer
D. 1 alone or 2 alone
E. 1 and 2 together are not sufficient

5. Can a polygon be divided into three triangles?

(1) It is a pentagon
(2) It has five sides

A. 1 alone, not 2 alone
B. 2 alone, not 1 alone
C. 1 and 2 together (need both)   Answer
D. 1 alone or 2 alone
E. 1 and 2 together are not sufficient

6. Is x positive?

(1) $x^3 < 0$
(2) $x^5 < 0$

A. 1 alone, not 2 alone
B. 2 alone, not 1 alone
C. 1 and 2 together (need both)   Answer
D. 1 alone or 2 alone
E. 1 and 2 together are not sufficient

7. How many sides does a regular polygon have?

    (1)   The total sum of all the interior and exterior angles = 1,800°

    (2)   The sum of its exterior angles = 360°

    A.   1 alone, not 2 alone

    B.   2 alone, not 1 alone

    C.   1 and 2 together (need both)   Answer

    D.   1 alone or 2 alone

    E.   1 and 2 together are not sufficient

8. Is x negative?

    (1) $xy = 3$

    (2) $x^2 = y$

    A.   1 alone, not 2 alone

    B.   2 alone, not 1 alone

    C.   1 and 2 together (need both)   Answer

    D.   1 alone or 2 alone

    E.   1 and 2 together are not sufficient

9. Are two triangles similar?

    (1)   Corresponding sides are in the same ratio

    (2)   Two pairs of angles are similar

    A.   1 alone, not 2 alone

    B.   2 alone, not 1 alone

    C.   1 and 2 together (need both)   Answer

    D.   1 alone or 2 alone

    E.   1 and 2 together are not sufficient

10. Is n divisible by 8 with no remainder?

    (1)   n + 8 is divisible by 8 with integer result

    (2)   n + 16 is divisible by 8 with integer result

    A.   1 alone, not 2 alone

    B.   2 alone, not 1 alone

    C.   1 and 2 together (need both)   Answer

    D.   1 alone or 2 alone

    E.   1 and 2 together are not sufficient

11. Two shapes are congruent (identical)

    (1) The angles in one shape are equal to the corresponding angles of the other
    (2) All pairs of corresponding sides are the same size

    A. 1 alone, not 2 alone
    B. 2 alone, not 1 alone
    C. 1 and 2 together (need both)   Answer ☐
    D. 1 alone or 2 alone
    E. 1 and 2 together are not sufficient

12. Is n divisible by 3 with no remainder?

    (1) $n - 3$ is divisible by 3 with integer result
    (2) $n - 21$ is divisible by 3 with integer result

    A. 1 alone, not 2 alone
    B. 2 alone, not 1 alone
    C. 1 and 2 together (need both)   Answer ☐
    D. 1 alone or 2 alone
    E. 1 and 2 together are not sufficient

13. How many sides does a regular polygon have?

    (1) The sum of its exterior angles $= 360°$
    (2) The total sum of all the interior and exterior angles $= 1,800°$

    A. 1 alone, not 2 alone
    B. 2 alone, not 1 alone
    C. 1 and 2 together (need both)   Answer ☐
    D. 1 alone or 2 alone
    E. 1 and 2 together are not sufficient

14. Is n divisible by 8 with remainder 6?

    (1) $n/2$ is divisible by 4 with remainder 3
    (2) n is divisible by 2 with integer result

    A. 1 alone, not 2 alone
    B. 2 alone, not 1 alone
    C. 1 and 2 together (need both)   Answer ☐
    D. 1 alone or 2 alone
    E. 1 and 2 together are not sufficient

15. Is a triangle right-angled?

   (1) A line drawn from the vertical angle to meet the base divides it at the mid-point
   (2) The length of the sides are a multiple of 5, 12, 13

   A. 1 alone, not 2 alone
   B. 2 alone, not 1 alone
   C. 1 and 2 together (need both)   Answer
   D. 1 alone or 2 alone
   E. 1 and 2 together are not sufficient

16. Is n divisible by 3 with remainder 2?

   (1) n – m is divisible by 3 with no remainder
   (2) m is divisible by 2 with integer result

   A. 1 alone, not 2 alone
   B. 2 alone, not 1 alone
   C. 1 and 2 together (need both)   Answer
   D. 1 alone or 2 alone
   E. 1 and 2 together are not sufficient

17. What is the surface area of the cone?

   (1) L = 7 cm and the base is 6 cm wide
   (2) The cone has a height of 4 cm and the base a radius of 3 cm

   A. 1 alone, not 2 alone
   B. 2 alone, not 1 alone
   C. 1 and 2 together (need both)   Answer
   D. 1 alone or 2 alone
   E. 1 and 2 together are not sufficient

18. Is the shape is a parallelogram?

   (1) The diagonals bisect each other
   (2) It has four sides

   A. 1 alone, not 2 alone
   B. 2 alone, not 1 alone
   C. 1 and 2 together (need both)   Answer ☐
   D. 1 alone or 2 alone
   E. 1 and 2 together are not sufficient

19. Which of these two is the greater, x or y?

   (1) $x = 2a$
   (2) $y = 5a$

   A. 1 alone, not 2 alone
   B. 2 alone, not 1 alone
   C. 1 and 2 together (need both)   Answer ☐
   D. 1 alone or 2 alone
   E. 1 and 2 together are not sufficient

20. A bar of soap costs 60 cents, how much would a similar bar cost?

   (1) The similar bar has dimensions $^4/_5$ of the original
   (2) The original weighs 6oz

   A. 1 alone, not 2 alone
   B. 2 alone, not 1 alone
   C. 1 and 2 together (need both)   Answer ☐
   D. 1 alone or 2 alone
   E. 1 and 2 together are not sufficient

21. Which of these two is the greater, x or y?

   (1) x is divisible by 4 with integer solution
   (2) y is divisible by 4 with remainder 1

   A. 1 alone, not 2 alone
   B. 2 alone, not 1 alone
   C. 1 and 2 together (need both)   Answer ☐
   D. 1 alone or 2 alone
   E. 1 and 2 together are not sufficient

22. Is the shape a kite?

    (1) The diagonals are perpendicular
    (2) Two pairs of sides are equal

    A. 1 alone, not 2 alone
    B. 2 alone, not 1 alone
    C. 1 and 2 together (need both)   Answer
    D. 1 alone or 2 alone
    E. 1 and 2 together are not sufficient

23. Which of these two is the greater, x or y?

    (1) $x - y < 0$
    (2) $x + y > 0$

    A. 1 alone, not 2 alone
    B. 2 alone, not 1 alone
    C. 1 and 2 together (need both)   Answer
    D. 1 alone or 2 alone
    E. 1 and 2 together are not sufficient

24. Is the quadrilateral a square?

    (1) All angles equal 90°
    (2) The diagonals divide the shape into 4 identical triangles

    A. 1 alone, not 2 alone
    B. 2 alone, not 1 alone
    C. 1 and 2 together (need both)   Answer
    D. 1 alone or 2 alone
    E. 1 and 2 together are not sufficient

25. Which of these two is the greater, x or y?

    (1) $x/3 > y$
    (2) $x^3 > y^3$

    A. 1 alone, not 2 alone
    B. 2 alone, not 1 alone
    C. 1 and 2 together (need both)   Answer
    D. 1 alone or 2 alone
    E. 1 and 2 together are not sufficient

26. If a ball bearing is dropped into a beaker of water 3 cm deep, by how much does the water rise?

    (1) The radius of the ball bearing is 7 mm
    (2) The radius of the beaker is 5 cm

    A. 1 alone, not 2 alone
    B. 2 alone, not 1 alone
    C. 1 and 2 together (need both)   Answer
    D. 1 alone or 2 alone
    E. 1 and 2 together are not sufficient

27. Which of these two is the greater, x or y?

    (1) $1/x > 1/y$
    (2) Both are negative

    A. 1 alone, not 2 alone
    B. 2 alone, not 1 alone
    C. 1 and 2 together (need both)   Answer
    D. 1 alone or 2 alone
    E. 1 and 2 together are not sufficient

28. How far up the wall does the ladder reach?

    (1) The ladder is on horizontal ground and the wall is vertical
    (2) The angle between the ladder and the ground is 80°

    A. 1 alone, not 2 alone
    B. 2 alone, not 1 alone
    C. 1 and 2 together (need both)   Answer
    D. 1 alone or 2 alone
    E. 1 and 2 together are not sufficient

29. A sequence of numbers a_1, a_2, a_3 etc. is generated using the following algorithm: $a_{n+1} = (a_n)^2$. Does the number 9 appear in the sequence if:

    (1) $a_1 = 3$
    (2) $a_3 = 81$

    A. 1 alone, not 2 alone
    B. 2 alone, not 1 alone
    C. 1 and 2 together (need both)   Answer
    D. 1 alone or 2 alone
    E. 1 and 2 together are not sufficient

30. How big is each angle in the pentagon?

  (1) One angle is 100°
  (2) Four angles are equal

  A. 1 alone, not 2 alone
  B. 2 alone, not 1 alone
  C. 1 and 2 together (need both)   Answer
  D. 1 alone or 2 alone
  E. 1 and 2 together are not sufficient

31. A sequence of numbers a_1, a_2, a_3 etc. is generated using the following algorithm: $a_{n+1} = (a_n)^2$. Does the number 36 appear in the sequence if:

  (1) $a_2 = \sqrt{6}$
  (2) 1,296 appears in the sequence

  A. 1 alone, not 2 alone
  B. 2 alone, not 1 alone
  C. 1 and 2 together (need both)   Answer
  D. 1 alone or 2 alone
  E. 1 and 2 together are not sufficient

32. What is the size of the non-shaded area?

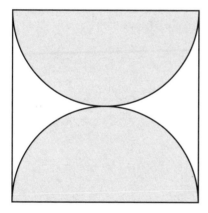

  (1) The square has sides 10 cm long
  (2) The semicircle has a radius of 5 cm

  A. 1 alone, not 2 alone
  B. 2 alone, not 1 alone
  C. 1 and 2 together (need both)   Answer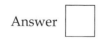
  D. 1 alone or 2 alone
  E. 1 and 2 together are not sufficient

33. A sequence of numbers a_1, a_2, a_3 etc. is generated using the following algorithm: $a_{n+1} = a_n/2$. Does the number 2 appear in the sequence if:

(1) a_1 is not 0
(2) There are no numbers in the sequence between 17 and 31 inclusive

A. 1 alone, not 2 alone
B. 2 alone, not 1 alone
C. 1 and 2 together (need both)   Answer ☐
D. 1 alone or 2 alone
E. 1 and 2 together are not sufficient

34. A disc revolves at 75 revolutions a minute. What is the speed at which a point on the disc is rotating?

(1) The disc has a circumference of 12 in
(2) The point on the disc is 2 in from the center

A. 1 alone, not 2 alone
B. 2 alone, not 1 alone
C. 1 and 2 together (need both)   Answer ☐
D. 1 alone or 2 alone
E. 1 and 2 together are not sufficient

35. A sequence of numbers a_1, a_2, a_3 etc. is generated using the following algorithm: $a_{n+1} = a_n + m$. Does the number 2 *not* appear in the sequence if:

(1) $m = -2$
(2) a_{16} is a positive even number

A. 1 alone, not 2 alone
B. 2 alone, not 1 alone
C. 1 and 2 together (need both)   Answer ☐
D. 1 alone or 2 alone
E. 1 and 2 together are not sufficient

36. Are the shapes similar?

(1) All pairs of corresponding sides are in the same ratio
(2) The shape is not a triangle

A. 1 alone, not 2 alone
B. 2 alone, not 1 alone
C. 1 and 2 together (need both)   Answer ☐
D. 1 alone or 2 alone
E. 1 and 2 together are not sufficient

37. Is $x^2 > y^2$?

    (1) $x > y$
    (2) $x/y > 0$

    A. 1 alone, not 2 alone
    B. 2 alone, not 1 alone
    C. 1 and 2 together (need both)   Answer
    D. 1 alone or 2 alone
    E. 1 and 2 together are not sufficient

38. Is $x^3 > y^3$?

    (1) $x > y$
    (2) $x/y > 0$

    A. 1 alone, not 2 alone
    B. 2 alone, not 1 alone
    C. 1 and 2 together (need both)   Answer
    D. 1 alone or 2 alone
    E. 1 and 2 together are not sufficient

39. How high is the building with a shadow 19 m long?

    (1) We look up on the internet the angle of the sun for that time and place
    (2) At the same time, a gatepost of known height casts a shadow 1.5 m long

    A. 1 alone, not 2 alone
    B. 2 alone, not 1 alone
    C. 1 and 2 together (need both)   Answer
    D. 1 alone or 2 alone
    E. 1 and 2 together are not sufficient

40. Is $x^2 > y$?

    (1) $0 < x < 1$
    (2) $x > y$

    A. 1 alone, not 2 alone
    B. 2 alone, not 1 alone
    C. 1 and 2 together (need both)   Answer
    D. 1 alone or 2 alone
    E. 1 and 2 together are not sufficient

41. How high is the kite from the ground?

    (1) It is on a string 70 ft long
    (2) The person holding the string calculated that the angle of elevation is 70°

    A. 1 alone, not 2 alone
    B. 2 alone, not 1 alone
    C. 1 and 2 together (need both)   Answer
    D. 1 alone or 2 alone
    E. 1 and 2 together are not sufficient

42. Is $1/x^2 + 1/y^2 > 0$?

    (1) $y < x$
    (2) x and $y \neq 0$

    A. 1 alone, not 2 alone
    B. 2 alone, not 1 alone
    C. 1 and 2 together (need both)   Answer
    D. 1 alone or 2 alone
    E. 1 and 2 together are not sufficient

43. Is $x/8 > y/12$?

    (1) $3x > 2y$
    (2) $x < y$

    A. 1 alone, not 2 alone
    B. 2 alone, not 1 alone
    C. 1 and 2 together (need both)   Answer
    D. 1 alone or 2 alone
    E. 1 and 2 together are not sufficient

44. Is $x/8 > y/12$?

    (1) $y = 0$
    (2) $x > 1$

    A. 1 alone, not 2 alone
    B. 2 alone, not 1 alone
    C. 1 and 2 together (need both)   Answer
    D. 1 alone or 2 alone
    E. 1 and 2 together are not sufficient

45. Is $1/x > 1/y$?

    (1) $(1/x) - (1/y) > 0$
    (2) $(y - x)/(xy) > 0$

    A. 1 alone, not 2 alone
    B. 2 alone, not 1 alone
    C. 1 and 2 together (need both)   Answer ⬜
    D. 1 alone or 2 alone
    E. 1 and 2 together are not sufficient

46. Is $y > 3x + 2$?

    (1) $y > 4x$
    (2) $x > 2$

    A. 1 alone, not 2 alone
    B. 2 alone, not 1 alone
    C. 1 and 2 together (need both)   Answer ⬜
    D. 1 alone or 2 alone
    E. 1 and 2 together are not sufficient

47. What is the value of xy?

    (1) $x + y = 6$
    (2) $2x + y = 10$

    A. 1 alone, not 2 alone
    B. 2 alone, not 1 alone
    C. 1 and 2 together (need both)   Answer ⬜
    D. 1 alone or 2 alone
    E. 1 and 2 together are not sufficient

48. What is the value of xy?

    (1) $1/x = 12$
    (2) $2/y = 10$

    A. 1 alone, not 2 alone
    B. 2 alone, not 1 alone
    C. 1 and 2 together (need both)   Answer ⬜
    D. 1 alone or 2 alone
    E. 1 and 2 together are not sufficient

49. What is the value of xy?

    (1) $x^2y^2 = 16$
    (2) $y^2 = 6$

    A. 1 alone, not 2 alone
    B. 2 alone, not 1 alone
    C. 1 and 2 together (need both)   Answer
    D. 1 alone or 2 alone
    E. 1 and 2 together are not sufficient

50. What is the value of xy?

    (1) $x^3y^3 = 8$
    (2) $5x + 10y = 25$

    A. 1 alone, not 2 alone
    B. 2 alone, not 1 alone
    C. 1 and 2 together (need both)   Answer
    D. 1 alone or 2 alone
    E. 1 and 2 together are not sufficient

51. What is the value of xy?

    (1) $(x + y)^2 = 8$
    (2) $(x - y)^2 = 6$

    A. 1 alone, not 2 alone
    B. 2 alone, not 1 alone
    C. 1 and 2 together (need both)   Answer
    D. 1 alone or 2 alone
    E. 1 and 2 together are not sufficient

52. What is the value of x?

    (1) $x/y = 4$
    (2) $xy = 4$

    A. 1 alone, not 2 alone
    B. 2 alone, not 1 alone
    C. 1 and 2 together (need both)   Answer
    D. 1 alone or 2 alone
    E. 1 and 2 together are not sufficient

53. What is the value of x?

   (1) $x^2 = 4$
   (2) $xy = 4$

   A.   1 alone, not 2 alone
   B.   2 alone, not 1 alone
   C.   1 and 2 together (need both)   Answer ☐
   D.   1 alone or 2 alone
   E.   1 and 2 together are not sufficient

54. What is the value of x?

   (1) $1/x + x/y = 5/12$
   (2) $3x/xy - 2x/y = 1/y$

   A.   1 alone, not 2 alone
   B.   2 alone, not 1 alone
   C.   1 and 2 together (need both)   Answer ☐
   D.   1 alone or 2 alone
   E.   1 and 2 together are not sufficient

55. What is the value of x?

   (1) $x^3 - 3x^2 + 3x = 1$
   (2) $(x - 1)^2 = 0$

   A.   1 alone, not 2 alone
   B.   2 alone, not 1 alone
   C.   1 and 2 together (need both)   Answer ☐
   D.   1 alone or 2 alone
   E.   1 and 2 together are not sufficient

56. Is x positive or negative?

   (1) $x^3 + 8 = 0$
   (2) $x^2 - 4 = 0$

   A.   1 alone, not 2 alone
   B.   2 alone, not 1 alone
   C.   1 and 2 together (need both)   Answer ☐
   D.   1 alone or 2 alone
   E.   1 and 2 together are not sufficient

57. Is x positive or negative?

   (1) $x^2 > y^2$
   (2) $y > 0$

   A. 1 alone, not 2 alone
   B. 2 alone, not 1 alone
   C. 1 and 2 together (need both)
   D. 1 alone or 2 alone
   E. 1 and 2 together are not sufficient

Answer

Warm up questions for the verbal sub-test

In the GMAT®, the verbal sub-test comprises 41 questions, and you are allowed 75 minutes in which to attempt them. The verbal test is comprised of three sorts of questions: sentence correction, reading comprehension and critical reading. The computer will present the questions in any order, however. So be prepared, for example, for a sentence correction question to be followed by a passage and a short series of reading comprehension and critical reasoning questions.

Sentence correction questions

These questions are a test of your command of English usage. Each question comprises a sentence, all of which, or a part of which, is underlined. Below the question are five suggested answers, the first of which is an exact copy of the under-lined part of the question. Your task is to identify which of the suggested answers is correct. It may be a problem of grammar, sense, style or sentence construction. Below, you will find 64 practice questions of this type:

Example question

Q1. It said on the bottle that drinking was bad for you <u>and he drank so much he was drunk</u>.

    A. and he drank so much he was drunk.
    B. he drunk so much he was drunk.
    C. he drank so much he was drank.   Answer   A
    D. he drunk so much he was drank.
    E. he drink so much he was drink.

Explanation: The verb to drink is irregular and the past simple form is drank, and the past participle, drunk.

Q2. The sum is still outstanding and <u>you ought to</u> paid it last week.

    A. you ought to
    B. you must have
    C. you should to have   Answer
    D. you ought to have
    E. you should to

Q3. The book is <u>about Sardinia, and the author has been all about</u> that beautiful island.

    A. about Sardinia, and the author has been all about
    B. around Sardinia, and the author has been all around
    C. about Sardinia, and the author has been all around   Answer
    D. around Sardinia, and the author has been all about
    E. round Sardinia, and the author has been all round

Q4. It's surprising that the President overruled the recommendations of the Committee.

   A. It's surprising that the
   B. It surprises that the
   C. It surprises the   Answer ☐
   D. It's surprising the
   E. It takes a lot to surprise the

Q5. The company has been trading for almost 25 years and already has plenty of life left in it.

   A. almost 25 years and already
   B. already 25 years and almost
   C. nearly 25 years and already   Answer ☐
   D. almost 25 years and still has
   E. already 25 years and nearly

Q6. It's the resignation of the Finance Director caused the fall in stock price.

   A. It's the
   B. It's that the
   C. There's no question that the   Answer ☐
   D. There's no good that the
   E. The question is that the

Q7. After his wife left him it was to his family why he turned for support.

   A. why he
   B. how he
   C. what he   Answer ☐
   D. when he
   E. that he

Q8. I met a new friend at the beach today.

   A. I met a new friend
   B. I meet a new friend
   C. I made a new friend   Answer ☐
   D. I make a new friend
   E. I come to a new friend

Q9. You could barely imagine <u>any worse news, and it was impossible for the reporter to say anything positive</u>.

   A. any worse news, and it was impossible for the reporter to say anything positive.
   B. any worse news, and it was impossible for the reporter to say something positive.
   C. some worse news, and it was impossible for the reporter to say anything positive.
   D. some worse news, and it was impossible for the reporter to say something positive.
   E. any worse news, and it was impossible for the reporter to say the positive.

   Answer ☐

Q10. <u>She wanted to lend her brother's car and even asked him if he would take it to her house the next day</u>.

   A. She wanted to lend her brother's car and even asked him if he would take it to her house the next day.
   B. She wanted to borrow her brother's car and even asked him if he would bring it to her house the next day.
   C. She wanted to lend her brother's car and even asked him if he would bring it to her house the next day.
   D. She wanted to borrow her brother's car and even asked him if he would take it to her house the next day.
   E. She wanted to borrow her brother's car and even asked him if he would go with it to her house the next day.

   Answer ☐

Q11. <u>Why I left that employment</u> before the contract ended was because I did not like my boss.

   A. Why I left that employment
   B. What I left that employment
   C. When I left that employment   Answer ☐
   D. When I left my employment
   E. The reason why I left that employment

Q12.   The letter <u>could be genuine</u>, as the writer was dead a good 10 years before the
       date it was supposedly written.

    A. could be genuine,
    B. might not be genuine,
    C. cannot be genuine,   Answer
    D. might be genuine,
    E. was genuine,

Q13.   The Asia-Pacific Index rose to <u>the worst possible</u> level in 17 years.

    A. the worst possible
    B. a fairly high
    C. the highest   Answer
    D. the completely high
    E. the highest possible

Q14.   Have a close look at <u>that one here. It is a facsimile, while those on the table are
       original and those in the library</u> across town are all rather poor-quality fakes.

    A. that one here. It is a facsimile, while those on the table are original and
       those in the library
    B. this one here. It is a facsimile, while those on the table are original and
       these in the library
    C. this one here. It is a facsimile, while these on the table are original and
       those in the library
    D. that one here. It is a facsimile, while that on the table are original and
       those in the library
    E. this one here. It is a facsimile, while these on the table are original and that
       one in the library

                                      Answer

Q15.   <u>Little did I</u> realize that the stock would become so valuable.

    A. Little did I
    B. Mostly did I
    C. Not did I   Answer
    D. Only did I
    E. Little do I

Q16. <u>Certain, today's television series are very different from the series shown when I was a child</u>.

  A. Certain, today's television series are very different from the series shown when I was a child.
  B. Yes, today's television series are very different than the series shown when I am a child.
  C. Certainly, today's television series are very different from the series shown when I am a child.
  D. Sure, today's television series are very different than the series shown when I was a child.
  E. No doubt, when I was a child the television shown today were very different.

Answer ☐

Q17. <u>Congratulations, your run was not fast enough to qualify for the Olympics</u>.

  A. Congratulations, your run was not fast enough to qualify for the Olympics.
  B. Congratulations, your run was too much to qualify for the Olympic team.
  C. Congratulations, you ran well sufficiently to qualify for the Olympics.
  D. Congratulations, your run was sufficient not enough to qualify.
  E. Congratulations, you ran well enough to qualify for the Olympic team.

Answer ☐

Q18. When I worked there it was a really friendly place, <u>and everywhere possible would do everything</u> to help each other.

  A. and everywhere possible would do everything
  B. and everybody would do everywhere
  C. and everything and everywhere possible
  D. and everyone would do everything possible
  E. and everyone would do possible everything

Answer ☐

Q19. After so many delays and false starts it is such a relief to witness the <u>starting of</u> full-scale production.

  A. starting of
  B. beginning of
  C. start of
  D. doing of
  E. begin of

Answer ☐

Q20. They were careful to make the offer to only <u>a few</u> very select clients.

  A. a few
  B. not many
  C. fewer   Answer
  D. little
  E. few

Q21. The course would last <u>for a month, and I waited for all</u> day to hear whether or not I had been offered a place on it.

  A. for a month, and I waited for all
  B. for a month, and I waited all for
  C. a month, and I waited for all   Answer
  D. for a month, and I waited all
  E. a month, and I waited all for

Q22. The cake was only <u>three-quarters as big as the last one, and to make it the children used an extra one and half</u> eggs and half the sugar.

  A. three-quarters as big as the last one, and to make it the children used an extra one and half
  B. a three-quarters as big as the last one, and to make it the children used an extra one and a half
  C. three-quarters as big as the last one, and to make it the children used an extra one and a half
  D. a three-quarters as big as the last one, and to make it the children used an extra one and half
  E. three-quarters of as big as the last one, and to make it the children used an extra one and half

                Answer

Q23. In the first few moments of the Big Bang, the universe <u>consisted of only</u> quarks and gluons.

  A. consisted of only
  B. consists only of
  C. consisting of only   Answer
  D. according to some physicists, consists of only
  E. according to some physicists, consisting only of

Q24. <u>He may be going to go</u> to the party.

  A. He may be going to go
  B. He may be going
  C. He is be going   Answer
  D. He going to go
  E. He be going to go

Q25. When the current stock is eventually sold, we did not reprint, as so few copies of the book have been purchased.

  A. When the current stock is eventually sold, we did not reprint, as so few copies of the book have been purchased.

  B. If the current stock is eventually sold, we did not reprint, as so few copies of the book have been purchased.

  C. When the current stock is eventually sold, we will not reprint, as so few copies of the book has been purchased.

  D. When the current stock is eventually sold, we will not reprint, as so few copies of the book had been purchased.

  E. If the current stock is eventually sold, we will not reprint, as so few copies of the book have been purchased.

Answer

Q26. He used to run very good, but since the injury last year he has not been good at running.

  A. run very good, but since the injury last year he has not been good at running.

  B. be a good runner, but since the injury last year he has not run so well.

  C. run very well, but since the injury last year he has not run any good.

  D. run very good, but since the injury last year he has not run so good.

  E. be a very good runner, but since the injury last year he used to be better.

Answer

Q27. There used not to be an effective treatment for Alzheimer's disease. However, recent advances in medical science have led to a cautious optimism that one will be found in the foreseeable future.

  A. There used not to be

  B. There might have been

  C. There may not be   Answer

  D. There could not be

  E. There ought to be

Q28. He came top in the national exams. He could well be the least clever man in the whole country.

  A. the least clever man

  B. the most clever man

  C. the more clever man   Answer

  D. more than any other the cleverest man

  E. the less clever man

Q29. <u>When I look into the freezer the water had become ice</u>.

    A. When I look into the freezer the water had become ice.
    B. When I look into the freezer the water became ice.
    C. When I'm looking into the freezer the water has become ice.
    D. When I looked into the freezer the water had become ice.
    E. I'm looking into the freezer and the water became ice.

Answer [ ]

Q30. They went <u>in</u> church on foot.

    A. in
    B. to
    C. in front of   Answer [ ]
    D. at
    E. on

Q31. When I saw the job advertisement I immediately knew it was the role <u>I have been looking for</u>.

    A. I have been looking for.
    B. I had to have been looking for.
    C. I have been looking for.   Answer [ ]
    D. I have be look for.
    E. I had been looking for.

Q32. <u>No matter that</u> the pilgrims stepped off the *Mayflower*, than the harsh New England winter set in.

    A. No matter that
    B. No longer had
    C. At no time at all   Answer [ ]
    D. No sooner had
    E. No way had

Q33. <u>I think I'm offering</u> the job to the candidate with the highest test score.

    A. I think I'm offering
    B. I have decided I would offer
    C. I think I have a willingness to offer   Answer [ ]
    D. I think I might offering
    E. I have decided I'll offer

Q34. <u>The assessment of the Director was pessimistic ago two weeks</u>.

    A. The assessment of the Director was pessimistic ago two weeks.
    B. The Director's assessment was pessimistic before two weeks.
    C. Two weeks before the assessment of the Director was pessimistic.
    D. Two weeks ago the Director's assessment is pessimistic.
    E. Two weeks ago the assessment of the Director was pessimistic.

Answer ☐

Q35. Given the adverse decision of the regulatory authority, the company <u>will to make</u> another takeover attempt.

    A. will to make
    B. won't be making
    C. wants not to make
    D. made not
    E. will not be made

Answer ☐

Q36. If interest rates <u>remains</u> too low, is the main effect inflation or an imbalance between saving and investments?

    A. remains
    B. be
    C. grow
    D. stay
    E. becomes

Answer ☐

Q37. Two reasons were given for the less than promising performance of the banking system, <u>both which could take two to three years'</u> intensive work to improve.

    A. both which could take two to three years'
    B. most of which could take two to three years'
    C. both at which could take two or three years'
    D. both of which could take two to three years'
    E. which could take two to three years'

Answer ☐

Q38. Malaria and dysentery kill millions worldwide, yet spending just <u>$10 million on each</u> of the next 10 years would cut deaths in half and cost only $100 million.

    A. $10 million on each
    B. $10 million at each
    C. $10 million in each
    D. $10 million of each
    E. $10 million to each

Answer ☐

Q39. In answer to the candidate's query, the test administrator said that <u>dictionaries may not be taken</u> into the examination room.

    A. dictionaries may not be taken
    B. dictionaries can't not be taken
    C. dictionaries cannot be taken
    D. dictionaries have got not to be taken
    E. dictionaries be not allowed into

Answer [ ]

Q40. Enjoy <u>yourself</u> at the party everyone.

    A. yourself
    B. himself
    C. themselves
    D. yourselves
    E. ourselves

Answer [ ]

Q41. <u>There aren't any people</u> who see price stability as the main objective of monetary policy.

    A. There aren't any people
    B. There aren't some people who
    C. Aren't some people
    D. There aren't many people
    E. There aren't people

Answer [ ]

Q42. The train was moving <u>away from the track and the passengers saw the girl jump off the bridge in the river</u>.

    A. away from the track and the passengers saw the girl jump off the bridge in the river.
    B. on the track and the passengers saw the girl jump at the bridge to the river.
    C. along the track and the passengers saw the girl jump off the bridge into the river.
    D. along the track and the passengers saw the girl jump out of the bridge to the river.
    E. on the track and the passengers saw the girl jump off the bridge in the river.

Answer [ ]

Q43. <u>The women doctor only treats women</u>.

    A. The women doctor only treats women.
    B. The women's doctor only treats women.
    C. The womens doctor only treats women.
    D. The women doctor only treats woman.
    E. The women's doctor only treats woman.

Answer [ ]

Q44. <u>One of the most interest and enduring questions in ecology is why greater</u> biodiversity (as well as biomass) is found in the tropics compared with the temperate regions of the earth.

A. One of the most interest and enduring questions in ecology is why greater
B. One of the most interesting and endure questions in ecology is why great
C. One of the most interesting and enduring questions in ecology is why greater
D. One of the most interesting and enduring question in ecology is why greater
E. One of the most interesting and enduring questions in ecology is why great

Answer ☐

Q45. Metal prices continue to soar and <u>have scarcely risen so</u> high in over 25 years.

A. have scarcely risen so
B. have rarely raised so
C. have scarcely raised so
D. have rarely risen so
E. have rarely rising so

Answer ☐

Q46. During <u>the latter half of the Second World War the German Army relied from the processing of coal to produce liquid fuels; now that the cost of crude</u> oil is so high the technology may once again be used.

A. the latter half of the Second World War the German Army relied from the processing of coal to produce liquid fuels; now that the cost of crude
B. the latter half of the Second World War the German Army relied in the processing of coal to produce liquid fuels; now that the cost of crude
C. the latter half of the Second World War the German Army relied on the processing of coal to produce liquid fuels; now that the price of crude
D. the later half of the Second World War the German Army relied on the processing of coal to produce liquid fuels; now that the cost of crude
E. the later half of the Second World War the German Army relied from the processing of coal to produce liquid fuels; now that the price of crude

Answer ☐

Q47. <u>It is someone else's car, and they will be back in a day or so</u>.

A. It is someone else's car, and they will be back in a day or so.
B. It is someone else car, and they will be back in a day or so's time.
C. It is someone elses car, and they will be back in a day or so time.
D. It is someone elses' car, and they will be back in a day or so's time.
E. It is someone elses car, and they will be back in a day or so.

Answer ☐

Q48.   The Japanese lead in the science of robotics, and <u>Peter accepted with them</u> <u>that the last android was surprisingly good in it</u> human likeness.

    A.   Peter accepted with them that the last android was surprisingly good in it
    B.   Peter agreed with them that the latest android was surprisingly good in terms of its
    C.   Peter accepted that the latest android was surprisingly good in terms of it
    D.   Peter agreed that the latest android was surprisingly good in terms of its
    E.   Peter agreed that the last android was surprisingly good in terms of it's

Answer ☐

Q49.   She warned the three <u>individuals that they needed to take more care,</u> <u>otherwise they would loose</u> their possessions.

    A.   individuals that they needed to take more care, otherwise they would loose
    B.   individuals that they needed to take more care, otherwise they would lose
    C.   people that they needed to take more care, otherwise they would loose
    D.   persons that they needed to take more care, otherwise they would loose
    E.   people that they needed to take more care, otherwise they would lose

Answer ☐

Q50.   <u>The pen is her's but it's not working.</u>

    A.   The pen is her's but it's not working.
    B.   The pen is hers but its not working.
    C.   The pen is her's but it has not working.   Answer ☐
    D.   The pen is hers but it's stopped working.
    E.   The pen is hers' but its' stopped working.

Q51.   I have <u>know her for so long because we have live</u> next door to each other for 12 years.

    A.   know her for so long because we have live
    B.   know her for so long because we have lived
    C.   known her for so long because we have living   Answer ☐
    D.   know her for so long because we have been living
    E.   known her for so long because we have lived

Q52. My boss has a <u>shut mind when it comes to new ways of working. No matter how much I try I can't seem</u> to get him to appreciate the potential benefits.

   A. shut mind when it comes to new ways of working. No matter how much I try I can't seem
   B. closed mind when it comes to new ways of working. No matter how much I try I can't appear
   C. shut mind when it comes to new ways of working. No matter how much I try I can't appear
   D. closed mind when it comes to new ways of working, No matter how much I try I can't seem
   E. open mind when it comes to new ways of working. No matter how much I try I can't seem

Answer ☐

Q53. <u>None of the delegates no longer could</u> support the chairperson.

   A. None of the delegates no longer could
   B. No one of the delegates no more could
   C. None of the delegates could any more
   D. Not one of the delegates could no longer
   E. None of the delegates could any longer

Answer ☐

Q54. A heated discussion <u>arose since</u> the possibility of a computer made from DNA and enzymes is such a controversial subject.

   A. arose since
   B. arise because
   C. arose because
   D. arose as
   E. rose as

Answer ☐

Q55. At first they thought the problem had been solved, but the next day the machine <u>would not begin and so they had to take it again to the shop</u>.

   A. would not begin and so they had to take it again to the shop.
   B. would not begin again and so they had to take it to the shop again.
   C. would not start and so they had to take it to the shop again.
   D. would not start and so they had to take it back to the shop.
   E. would not begin and so they had to take it back to the shop.

Answer ☐

Q56.   She speaks five European languages <u>except</u> her native tongue.

    A. except
    B. besides
    C. accept   Answer
    D. but
    E. save

Q57.   In those days you had no real alternative but <u>too enter the same trade or profession as your father</u>.

    A. too enter the same trade or profession as your father.
    B. to enter the same trade or profession as your father.
    C. to enter the trade or profession like your father.   Answer
    D. enter the trade or profession same as your father.
    E. take up the trade or profession equal to your fathers.

Q58.   <u>While many</u> Americans are complaining of high gasoline prices, the government decided to lower taxes so that they got a better deal at the pump.

    A. While many
    B. When many
    C. Scarcely any   Answer
    D. Hardly many
    E. Because many

Q59.   <u>I can know he's worried about something because he normally really cares about his appearance</u>.

    A. I can know he's worried about something because he normally really cares about his appearance.
    B. I can know he's worried about something because he normally really cares for his appearance.
    C. I can tell hes' worried about something because he normally really cares less about his appearance.
    D. I can tell he's worried about something because he normally really cares about his appearance.
    E. I can know he's worried about something because he's normally caring for his appearance.

                                      Answer

Q60.   He was totally engrossed in his work <u>when</u> the telephone started to ring.

    A. when
    B. while
    C. hardly   Answer
    D. because
    E. as

Q61. My wife and <u>I hadn't</u> decided if we want to move.

    A. I hadn't
    B. I haven't
    C. aren't   Answer ☐
    D. I doesn't
    E. I hasn't

Q62. It was an expensive place to <u>live, but on the opposite</u> it was very central.

    A. live, but on the opposite
    B. live, but on the contrary
    C. life, but on the other hand   Answer ☐
    D. live, but on the other hand
    E. life, but on the contrary

Q63. In Central America the staple foods are <u>rice and bean</u>.

    A. rice and bean
    B. bean and rices
    C. rice and beans   Answer ☐
    D. rices and beans
    E. beans and rices

Q64. She loved to <u>travels to exotic locations but found the long journey</u> tiresome.

    A. travels to exotic locations but found the long journey
    B. travel to exotic locations but often found the long journeys
    C. travel to exotic location but often found the long journey
    D. travels to exotic locations but often found the long journeys
    E. traveling to exotic locations but often found the long journeying

                                      Answer ☐

Reading comprehension and critical reasoning questions

The reading comprehension and critical reasoning questions in the verbal sub-test require you to answer a series of questions by referring to a passage. The questions require you to comprehend meaning and significance, assess logical strength, identify valid inference, distinguish a main idea from subordinate ones, single out the correct summary, evaluate interpretations, detect reasonable conclusions, pinpoint the writer's intention or determine the most likely conjectures and hypotheses.

    The passages in a real verbal sub-test comprise around 350 words. The subjects covered may be drawn from science, business and current affairs. Typically, questions ask you to, for example, identify the key point, supporting points, reasons given, statements the author might agree or disagree with, the best summary of the passage or its conclusions. Five suggested answers will be offered and your task is to select one as correct. Note that in these warm up questions you have to choose from four possible answers.

Be careful. If you know something of the subject you should not bring any information not contained in the passage to the question. Even if you consider the passage factually incorrect take the information as given and use it to answer the questions. Be extra careful if it is a subject on which you hold strong views. It is not your task to offer a critique of the passage. Stick strictly to the content of the passage and what can be inferred from it.

Practice at these questions will help you to realize the demands of this part of the verbal sub-test. You may also need to build your vocabulary. Do this by reading quality daily newspapers and weekly current affairs and scientific journals. Get yourself a quality dictionary and thesaurus and discipline yourself to check every word you are unsure about.

Some of the passages below are longer and others shorter than those that occur in a real GMAT®. Below, there are seven passages and 55 practice questions, which are a mix of reading comprehension and critical reasoning.

Passage 1
(443 words)

Recent research has provided further stark evidence of the educational apartheid dividing the achievements of bright children from low- and high-income families. The study followed for many years the progress of a sample of almost 40,000 of the brightest children. Two-thirds were drawn from low-income families. The research found that almost all the able children from high-income families achieved three or more A grades in exams at the age of 18 years. But it was found that only one in four of the most able children from low-income families achieved similar grades. The effect of this inequality puts the low-income, bright child at a considerable disadvantage. A bright child from a high-income family was found to have a one in two chance of gaining a place at one of the best universities. A bright child from a low-income family had only a 1 in 10 chance of gaining such a place. The bright children from high-income families were themselves very likely to enjoy a high income in their working life. A significant majority of the bright children from low-income families failed to earn above the national average wage.

An acrimonious debate among political parties and educational commentators raged. Widespread anger was voiced over the sheer waste of talent and the cost to the economy of failing to nurture so many of the nation's gifted children. The greatest criticism was directed at the schools responsible for their education. Most low-income children attend schools funded by the state and it was concluded that these institutions were badly failing bright pupils. The contrast in performance between state and private schools received renewed public scrutiny and was described as a first-class/second-class education system. This divide had been known about for many years, however, the new research portrayed it in a new and even worse light. For now on it had to be seen as not merely a divide between achievement in state and private education but as a divide between the achievement of children of similar standard.

In defense of the state schools some commentators pointed out the important contribution that home life makes to achievement. It was argued that a child needed parental encouragement and resources such as a quiet place to study, books and internet access if they were to realize their full potential and that many low-income families were unable to provide such an environment. Others pointed out the far higher level of funding enjoyed by private schools and the autonomy they enjoy with respect to key functions such as admissions and curriculum.

Example question

Q1. Which of the following statements best expresses the main theme of the passage?

A. The brightest children from poor homes are failing to get places in top universities.

B. Bright children in state schools are failing to get as good grades in national exams as children in independent schools.

C. The brightest children at state school are failing to get places in top universities.

D. Bright children from poor homes are failing to get the same grades as their rich counterparts.

Answer | D

Explanation: The main theme of the passage is the failure of bright children from low-income homes to achieve the same grades as bright children from high-income families. The passage is implying that children from both backgrounds are, in fact, equally bright.

Q2. Which of the following statements is offered in support of the main theme?

A. A significant majority of the bright children from low-income families failed to earn above the national average wage.

B. Most low-income children attend schools funded by the state and it was concluded that these institutions were badly failing bright pupils.

C. Almost all the able children from high-income families achieved three or more A grades in exams at the age of 18 years. But it was found that only one in four of the most able children from low-income families achieved similar grades.

D. Bright children from high-income families were themselves very likely to enjoy a high income in their working life.

Answer

Q3. Which of the following statements best captures the key point of the passage?

    A. Recent research has provided further evidence of the educational divide between the achievements of bright children from low- and high-income families.

    B. Research has provided stark evidence of the educational divide in the achievements of bright children from low- and high-income families.

    C. A stark divide exists between the educational achievements of children of similar standard from different backgrounds.

    D. Bright kids from low-income homes get far lower grades than bright kids from high-income homes.

Answer ☐

Q4. Which of the following statements best summarizes the primary objective of the passage?

    A. to report the findings and the reaction to the recent research

    B. to contrast the educational achievements of gifted students from rich and poor backgrounds

    C. to solve the problem of the disparity of grades achieved by rich and poor students

    D. to disseminate the findings of recent research

Answer ☐

Q5. Which of the following points is made in the passage?

    A. The findings led to the proposal of a raft of reforms.

    B. The divide in the educational achievement of rich and poor children was already known about.

    C. Extra funding was found for the state education sector.

    D. Many felt that higher funding could only be turned into higher standards of achievement if it went hand in hand with other reforms.

Answer ☐

Q6. The tone of the passage is:

    A. dogmatic

    B. anecdotal

    C. indignant   Answer ☐

    D. detached

    E. journalistic

Q7. In the context of the passage the word apartheid means:

    A. the system of segregation in force in South Africa between 1948–91
    B. discrimination on the grounds of educational achievement
    C. discrimination
    D. a system of discrimination on the grounds of race or background

Answer ☐

Q8. It can be inferred from the passage that:

    A. Most low-income children attend schools funded by the state.
    B. Higher funding and great autonomy for state schools would help close the achievement gap in education.
    C. A child needed parental encouragement and resources such as a quiet place to study to realize their educational potential.
    D. More bright children from rich families win places at top universities than bright children from poor families.

Answer ☐

Q9. Which of the following questions is answered in the passage?

    A. Would initiatives such as homework clubs and the imposition of quotas for the intake of students from state schools into top universities help address the inequality?
    B. Why does there exist a divide between the educational achievements of bright children from high- and low-income families?
    C. What did new research find in respect of the educational achievements of bright children from high- and low-income families?
    D. What can be done to address the inequality and reduce the cost to the economy of the failure to nurture so many of the nation's gifted children?

Answer ☐

Q10. Which of the following points is not made in the passage?

    A. Some commentators pointed out the important contribution that home life makes to achievement.
    B. Greatest criticism fell to the schools responsible for the education of low-income children.
    C. The status quo puts low-income, bright children at a considerable disadvantage.
    D. Most children from high-income families were very likely to enjoy a high income in their working life.

Answer ☐

Passage 2
(507 words)

It is obvious, if you think about it for a moment, that the quality of justice is dependent on where and when you live. In some parts of the world and at some points in history, justice is determined by the rule of the mob rather than the rule of law. But, even in the parts of the world where today we might assume the quality of justice to be high, a more careful look reveals significant variations.

If you were unfortunate enough to become the victim of a serious crime in a Western democratic country you might be of the view that you have a high chance of seeing justice to be done. But, the factors that determine the performance of a judicial system are complex and there are many points in the process where justice can be denied. First, the police must conduct a successful investigation and make an arrest. Then prosecutors must correctly interpret guidelines for pressing criminal charges and draw up a competent case to be presented in a court of law. In that court, the defense lawyer must be able to present the accused's defense.

Given the very complex nature of the judicial process, the quality of justice is not only dependent on the point of history and country in which you live but also where you live within that country. You may be the victim of a crime in a country that nationally enjoys a good judicial system, but the area where you were the victim of crime has an incompetent police force or prosecution service. The result may be that justice is not done, but had the crime occurred in another part of the country it may well have been.

Local variations in the quality of justice can be massive. Studies that compare case outcomes of a country by area have shown that for some crimes, the conviction rate can be 10 times higher in one part of a country than another. One study showed that this was true for even serious crimes including murder. In some areas, a 100 percent conviction rate for murder was realized, while in other parts of the same country the conviction rate was as low as 60 percent. Strangely, this was not found to be the case for offences relating to drugs. In relation to this charge, all areas of the country were found to achieve the same high conviction rate. This might be explained by the fact that most charges relate to the possession of illegal substances.

Perhaps it is inevitable that justice will be delivered in an unpredictable and inconsistent way. But in each case where the system fails, a victim is denied justice.

An unjust system can also mean false convictions and the imprisonment or punishment of the innocent. Should we judge a 100 percent conviction rate as a sign of a successful or failing judicial system? It is surely inevitable, desirable even, that some cases will be brought that fail at trial.

Example question

Q11.   Which of the following statements is validly inferred from the passage?

A. The quality of justice is not only dependent on the point of history and country in which you live but also where you live within that country.
B. The author would not want to live in a country where the national conviction rate was 100 percent.
C. Failing officials in the judicial system should be prosecuted.
D. Local variations in the quality of justice can be massive.

Answer | B |

Explanation: Answers A and D are explicitly stated in the passage and so are not inferred from the passage. Answer C is not stated or inferred.

Q12.   It is clear that the author does not agree that:

A. A 100 percent conviction rate is a sign of a failing judicial system.
B. There are many points in the process where justice can be denied.
C. Justice should depend on where you live.
D. The quality of justice is only dependent on the point of history and country in which you live.

Answer | |

Q13.   In the passage the point is made that:

A. The varying abilities of local police is one reason for the difference in justice.
B. Difference in conviction rates can be explained by the fact that some areas of a country are culturally and socially very different from others.
C. The lower the conviction rates, the more victims are denied justice.
D. The more convictions secured, the greater the justice.

Answer | |

Q14.   Which statement, if true, would most weaken the case made in the passage?

A. Guilty criminals are more likely to go free in some parts of a country than others.
B. The area of a country that comes bottom in a league table of conviction rates is inevitably found to be failing most to provide justice.
C. The reasons for differences in convictions rates in various parts of a country are complex.
D. Local variations in the quality of justice is minimal.

Answer | |

Q15.   To support the main point in the passage the author relies on:

   A.   a critique of an opposing view
   B.   the findings of experimental research   Answer ☐
   C.   a comparative survey of data
   D.   an in-depth knowledge of the complexities of legal systems generally

Q16.   Which of the following sentences would best follow on from the penultimate paragraph?

   A.   In a failing part of the country this can soon mean that hundreds of victims are being denied justice.
   B.   If consistent rates of convictions can be realized for drug-related offences, then it should be possible to realize such consistency across all types of serious crime.
   C.   This could soon result in the rule of the mob rather than the rule of law.
   D.   Regional disparity in conviction rates is evidence of a failed judicial system.

   Answer ☐

Q17.   Which of the following is given as a reason for the main point in the passage?

   A.   If you were unfortunate enough to become the victim of a serious crime in a Western democratic country you might be of the view that you have a high chance of seeing justice to be done.
   B.   You may be the victim of a crime in a country that nationally enjoys a good judicial system but the area where you were the victim of crime has an incompetent police force or prosecution service.
   C.   One study showed that this was true for even serious crimes including murder.
   D.   This might be explained by the fact that most charges relate to the possession of these illegal substances.

   Answer ☐

Q18.   Which of the following sentences would best follow on from the fourth paragraph?

   A.   And if you are found in possession then to deny your guilt is rather pointless.
   B.   And if you are found to be a drug dealer you are guilty of a serious crime.
   C.   And if you are found in possession of drugs you deserve punishment.
   D.   And if you are found under the influence of illegal substances then your guilt can be proved with a drug test.

   Answer ☐

Q19. Which of the following is not mentioned?

  A. mob rule
  B. guilty criminals
  C. arrest
  D. prosecution service

Answer ☐

Q20. Which of the following sentences would best follow on from the second paragraph?

  A. The differences mean that there is a new surge of cases doomed to fail.
  B. The same factors have produced striking anomalies that cannot be explained by the obvious differences between regions.
  C. Under a jury system the people deciding guilt or innocence must attempt to OR be able to OR are theoretically meant to be able to put aside their own views and prejudices and arrive at a fair decision on the basis of the evidence presented to them.
  D. The reasons are not easily understood and there is no easy way to obtain more convictions while ensuring the system remains a just one.

Answer ☐

Passage 3
(445 words)

The building of new nuclear power stations is a necessary step if global warming is to be held back. This is the view of an environmental scientist who has previously campaigned against the proliferation of nuclear power as a means to generate electricity. It is a viewpoint that is starting to win favor and convert other long-term opponents.

Nuclear power generation is being reconsidered because so many industrialized countries are failing to reduce the level of their carbon emissions through energy efficiencies or renewable power. Some advisors therefore feel that the industrialized world has no alternative but to return to nuclear power, at least until renewable alternatives become available. Nuclear power, which can generate electricity without emitting CO_2, is seen as a necessary evil that can help governments meet future and seemingly ever-increasing demand for more power without increasing the level of carbon emissions.

Proposals to look to nuclear power as a means to address global warming have not been welcomed by all environmental scientists and campaigners. Many argue that nuclear power is far from clean and at some stages of its life-cycle, for example when the uranium is mined and refined, is not carbon-free. They raise the well-known objections to nuclear power of waste storage, the risk of radioactive leaks, the threat of terrorism, the cost of decommissioning and the risk of the spread of nuclear weapons.

The public has also been willing to reconsider nuclear power in a way that would have seemed impossible only a few years ago. Part of the reason for this change of heart is that they now better understand renewable sources and they realize that these alternatives also bring unwelcome consequences. They are also increasingly unwilling to pay the personal price of what environmentalists mean by energy efficiencies. Sustained opposition to wind turbines has emerged. The public has become extremely reluctant to forego cherished features of modern life such as a family car in the name of energy efficiency.

The decision by some environmentalists to reconsider their stance towards nuclear power will certainly mean that the case for renewable energy is also re-examined. It is possible that this review will bring greater investment to these alternatives and speed up their development. The dilemma that nuclear power generation presents for environmentalists is that it is arguably the only technology currently capable of filling an emerging energy gap without contributing to climate change. If this is correct then the choice for environmentalists is a stark one. They must either reject the nuclear option now and risk further increases in greenhouse emissions or accept it's a far from perfect carbon-free contribution until better alternatives become available.

Example question

Q21. Which of the following points is made in support of the main theme of the passage?

A. Environmentalists now realize that renewable alternative sources also bring unwelcome consequences.

B. The fact that so many respected commentators have changed their mind on such a controversial issue is down to the search for ways to reduce carbon emissions and resolve climate change and global warming.

C. Nuclear power is far from clean and at some stages of its life-cycle, for example when the uranium is mined and refined, is not carbon-free.

D. So many industrialized countries are failing to reduce the level of their carbon emissions through energy efficiencies or renewable power.

Answer | D |

Explanation: The passage states this point in support for the theme that the industrialized world may have no alternative but to return to nuclear power.

Q22. Which of the following statements best expresses the main point made in the ultimate paragraph?

A. Most environmentalists are still strongly opposed to the view that nuclear power is necessary if global warming is to be stopped.
B. Environmentalists may have to accept either a temporary return to nuclear power or continuing increases in greenhouse emissions.
C. Environmentalists must accept that only nuclear power can prevent climate change.
D. In the short term, nuclear power is the only way that countries are to meet their targets for reducing carbon emissions.

Answer ☐

Q23. Which of the following statements best expresses the main theme of the passage?

A. Nuclear power generation is being reconsidered.
B. Many respected commentators have changed their mind on nuclear power.
C. The industrialized world may have no alternative but to return to nuclear power.
D. The building of new nuclear power stations is a necessary step if global warming is to be held back.

Answer ☐

Q24. Which of the following reasons are given in the passage for the public change of heart?

A   They accept the urgency of tackling global warming.
B. They raise the well-known objections to nuclear power of waste storage.
C. They now better understand renewable sources.
D. They must either reject the nuclear option now and risk further increases in greenhouse emissions or accept its far from perfect carbon-free contribution.

Answer ☐

Q25. Which of the following claims in the passage most divide the environmental lobby?

A. Uranium production is not carbon-free.
B. Nuclear power is renewable.   Answer ☐
C. Nuclear power can help to reduce greenhouse emissions.
D. The argument has divided the environmental lobby.

Q26. Which of the following statements, if true, would most weaken the case made in the passage?

  A. Long-term opponents are unconvinced by the carbon-free credentials of nuclear power.
  B. Viable renewable alternative sources of energy are available now.
  C. Nuclear power is not CO_2-free at some stages of its life-cycle.
  D. A renewed enthusiasm for nuclear power could ultimately lead to the spread of nuclear weapons.

Answer ☐

Q27. It can be inferred from the fourth paragraph of the passage that the public would not want to give up:

  A. the right to free speech
  B. subsidized public transport
  C. frequent air travel
  D. freedom of association

Answer ☐

Q28. Which of the following sentences could best follow on from the end of the third paragraph?

  A. All commentators accept that nuclear power has to be considered as a future option and many accept that a case exists for a temporary return to reliance on nuclear power.
  B. They argue that nuclear power has to be considered as a future option.
  C. They argue that the proliferation of nuclear power stations is not necessary if global warming is to be contained and that the public opposition to wind farms will reduce as the public's better understanding of the case for renewable sources of energy increases.
  D. They accept the urgency of tackling global warming but believe the answer lies not in nuclear power but greater efforts and investment in renewable sources such as wind, wave and tidal power and in more energy efficiency.

Answer ☐

Q29. In the context of the passage the term 'necessary evil' means:

  A. Nuclear power is harmful or likely to harm.
  B. Nuclear power is believed to cause harm.
  C. Nuclear power is undesirable but needed.
  D. Nuclear power is unavoidable but wicked.

Answer ☐

Q30. So many respected commentators have changed their mind on such a contro-versial issue because of:

    A. the urgent need to reduce carbon emissions and the absence of a viable alternative

    B. the need to reduce carbon emissions against a background of rising energy demand

    C. the failure of industrialized countries to reduce carbon emissions

    D. the public's unwillingness to make energy efficiencies

Answer ☐

Passage 4
(444 words)

Planning and then recording in a last will and testament how we would wish our assets and affairs to be dealt with on our death is something more of us should do. Normally in a will, a person details their preference for how they would like their funeral to be arranged, whether or not they wish to donate organs, details specific gifts for friends and relatives, makes charitable donations and, most importantly perhaps, specifies who they wish to look after any dependent children should both parents not survive.

Writing a will is something we all mean to do but it is something that only one in three of us have actually got around to doing. The thought of our own mortality is something few people find comfortable and this, along with the fact that many people believe they have nothing to leave, is probably the reason why so many of us have not yet made a will.

Even someone who feels they have few or no assets should write a will if they have dependent children or a preference in terms of how their funeral should be organized. In the case of someone with assets or someone lucky enough to have assets of a significant value, then a will becomes an important means to ensure the tax-efficient transfer of those assets. In such a case, professional advice can help ensure that assets are transferred without incurring the widely resented inheritance tax. In some cases, where there is no will, this lack of will means that the assets go to the state. This is more widespread than people imagine and every year the Treasury receives many tens of millions from estates where a will was not made and no relative found.

For the majority of us with straightforward affairs and modest assets, a 'do it yourself' will may suffice. These can be purchased online or at many bookshops or even supermarkets for a small sum and should ensure that your wishes are respected after your death.

Anyone unmarried who lives with a partner should definitely make a will if they would want that partner to inherit their estate. Unmarried partners are not recog-nized by law, and there are many instances when a death means the surviving partner receives nothing while an ex-husband or wife or blood relatives inherits.

If you are one of the many people these days with more complex affairs, for example, someone with dependent children from more than one marriage, then a will is essential and probably requires the services of a professional if it is to be drawn up in a way that ensures that it survives your death unchallenged.

Example question

Q31. Which of the following is a reason given for the main point of the second paragraph?

   A. People's reluctance to dwell on their own death.
   B. People find death a subject best avoided.
   C. People find lawyers uncomfortable company.
   D. People find the subject of mortality uncomfortable.

Answer A

Explanation: D and B are wrong because it is one's own mortality, not mortality in general that the passage states people find uncomfortable. Answer C is wrong, as lawyers are not mentioned in this paragraph.

Q32. The passage states that someone with no assets should write a will if:

   A. they have children
   B. they do not want the state to inherit
   C. they have dependent children   Answer
   D. they are unmarried and live with a partner

Q33. It can be inferred from the passage that someone with no assets should write a will if:

   A. they are uncomfortable with the thought of their own mortality
   B. they wish to make charitable donations
   C. they wish their funeral to be organized in a particular way
   D. they wish to donate organs

Answer

Q34. The passage states that anyone unmarried should make a will if:

   A. they live with someone and they have something to leave
   B. they live with a partner who is not recognized in law
   C. they live with a partner and want them to inherit their estate
   D. they want their blood relatives to inherit their estate

Answer

Q35. Which of the suggested answers is the most suitable follow-on sentence for the third paragraph?

    A. It is inconceivable that these people intended the state to inherit their estate and wrong that the state should benefit from people's oversight.

    B. It is conceivable that in some cases the deceased intended the state to be the benefactor.

    C. The deceased should have a say as to whom their estate goes.

    D. But in most cases surely people would have preferred to have determined to whom their estate goes.

                            Answer ☐

Q36. The primary motive of the passage is to:

    A. encourage more of us to prepare a will

    B. explain why people with dependent children need to write a will

    C. convince people with an estate that writing a last will and testament is worthwhile

    D. encourage more of us to prepare a do-it-yourself last will and testimony

                             Answer ☐

Q37. Which of the following topics are not touched upon in the passage?

    A. the cost of writing one

    B. how many people have one

    C. why someone with nothing might want to write one   Answer ☐

    D. how to make a charitable donation through one

Q38. Which of the following sentences correctly sums up the conclusion of the passage?

    A. Writing a will is something we all mean to do but it is something that only one in three of us has actually got around to doing.

    B. Planning and then recording in a last will and testament how we would wish our assets and affairs to be dealt with on our death is something more of us should do.

    C. Even someone who feels they have few or no assets should write a will if they have dependent children or a preference in terms of how their funeral should be organized.

    D. For the majority of us with straightforward affairs and modest assets a 'do-it-yourself' will may suffice.

                             Answer ☐

Q39. According to the author you should probably use the services of a professional to draw up a will if you:

    A. wish to donate organs or specify who you wish to look after dependent
children
    B. wish to leave your estate to a partner to whom you are not married
    C. have dependent children from more than one marriage
    D. have dependent children

Answer ▢

Q40. Which of the suggested answers would be the most suitable follow-on
sentence for the penultimate paragraph?

    A. This easily avoided situation can leave a grieving partner in great hardship.
    B. Otherwise a great deal of inheritance tax could be due.
    C. In these cases a great deal of expense can be incurred challenging the will
so that the partner can in fact inherit.
    D. In such a case professional advice can help ensure that assets are transferred.

Answer ▢

Passage 5
(285 words)

Official statistics produced by national statistical offices are treated with a deal of
cynicism by the general public in many countries. This skepticism is total and born
both from the belief that the figures are inaccurate and that they are subject to
political interference.

The vast majority of citizens do not have a sufficient grasp of statistics to tell
whether or not the figures produced by their government are correct or being used
correctly. This lack of numerical skills means that commentators can misinterpret
figures with impunity and take them to signify something else entirely. They do this
safe in the knowledge that they are very unlikely to be rumbled by the vast majority
of listeners. Governments, opposition parties and pressure groups are all guilty of
using statistics in widely misleading ways in order to support their particular take
on a policy. Governments use them to make the best possible case, while the opposition takes the least favorable interpretation. Pressure groups will only select the
figures that prove their point. The media is just as guilty. Bad news is always much
more newsworthy than good news and so we hear a constant stream of numerical
'facts' purporting to show that life is indeed grim. Debate all too often degenerates
into a dispute about the fact of the matter, making informed discussion and
consensus almost impossible. Because most people lack the skills to tell when
statistics are being used correctly and they witness the way in which the same
figures can be used in a debate to support entirely different conclusions, it is no

wonder they cast a world-weary eye on them all and that so many have become entirely disillusioned with both official statistics and politics.

Example question
Q41. People distrust statistics because:

A. They are unable to tell if they are being used correctly.
B. They do not have the necessary skills to tell if the statistics are being used correctly.
C. They believe the same figures can be used to support entirely different points of view.
D. They believe the figures are not correct and are politically manipulated.

Answer $\boxed{\text{D}}$

Explanation: This is the reason given in the first paragraph for people's distrust. Suggested answers B and C are given in the last paragraph as reasons why people become disillusioned.

Q42. According to the author what is the media just as guilty of?

A. producing inaccurate figures and making informed discussion almost impossible
B. using statistics in a misleading way
C. misinterpreting figures with impunity
D. subjecting statistical figures to political interference

Answer ☐

Q43. It can be inferred from the passage that:

A. No one can control how statistics are used in debate.
B. Eventually the truth will prevail.
C. People become disillusioned with official statistics.
D. Politicians using official statistics are the worst offenders.

Answer ☐

Q44. In the context of the passage 'cynicism' means:

A. The public are motivated by self-interest and are world-weary.
B. Politicians are motivated by self-interest irrespective of accepted standards.
C. Distrust.
D. Put to a self-interested end irrespective of accepted standards.

Answer ☐

Q45. In reaching his conclusion the author fails to consider:

A. the state of affairs in other countries
B. the role of the media
C. in the current climate whether or not consensus could ever be possible
D. what could be done about it

Answer ☐

Passage 6
(203 words)

To produce the official annual inflation rate each year, government statisticians monitor the price of a basket of 650 goods and services sold at a total of 120,000 outlets. To ensure that the rate is representative of consumer trends, the civil servants review the items included in the basket and delete items judged no longer popular and include items that are thought to better reflect new consumer tastes.

A major difficulty faced by the officials is how to balance the long-term divide between deflation in the price of goods, and inflation in the price of services. For over 10 years, there has been a dramatic undertone of inflation in the price of hi-tech goods, even while quality has improved. Services on the other hand, have experienced at times souring and resilient inflation. These two trends offset each other in the official inflation rate. For this reason, commentators look with interest at the items deleted or added to the basket of goods and services monitored. The inclusion of more goods that are likely to fall in price and the removal of some inflationary services could result in a lower official rate of inflation, a reduced rate of interest and, in turn, looser monetary policy.

Q46. Which of the following sentences best follows the final paragraph?

A. The inclusion of these goods raises the issue of how to adjust the rate of inflation to take into account improvements in quality.
B. Conversely, shopping trends that are deemed to include more inflationary services than deflationary goods could result in baskets of goods that give rise to a higher official rate, and tighter monetary policy and more expensive borrowing.
C. Equally, the inclusion of goods more likely to fall in price than those removed from the basket could result in lower inflation.
D. Conversely, the inclusion of goods more likely to increase in price than those removed from the basket could result in higher inflation.

Answer ☐

Q47. From which of the following actions can it be inferred that the most inflationary pressure will result?

    A. removing the cost of after-school clubs from the basket
    B. adding the price of flat screen TVs to the basket
    C. removing from the basket the price of a loaf of bread   Answer
    D. adding to the basket the price of banking services

Q48. In the context of the passage the author means by offset:

    A. co-occur
    B. invalidate
    C. nullify   Answer
    D. contract

Q49. Which of the following extracts from the passage is an oxymoron?

    A. a dramatic undertone
    B. pressure groups
    C. deemed to include   Answer
    D. a major difficulty

Q50. Which of the extracts from the passage contains a tautology?

    A. give rise to a higher official rate
    B. souring and resilient inflation
    C. result in a lower official rate of inflation, a reduced rate of interest
    D. the official annual inflation rate each year

    Answer

Passage 7
(225 words)

No one can control how statistics are used in debate and it would be undesirable to attempt such control. Imagine if some statistician were to be elevated to the position of judge in every debate and intervened to endorse or reject contesting interpretations put onto official figures. We can't insist that the general public go back to school and attend classes on statistical error and the meaning of data and how far it can be taken.

    Public trust in official data is at an all-time low. What can be done to improve the credence of official statistics? One suggestion is to make statistical offices entirely independent of government. Then it will be possible to argue that political interference in the production of the figures has not taken place. This at least might convince the general public that the figures are objective. To add to the sense of impartiality it would be important that the government did not receive the figures any earlier than other parties, nor should government have any say over what statistics are produced. An independent office might partially address the public distrust of the interpretation of statistics if it were able to provide alongside its publication an indication of what the figures signify and the limits to what can be inferred from them and what they can be taken to mean.

Q51. The author wants:

    A. the data produced by the state to be clearer
    B. the data produced by the state to be more accurate
    C. the state's data to be produced by independents   Answer
    D. the state's data to be produced by a single office

Q52. In reaching his conclusions the author fails to consider:

    A. independent quality audits of the state statistics
    B. educating the general public in the interpretation of data
    C. independent production of the state's statistics   Answer
    D. independent interpretation of the state's statistics

Q53. Which of the following findings of a survey, if true, would most weaken the case made by the author?

    A. A majority of people do not believe their government uses statistics honestly.
    B. Most people felt they could not tell if the figures produced by their government were accurate.
    C. Most people feel that official figures are impartial.
    D. Few people feel that their government's statistics are free of inaccuracy.

    Answer

Q54. Which of the following justifications for independence are not given in the passage?

    A. the public distrust of statistics
    B. the view that political interference in the production of the figures takes place
    C. the public distrust of the interpretation of statistics
    D. the accuracy of official statistics

    Answer

Q55. Which of the following would most logically follow on from the passage as the next sentence?

    A. Any government statements on the figures should be released before the publication of these interpretations.

    B. Government statements relating to the figures should be published after the release of these interpretations.

    C. Government approval for these interpretations could be obtained before their publication.

    D. Government approval for the interpretations should be obtained after their publication.

Answer ☐

Twenty mini-tests to help you get off to a flying start

This chapter comprises 100 questions organized as 20 practice starts for the GMAT® (10 quantitative and 10 verbal). It is far better to practice little and often when preparing for a test and most people can find 10 minutes without distraction to undertake one of these mini-tests.

You know the level of difficulty of your first question in a real GMAT® test (a question that 500+ candidates should get right), but you will not know what type or mix of question you will get at the start of your real GMAT®. Your quantitative sub-test may start with a geometry question, a question of algebra; the first question may be either a problem-solving question or a data sufficiency question. Your verbal sub-test may start with a sentence correction, reading comprehension or critical reasoning question.

The practice starts below are a mix of possible combinations of starts but they do not include all possible combinations, and in your real GMAT® you may face a combination that is not covered in this chapter. You may get a lucky break and your real GMAT® might start with the questions at which you excel. It is also just as possible that your real GMAT® starts with the questions that you find the most challenging.

Each of the following practice starts contains five multiple-choice questions. The first is of average difficulty and they become progressively harder. This is exactly what would happen in the real GMAT CAT®, assuming that you get each of the opening questions right! Use these questions to get down to some really serious score-improving practice and be sure of the very best start in your real GMAT®.

Set yourself the time limit of 10 minutes in which to complete each practice start. Read each question carefully, calculate your answer and then re-read the question again. Only when you are sure about your answer should you submit it and move onto the next question. Remember, in the real GMAT CAT® there is no going back. So adopt and practice this same no-going-back requirement here, then the practice will be more realistic and you will develop an effective GMAT® exam technique.

The real GMAT® is obviously administrated on a computer and to select an answer you must click on the appropriate box. This practice test is, of course, undertaken with paper and pen, so put a tick by the correct answer and before filling in the box, recheck your choice and move onto the next question. Do not be tempted to review your answers once you have moved to the next question.

Get the most out of this practice by setting yourself the personal challenge of trying to beat your last score each time you take one of these mini-tests. You will need to try very hard and take the challenge seriously if you are to succeed in beating your previous best score. That way you will create a realistic real test feel.

If you keep getting one sort of question wrong, then focus your practice on that type of question until you overcome the personal challenge it represents. Then return to these mini-tests. Keep practicing until you consistently get all five questions in these mini-tests right. Achieve this and you can take strength from the fact that you are likely to make a very good start in your real GMAT®. The only thing then left to do is to keep up that rate of success through to the end of the real test!

Answers and explanations to these 100 practice questions are to be found in Chapter 6. They are all multiple-choice questions. Do not use a calculator.

GMAT® mini-test 1: quantitative

Q1. How many women graduates will NOT set up their own business if half the total of 800 graduates are women and 15% of all graduates start their own business?

    A.   120
    B.   90
    C.   60   Answer
    D.   340
    E.   360

Q2. If $2x - 6y = 9$, then $3y - x$ is:

    A.   4.5
    B.   −4.5
    C.   9   Answer
    D.   3
    E.   Cannot be determined

Q3. What is the difference in the areas of the square set inside the circle and the circle (take π as 3.14)?

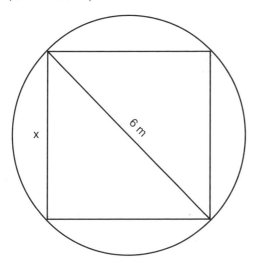

    A.   10 m²
    B.   28.26 m²
    C.   10.26 m²   Answer
    D.   18.26 m²
    E.   28 m²

Q4. Is x positive?

(1) $x^2 - 9 = 0$
(2) $x^3 - 27 = 0$

A.   1 alone, not 2 alone
B.   2 alone, not 1 alone
C.   1 and 2 together (need both)   Answer
D.   1 alone or 2 alone
E.   1 and 2 together are not sufficient

Q5. If $2x + 3y = 20$ and $6x + 2y = 46$ then y is:

A.   5
B.   7
C.   2   Answer
D.   9
E.   Cannot be determined

GMAT® mini-test 2: quantitative

Q1.

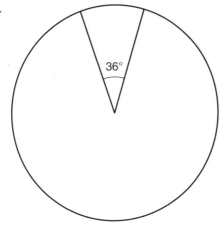

36°

If the circle has a radius of 5 cm and the point of the segment is at the center, what is the area of the segment (take π as 3.14)?

A. 78.5 cm²
B. 6.57 cm²
C. 7.85 cm²
D. 65.7 cm²
E. 2.5 cm²

Answer ☐

Q2. Which of the following inequalities is the solution to the inequality $2x + 1 > x + 2$?

A. $x > 0$
B. $x > 2$
C. $x > \frac{1}{2}$
D. $x > 1$
E. Cannot be determined

Answer ☐

Q3. If 85% of stock is sold, how much stock did we start with if 120 items remain?

A. 800
B. 680
C. 18
D. 120
E. 750

Answer ☐

Q4. Is n divisible by 2 with no remainder?

    (1) 2n is divisible by 4 with integer result
    (2) 4n is divisible by 2 with integer result

    A. 1 alone, not 2 alone
    B. 2 alone, not 1 alone
    C. 1 and 2 together (need both)   Answer
    D. 1 alone or 2 alone
    E. 1 and 2 together are not sufficient

Q5. If $x/2 + y/3 = x/3 + y/2$, then $x + y$ is:

    A. 2x 2y
    B. 0
    C. 6x   Answer
    D. 2x
    E. Cannot be determined

GMAT® mini-test 3: quantitative

Q1. Customers buy yellow, red and white cars in a ratio of 1:2:3. If, in total, 84 cars were sold, how many were red?

    A. 24
    B. 25
    C. 26   Answer ☐
    D. 27
    E. 28

Q2. If xy = 6, what percentage of x is 3x + y?

    A. 100/6
    B. 25
    C. 50   Answer ☐
    D. 200
    E. Cannot be determined

Q3.

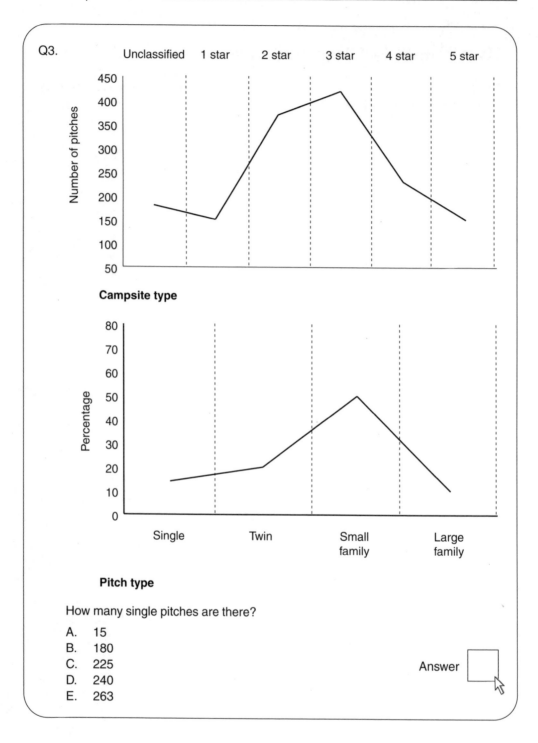

How many single pitches are there?

A.   15
B.   180
C.   225
D.   240
E.   263

Answer [ ]

Q4. If $x < 0$ and $y < 0$, then:

    A. $xy > 0$
    B. $xy < 0$
    C. $-x > y$ Answer
    D. $-x < y$
    E. $x < y$

Q5. Which of these two is the greater, x or y, if both are positive?

    (1) $(x/y) - 1 > 0$
    (2) $x/y < 1$

    A.   1 alone, not 2 alone
    B.   2 alone, not 1 alone
    C.   1 and 2 together (need both)   Answer
    D.   1 alone or 2 alone
    E.   1 and 2 together are not sufficient

GMAT® mini-test 4: quantitative

Q1. If each side of a square is increased by 30%, by how much does the area occupied by the square increase?

    A.   130%
    B.   98%
    C.   72%   Answer
    D.   70%
    E.   69%

Q2. If $x + y = 2$, $x - y = 98$, then x is:

    A.   50
    B.   100
    C.   98   Answer
    D.   2
    E.   102

Q3. A profit of $3,600 is to be divided by the ratio of how much each partner invested. How much does B get if A invested $5,000, B $4,500 and C $2,500?

    A. $1,500
    B. $750
    C. $1,350   Answer
    D. $2,250
    E. $1,200

Q4. A sequence of numbers a_1, a_2, a_3 etc. is generated using the following algorithm: $a_{n+1} = (a_n)^2 + 2$. Does the number 35 appear in the sequence if:

    (1)   0 appears in the sequence
    (2) $a_3 > a_2$

    A.   1 alone, not 2 alone
    B.   2 alone, not 1 alone
    C.   1 and 2 together (need both)   Answer
    D.   1 alone or 2 alone
    E.   1 and 2 together are not sufficient

Q5. The function *x returns the value of the highest integer smaller than x. What is *12.5 divided by *2.5?

    A.   4
    B.   5
    C.   6   Answer
    D.   10
    E.   5.5

GMAT® mini-test 5: quantitative

Q1. How many factors does the first number in a series of 3 consecutive numbers have, if that series has the sum of 57?

    A. 6
    B. 5
    C. 4   Answer ☐
    D. 3
    E. 2

Q2. What is the difference between the volumes of these shapes if they both have a radius of 3 cm (work to the nearest cm³ and treat π as 3.14)?

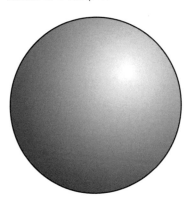

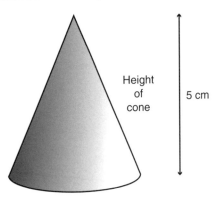

Height of cone   5 cm

Sphere   **Cone**

    A. 113 cm³
    B. 47 cm³
    C. 27 cm³   Answer ☐
    D. 84 cm³
    E. 66 cm³

Q3. If $x = y = z$ and $xyz = 216$, x is:

    A. 72
    B. 9
    C. 12   Answer ☐
    D 6
    E. 4

Q4. If $3a + b = 3$ and $b/a = 3$ what is $1/a + 3/b$?

    A. 1.5
    B. 4
    C. 3   Answer ☐
    D. 2.5
    E. 5

Q5. Is $x^2 > y^2$?

    (1) $x - y > 0$
    (2)   x is negative

    A.   1 alone, not 2 alone
    B.   2 alone, not 1 alone
    C.   1 and 2 together (need both)   Answer
    D.   1 alone or 2 alone
    E.   1 and 2 together are not sufficient

GMAT® mini-test 6: quantitative

Q1. What is the common factor that two numbers have if one of the numbers is 5 times the other and their sum is 30?

    A. 2
    B. 3
    C. 5   Answer
    D. 7
    E. 9

Q2. If the diameter of a circle is increased by 10%, by how much does the area of the circle increase?

    A. 5%
    B. 10.5%
    C. 14%   Answer
    D. 17.5%
    E. 21%

Q3. For which values of x is $x^2 - 4x + 4$ greater than 0?

    A. $2 < x$ and $x < 2$
    B. $x > 4$ and $x < 2$
    C. $2 < x < 4$ Answer
    D. $x > 2$
    E. $x > 1$

Q4. Is $x/8 > y/16$?

    (1) $x > y$
    (2) $2x > y$

    A. 1 alone, not 2 alone
    B. 2 alone, not 1 alone
    C. 1 and 2 together (need both)   Answer
    D. 1 alone or 2 alone
    E. 1 and 2 together are not sufficient

Q5. If $a - b = ¼$ and $a + b = -12$, then:

    A. $a = -12/4$
    B. $8a = -47$
    C. $8a = -38$ Answer
    D. $a = -6⅛$
    E. $a = -5.75$

GMAT® mini-test 7: quantitative

Q1.

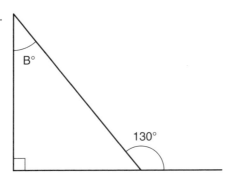

What is the value of angle B?

A.   40°
B.   50°
C.   60°   Answer
D.   70°
E.   80°

Q2. What is the probability of drawing two kings consecutively from a pack of 52 cards if there are 4 kings in the pack and the first card is replaced before the second is drawn?

A.   1/221
B.   1/104
C.   1/26   Answer
D.   1/169
E.   None of these

Q3. What is the value of xy?

(1) $x = y$
(2) $x/y = 1$

A.   1 alone, not 2 alone
B.   2 alone, not 1 alone
C.   1 and 2 together (need both)   Answer
D.   1 alone or 2 alone
E.   1 and 2 together are not sufficient

Q4. If $y - x < 0$, then:

A. $x > y$
B.   Both x and y are positive
C.   Only one of the two is negative   Answer
D. $x < y$
E.   None of the above

Q5. If $1/xy = 2/x + 1/2x$ and $x = 3$, then y is:

   A.   3/2
   B.   5/6
   C.   7/9
   D.   2/5
   E.   None of the above

Answer ☐

GMAT® mini-test 8: quantitative

Q1. If two ships leave port 1 hour apart and both sail at a constant speed of x on the same course, at what average speed must the second ship maintain if it is to catch the first ship after 2 hours?

    A.   3x
    B.   2.5x
    C.   2x   Answer
    D.   1.5x
    E.   1.25x

Q2. If you walk around a square that covers an area of 225 m², how far would you walk?

    A.   15 m
    B.   20 m
    C.   25 m   Answer
    D.   30 m
    E.   60 m

Q3. A man and a boy together dig 600 kg of earth in an hour (600 kg/hr) working independently but simultaneously. How long would the man take working alone?

    (1)   The man moves 200 kg/h more than the boy
    (2)   The boy works twice as long as the man

    A.   1 alone, not 2 alone
    B.   2 alone, not 1 alone
    C.   1 and 2 together (need both)   Answer
    D.   1 alone or 2 alone
    E.   1 and 2 together are not sufficient

Q4. If $3\pi + 3x = 21$ and $4y - 2x = -14$, then x is:

    A. $\pi/2$
    B. $-\pi/2$
    C.   7   Answer
    D. -2π
    E.   Cannot be determined

Q5. What is the value of x?

    (1) $x^3 = 8$
    (2) $x^2 + 2 = 6$

    A.   1 alone, not 2 alone
    B.   2 alone, not 1 alone
    C.   1 and 2 together (need both)   Answer
    D.   1 alone or 2 alone
    E.   1 and 2 together are not sufficient

GMAT® mini-test 9: quantitative

Q1. If you spent $30 on a book and a CD ROM and the CD ROM cost 50% more than the book, how much did the book cost?

    A. $12
    B. $13
    C. $17   Answer
    D. $18
    E. $19

Q2. What is the area of this isosceles triangle?

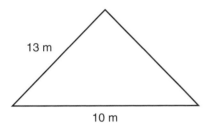

13 m

10 m

    A.   144 m²
    B.   66 m²
    C.   60 m²   Answer
    D.   12 m²
    E.   5 m²

Q3. A man, a woman and a girl take 5 hours to label 1,000 packages. How long would the woman take to label 100?

    (1)   The girl only works for the first $2\frac{1}{2}$ hours
    (2)   The man and the woman together label 400 in $2\frac{1}{2}$ hours

    A.   1 alone, not 2 alone
    B.   2 alone, not 1 alone
    C.   1 and 2 together (need both)   Answer
    D.   1 alone or 2 alone
    E.   1 and 2 together are not sufficient

Q4. Which of the following inequalities is the solution to the inequality $x/2 < x/3$?

    A. $x > 1/3$
    B. $x < 1/6$
    C. $x < -2/3$ Answer
    D. $x > -1$
    E. $x < 0$

Q5. Is x positive or negative?

    (1) $x^2 > 0$
    (2) $x^5 > x^4$

    A.   1 alone, not 2 alone
    B.   2 alone, not 1 alone
    C.   1 and 2 together (need both)   Answer
    D.   1 alone or 2 alone
    E.   1 and 2 together are not sufficient

GMAT® mini-test 10: quantitative

Q1. A girl wishes to spend as much of her $5 as possible on burger, fries or both burger and fries. Can she decide what to buy?

(1) 4 burgers would cost $4.20
(2) 8 portions of fries would cost $5.20

A. 1 alone, not 2 alone
B. 2 alone, not 1 alone
C. 1 and 2 together (need both)   Answer
D. 1 alone or 2 alone
E. 1 and 2 together are not sufficient

Q2. If you buy postage stamps for $1 each and you use $2/7$ of the stamps that you bought sending a package to your friends, what was the face value of stamps on the package if you have 15 stamps left?

A. $9
B. $8
C. $7   Answer
D. $6
E. $5

Q3. There are 200 students in one year divided into 10 groups. Is it possible to know the average score for all the year?

(1) The average score is known for each of the groups
(2) The group size is known for 9 of the groups

A. 1 alone, not 2 alone
B. 2 alone, not 1 alone
C. 1 and 2 together (need both)   Answer
D. 1 alone or 2 alone
E. 1 and 2 together are not sufficient

Q4. What is the probability of drawing the letters GM from a set of alphabetical cards (which comprises one card from each letter of the alphabet) if, once drawn, each card is not replaced?

A. 1/650
B. 1/676
C. 1/52   Answer
D. 1/51
E. None of these

Q5. If 3x + 3y = 2(x + y), then x + y is:

    A.   2/3

    B.   1

    C.   2x – 2y   Answer

    D.   0

    E.   Cannot be determined

GMAT® mini-test 11: verbal

Q1. <u>He didn't ride his bike since we lived here</u>.

    A.   He didn't ride his bike since we lived here.

    B.   He hasn't ridden his bike since we've lived here.

    C.   He hasn't rode his bike since we've lived here.   Answer

    D.   He has not rode his bike since we lived here.

    E.   He didn't ride his bike since we've lived here.

Passage

(231 words)

There is much talk of a hydrogen economy and one version of that future is described as based on dissociating water into hydrogen and oxygen with sunlight in photo-catalyst cells or films. If the rooftops of every house in the United States were covered in these cells, then every household would have at its disposal the hydrogen equivalent of over 10 liters of gasoline a day. The cells used would have to achieve the US Department of Energy's standard of 10 percent water-splitting efficiency before the investment would be worthwhile and the output would approach the 10 liter level. But this kind of efficiency has only been achieved under careful laboratory conditions using ultra-violet light. Sunlight comprises only 4 percent ultra-violet light and so the search is still on for a photo-catalyst that reaches the same level of efficiency using the whole sunlight spectrum.

Another technological approach to the dissociation of water relies on micro-organisms. Biologists have long known of the existence of single-celled plants that can break water molecules apart and release hydrogen and oxygen gas and the hope is that a micro-organism can be found capable of generating hydrogen gas in sufficient quantities. So far, the search has been disappointing and the levels of gas produced have fallen a long way short of the amount necessary to satisfy the US Department of Energy's standard of efficiency.

Q2. Which of the following sentences best expresses the general theme made in the passage?

    A.   The passage optimistically predicts that the hydrogen economy is just around the corner.

    B.   The passage is pessimistic regarding the likelihood of a hydrogen economy based on the dissociation of water.

    C.   The passage identifies a number of technological challenges that remain before a hydrogen economy is feasible.

    D.   The passage describes a number of challenges that must still be solved on the path to a hydrogen economy based on the dissociation of water.

    E.   The passage is downbeat regarding the prospects of finding an organic solution to the challenge of efficient dissociation of water.

    Answer

Q3. Which of the following subjects is not raised in the passage?

   A.   solar panels that split water for hydrogen
   B.   the dissociation of water with sunlight
   C.   hydrogen production using ultra-violet light   Answer ☐
   D.   photo-catalysts that generate hydrogen from water
   E.   bugs or organisms capable of generating hydrogen gas

Q4. Which of the following is the best description of the main conclusion of the passage?

   A.   deductive
   B.   inductive
   C.   presumptuous   Answer ☐
   D.   hypothetical
   E.   theoretical

Q5. <u>We has to get to some serious work in order to sort out the untidy office.</u>

   A.   We has to get to some serious work in order to sort out the untidy office.
   B.   We had to get down to a serious workout in order to sort out the untidy office.
   C.   We had to get to some serious work down in order to sort the untidy office.
   D.   We had to get down to some serious work in order to sort out the untidy office.
   E.   We had to get to some serious work in order to sort the untidy office out.

                                                              Answer ☐

GMAT® mini-test 12: verbal

Passage
(238 words)

It is natural to believe that the world's leading cities would be found to be in a constant state of change, evolving to accommodate new waves of immigrants, work/life balance, modes of transport and architectural style. With such a process of reinvention and renewal, and often sprawl, these places must become almost unrecognizable over long periods of time, say, for example, 100 years. However, when you get down to it and have a careful look at how these cities have changed over such a period, you are immediately struck not by the way they have changed but in the ways they haven't. In particular, most of the broad patterns of socio-economic class remain the same, as do many local socio-economic characteristics. Most of the poorest areas will still be found to be poor. The architectural style of slum may have changed; low-rise, multi-occupied hovels may well have been knocked down to be replaced with high-rise flats on sprawling heartless estates, but the social malaise caused by poverty and unemployment remains. A road that was notorious 100 years ago as a place frequented by drunks and members of the criminal class may well be found to suffer the same challenges. Only the language used to describe the nature of the problem will have changed and perhaps the problems will be attributed to drugs rather than alcohol and gangs of alienated youths rather than a criminal class.

Q1. Which of the suggested answers best expresses the key point of the passage?

    A.   The social geography of the world's leading cities changes over long periods less than you might expect.

    B.   In the last 100 years, the world's leading cities have changed beyond recognition architecturally, but socially they have hardly changed at all.

    C.   The world's leading cities are in a constant state of change, evolving to accommodate new waves of immigrants, work/life balance, modes of transport and architectural style.

    D.   When you get down to it and have a careful look at these cities you are struck not by the way they have changed, but in the ways they haven't.

    E.   The world's great cities are just that because they are in a constant state of flux.

Answer ☐

Q2. Which of the following statements would the author of the passage be most likely to disagree with?

A.   The architecture of the world's great cities is being constantly revamped.
B.   The language with which we describe the social geography of our great cities is constantly evolving.
C.   The social geography of our great cities is in a constant state of transformation.
D.   The social geography of our great cities appears invariable.
E.   Tomorrow's archeologists will find our architectural styles and modes of transport novel.

Answer [   ]

Q3. In the context of the passage, the word 'sprawl' means:

A.   spread out one's limbs
B.   disorganized expansion
C.   an ungainly movement
D.   an industrial area
E.   a mix of residential and industrial developments

Answer [   ]

Q4. The new compound was <u>comprise from</u> two very common elements.

A.   comprise from
B.   is comprised by
C.   comprised from
D.   was comprised in
E.   comprised of

Answer [   ]

Q5. He traveled all day first <u>by boat, then by plane, and finally, by foot</u>.

A.   by boat, then by plane, and finally, by foot.
B.   in boat, then in plane, and finally, by foot.
C.   on boat, then on plane, and finally, on foot.
D.   by boat, then by plane, and finally, on foot.
E.   in boat, then in plane, and finally, in foot.

Answer [   ]

GMAT® mini-test 13: verbal

Q1. When you first told me <u>he's considering to selling the business I did not believe you</u>.

- A.   he's considering to selling the business I did not believe you.
- B.   he's considering selling the business I did not believe you.
- C.   he's considering selling the business I'm not believing you.
- D.   he is considering selling the business I am believing you not.
- E.   he considers selling the business I did not believed you.

Answer [   ]

Passage
(207 words)

Countries are slowly realizing that there is no such thing as zero immigration and no such thing as a non-porous border. Until economic immigration was tightened in the 1970s most migrants went to their new home to work and brought with them valuable skills. Since then all efforts to protect jobs by stopping the inflow of people has succeeded only in changing the characteristic of the type of person arriving. The majority of migrants now comprise dependents of existing immigrants, political refugees and illegal immigrants. The proportion of skills held by these immigrant populations has consequently steadily fallen. Many of these people now face considerable hostility from their adopted country, most find themselves unable to compete for work and marginalized from the majority society, living in ghettos with little prospect of employment or integration. In response to these perceived problems, countries are starting to reintroduce skills-based immigration to encourage educated and skilful foreigners to emigrate and thereby bring benefits to the host country. At the same time, they are again cracking down on other immigrants and stepping up deportation. Another particularly contentious initiative is to restrict the entry of family members of existing immigrants unless the applicant can demonstrate sufficient income to support that family.

Q2. The primary objective of the passage is to:

- A.   make the case for a demand-led immigration policy
- B.   describe the move away from a policy of zero immigration
- C.   defend a policy that seeks to crack down on unskilled refugees
- D.   describe a shift towards selective immigration
- E.   air the views of right-wing bigots

Answer [   ]

Q3. Which of the following statements serves as a premise to the case made in the passage?

A.   Dependents of existing immigrants, political refugees and illegal immigrants have few useful skills.

B.   Zero immigration creates a system that lets in only those who have neither a job nor any useful skills.

C.   The described change in immigration policy is right wing.

D.   There is a sensible move towards a demand-led immigration policy.

E.   The dependents of existing immigrants and refugees have the same potential as anyone else in their host country.

Answer [   ]

Q4. The writer of the passage is describing:

A.   the findings of experimental research

B.   efforts to classify or define a subject

C.   the consequences of cause and effect

D.   attempts to solve a perceived problem

E.   attempts to solve a problem

Answer [   ]

Q5. <u>The rooms were full of bottles and each bottle was filled with water.</u>

A.   The rooms were full of bottles and each bottle was filled with water.

B.   The rooms were full of bottles and each was filled with water.

C.   The rooms were full with bottles and each bottle was filled with water.

D.   The rooms were full of bottles and each was full of water.

E.   The rooms were full of bottles and each was filled of water.

Answer [   ]

GMAT® mini-test 14: verbal

Passage
(230 words)

Bio-fuels, blended with ordinary fuel, are beginning to bring these green alternatives from obscurity. Brazil has, for many years, produced ethanol from sugar and used the high-octane alcohol as a substitute for gasoline. Vegetable oil derived from soya beans and rapeseed (called canola in the Americas) has been used to run tractors in many parts of the world. But these environmental alternatives to crude oil have until recently not been taken very seriously by the big consumer nations and their petro-corporations. But new laws requiring gasoline to contain 10 percent ethanol, and diesel to contain 6 percent vegetable oil by volume are changing all that. At the levels imposed, no new infrastructure is required in order to accommodate these changes as they can be dispensed at existing fuel stations and used to run existing cars, trucks and tractors. To go further, however, and, for example, run all cars exclusively on ethanol would require a new generation of engine and perhaps, more significantly, the scaling up of production of ethanol by a fantastic margin. A whole-scale switch to bio-diesel seems to carry fewer challenges. Its production is far less capital-intensive in the start-up phase. Most existing engines can burn the fuel or would be relatively easy to convert and farmers are very receptive to the idea of a new market (and better prices) for a product they already grow.

Q1. Which of the following sentences best expresses the key point made in the passage?

    A. As oil prices rise, policy-makers are turning to alternatives.
    B. New laws are beginning to lift bio-fuels from obscurity.
    C. Blending bio-fuels with traditional oil products is bringing them into prominence.
    D. Bio-fuels are about to take off.
    E. At the level imposed, no new infrastructure is required to accommodate the emergence of bio-fuels.

Answer ☐

Q2. Which of the following sentences would best conclude the passage?

A. Perhaps the greatest appeal of both bio-diesel and ethanol is the promise, for any country with the space to grow bio-fuel-producing crops, is independence from imported fuels and increased agricultural revenue.

B. Fear of global warming is partly driving this search for off-the-wall alternatives.

C. Skeptics argue that growing crops to produce ethanol will consume more gasoline than it will produce.

D. If bio-fuels do take off, environmentalists will raise as many concerns as they do currently.

E. Perhaps the greatest appeal of bio-fuels is the opportunity they represent for venture capitalists to break into the highly profitable but previously closed oil markets.

Answer

Q3. It can be inferred from the passage that:

A. Most cars could run on a fuel blend made of up to 85 percent ethanol.

B. Government policy is lifting bio-fuels from obscurity.

C. Demand for bio-fuels will soon outstrip supply.

D. Cars can handle a 10 percent ethanol blend.

E. Bio-fuels are not the only alternative to the current dependence on imported crude products.

Answer

Q4. According to the weather forecast <u>it can rain tomorrow</u>.

A. it can rain tomorrow.
B. it couldn't rain tomorrow.
C. it is able to rain tomorrow.
D. it could rain tomorrow.
E. it could hardly rain tomorrow.

Answer

Q5. <u>She persisted in her endeavor to win and insisted in</u> the very highest standards from the whole team.

A. She persisted in her endeavor to win and insisted in
B. She persisted in her endeavor to win and insisted on
C. She persisted with her endeavor to win and insisted in
D. She persisted to endeavor to win and insisted on
E. She persisted on her endeavor to win and insisted on

Answer

GMAT® mini-test 15: verbal

Q1. That man sitting <u>at the table, is he a relation of yours</u>?

    A.   at the table, is he a relation of yours?
    B.   at the table, is he a relation of you?
    C.   on the table, is he a relation of yours?   Answer
    D.   at the table, is he related of you?
    E.   at the table, is he related with you?

Passage

(259 words)

In some parts of Europe there is a tradition for families to send their children to a school where they board (have accommodation and only return home during the school holidays). This tradition has always been the preserve of the rich, as the fees for a place at boarding schools are very high. Today, most boarders are the children of rich families living overseas. Wealthy domestic families have, to a large extent, been put off by a number of high-profile cases of drug misuse and bullying within the boarding sector.

Perhaps surprisingly, the second largest group of boarders in this day and age are children who are in the care of the state. A number of charities pay the fees for these vulnerable children so that they may have the considerable benefit of small class sizes, strong discipline and high expectations promised by these schools. This kind of intervention most certainly seems to work. Only a relative handful of 16-year-old children in state care achieve good grades in their national exams, while over 50 percent of the hundreds of children in state care who are funded by these charities to attend boarding school achieve such grades. The case against this kind of intervention is expressed in terms of the potential harm that may result from taking very vulnerable children away from the few vestiges of family contact that may exist, as it is more difficult for families to see these children when they are at boarding schools as opposed to normal state care.

Q2. Which of the following statements best sums up the primary objective of the passage?

    A.   to demonstrate to the reader that children in state care would do better at boarding school
    B.   to investigate the question of whether or not children in state care would do better at boarding school
    C.   to prove the case that children in state care could be exposed to further harm if they were sent to boarding school
    D.   to inform the reader of the changing character of the children attending boarding school
    E.   to investigate whether or not boarding schools are a good thing

                        Answer

Q3. In the passage the author does not consider:

    A.   that the reader may not know what a boarding school is

    B.   how the low expectation of children in state care might be countered

    C.   what to do with the children in state care during the school holidays

    D.   why boarding schools have lost their appeal to the domestic rich

    E.   how children in state school who do not go to a boarding school do in state exams

Answer ☐

Q4. The author relies on which of the following assumptions?

    A.   that children in care will be happier at boarding school

    B.   that charities are willing to pay the fees for children in care to go to such schools

    C.   that schools qualify for tax breaks if they accept children in state care

    D.   that better exam results are evidence of children in care doing better in boarding schools

    E.   that there are substantial reasons for not sending children in state care to boarding school

Answer ☐

Q5. He heard a noise was from downstairs and he called out to see if there is anybody there?

    A.   He heard a noise was from downstairs and he called out to see if there is anybody there?

    B.   He heard there was a noise from downstairs and he called out 'Whose there?'

    C.   He heard a noise was from downstairs and he called out 'Is anybody there?'

    D.   There was a noise from downstairs and he called out is anybody from there?

    E.   He heard a noise from downstairs and he called out 'Is anyone there?'

Answer ☐

GMAT® mini-test 16: verbal

Q1. He was surprised for the fact that the first song was so similar to the second.

    A.   He was surprised for the fact that the first song was so similar to
    B.   He was surprised by the fact that the first song was so similar with
    C.   He was surprised for the fact that the first song was so similar with
    D.   He was surprised by the fact that the first song was so similar to
    E.   He was surprised at the fact that the first song was so similar with

Answer ☐

Q2. The poem was translated into five languages and in every case printed in red ink.

    A.   translated into five languages and in every case printed in
    B.   translated to five languages and in every case printed in
    C.   translated into five languages and in every case printed with
    D.   translated in five languages and in every case printed with
    E.   translated to five languages and in every case printed with

Answer ☐

Passage
(243 words)

The consequences that follow from the theft of valuable data cannot be over-estimated. Financial loss from fraud is perhaps the most obvious, but equally damaging can be the consequent loss of customer confidence. It is no wonder that information security has become a top business priority. Most people perceive the threat to be an external one, and most security products highlight the threat as originating externally, from the internet, viruses and spyware. But the threat is just as likely to come from within an organization. The criminal or malicious employee is in the perfect position to know what information is of most value and they are very well-placed to steal it. If that data includes customer credit card details or employee and personnel information, then there are criminal gangs willing to pay a great deal of money for it.

The security headache increases greatly when the widespread practice of mobile working is taken into consideration. Increasingly, staff work from a variety of locations, including home, and bring laptops to and from the corporate network. While away, the device can be connected to any number of insecure and unsafe systems and become compromised. The security risk arises on its return and reconnection to the corporate network. Employees on the move further add to the risk of data theft when, as inevitably happens, a laptop is left on a train or stolen along with all the sensitive data contained within it.

Q3. Which of the following statements best expresses the general theme of the passage?

A.   There are many information security issues facing organizations.

B.   There is no such thing as a secure network and the internal threat is potentially greatest.

C.   The theft of sensitive data can cause a loss of confidence as well as a financial loss.

D.   Information security has become a top priority for businesses.

E.   Organizations face unprecedented challenges to the security of their commercial data.

Answer ☐

Q4. Which of the following is not mentioned in the passage?

A.   laptops

B.   hackers

C.   Internet   Answer ☐

D.   viruses

E.   mobile working

Q5. Which of the following facts can best be inferred from the passage?

A.   The criminals are becoming more determined.

B.   The criminal employee is in the perfect position to know what information is of most value.

C.   Many companies are switching to systems that use encryption.

D.   Information theft by insiders is as common as theft from external threats.

E.   Loss of customer confidence is potentially as damaging as financial loss through fraud.

Answer ☐

GMAT® mini-test 17: verbal

Q1. Are you <u>satisfied of or shame about</u> the results of the investigation?

    A.   satisfied of or shame about
    B.   satisfaction of or ashamed of
    C.   satisfied for or ashamed in   Answer
    D.   satisfaction with or ashamed with
    E.   satisfied with or ashamed of

Passage
(197 words)

The author of *The Affluent Society* argued throughout his long and distinguished career for a better balance in advanced capitalist societies between private affluence and the evident public poverty. By public poverty he meant the impoverished disenfranchised citizens, but also the poor infrastructure such as inadequate roads, state school provision and the lack of state intervention to preserve the environment against the excesses of industry. The affluent society was to be achieved through measures (more active government, welfare programs, state planning and most controversially, the redistribution of wealth through taxation), which were very much out of favor during the brief period when monetarism dominated both politics and economics. Of course, Galbraith had been making the case for these policies long before monetarism and he continued to do so long after its demise; a demise that he most certainly hastened with his profound yet witty criticism of that ideology. For a European it is hard to understand why he did not embrace socialism, but he always advocated the mixed economy. Politically and as an adopted American he was a Democrat. Intellectually he was a lifelong disciple of Keynes and greatly influenced by the post-war American New Deal.

Q2. Which of the following statements best expresses the primary objective of the passage?

    A.   to expound Keynesian economics
    B.   to highlight the period of monetarism as brief and controversial
    C.   to put forward the theories of Galbraith
    D.   to set forth the case for greater state intervention and curtail the excesses of capitalism
    E.   to present the theories found in the classic title *The Affluent Society*

Answer

Q3. Which of the following statements can best be inferred from the passage?

    A.   Mr Galbraith was acclaimed for the way he made complex economic theory accessible to the person in the street.

    B.   Tax cuts should be opposed if the air is polluted.

    C.   The perfect society would be one where the rich accepted high rates of taxation.

    D.   Economic life is a bipolar phenomenon.

    E.   The benefits of tax cuts trickle down through the whole of society.

Answer ☐

Q4. Which of the following statements, if true, would add most to the main point of the passage?

    A.   Galbraith was disappointed with the collapse of communism.

    B.   Most people are content to accept public squalor and private affluence.

    C.   Galbraith met J.M. Keynes.

    D.   It is claimed that his fame was fading in the 1970s until he wrote his critique of the monetarist, Milton Freedman.

    E.   Galbraith was delighted by the collapse of communism.

Answer ☐

Q5. If price rises continue the Central Bank <u>will raise interest rates</u> in an attempt to stabilize the markets.

    A.   will raise interest rates

    B.   used to raise interest rates

    C.   would raise interest rates   Answer ☐

    D.   won't raise interest rates

    E.   wouldn't raise interest rates

GMAT® mini-test 18: verbal

Passage
(201 words)

There are plenty of careers that do not need a university degree. In law enforcement, administration, catering, retail, construction and transport, there are many highly paid careers to be had without the requirement of going to university. Take airline pilots, for example. No degree is necessary for this job and most are on salaries of over $100K. Anyone can achieve qualifications equally valued by employers through night school or college for a fraction of the cost of a degree. Many employers are complaining that they cannot find enough candidates of sufficient quality when they run graduate recruitment campaigns. So many graduates these days are simply not leaving university with the basic skills needed by employers. Poor spelling and grammar and weak mathematical ability means many graduate candidates cannot be left unsupervised without the risk of basic mistakes being made or e-mails or memos being sent out with crass errors. Employers complain that graduates lack experience of the world of work. Above all else, employers are looking for committed and conscientious staff with common sense and the hunger to succeed, and unfortunately universities do not teach these either. So why go to university?

Q1. Which of the following statements best sums up the general theme made in the passage?

   A.   You do not need a degree in order to get a good job.
   B.   A degree is no longer the route to a good job.
   C.   What is taught at university is not particularly relevant to employers.
   D.   There are many ways to get a top job without a degree.
   E.   A degree is no longer the guaranteed route into a good job that it used to be.

   Answer ☐

Q2. Which of the following statements, if true, would most weaken the case made in the passage?

   A.   Twenty percent of employers are dissatisfied with the communication skills of graduates.
   B.   Apart from the few more intellectually demanding jobs, a degree has little significance to your chances of getting a job.
   C.   Eighty percent of jobs by 2010 will need a degree.
   D.   One-third of employers complain that they cannot fill all their graduate positions.
   E.   Eighty percent of graduates by 2010 will be out of work.

   Answer ☐

Q3. Which of the following would be the most suitable sentence to follow on from the passage?

    A.   I am not sure of the significance of a degree to the world of work.

    B.   Many young people drift into university because they do not know what else to do.

    C.   The number of graduates is increasing at a faster rate than the number of graduate jobs.

    D.   It might well turn out to be the best three or four years of your life but it will probably not be the sure-fire route to a great job that it used to be.

    E.   When so many are leaving without a job.

Answer ☐

Q4. Historically, an increase in the level of production <u>virtually always leads to a reduction</u> in unit cost.

    A.   virtually always leads to a reduction

    B.   are going to lead to a reduction

    C.   would lead to a reduction   Answer ☐

    D.   mustn't lead to a reduction

    E.   may lead to a reduction

Q5. He left his speech on the plane and so was <u>unable of giving his presentation; all the same he insisted to go</u> to the conference.

    A.   unable of giving his presentation; all the same he insisted to go

    B.   unable to giving his presentation; all the same he insisted on go

    C.   unable of giving his presentation; all the same he insisted on going

    D.   unable to give his presentation; all the same he insisted on going

    E.   unable to give his presentation; all the same he insisted to going

Answer ☐

GMAT® mini-test 19 – verbal

Q1. He was <u>fond to swim but preferred to swim</u> in the sea.

  A. fond to swim but preferred to swim
  B. fond of swimming but preferred to swim
  C. fond of swimming but preferred of swim
  D. fond to swim but preferred of swimming
  E. fond to swimming but preferred to swimming

Answer

Q2. <u>There aren't</u> no formal objections, the resolution was adopted by the committee.

  A. There aren't
  B. There weren't
  C. There be
  D. There is
  E. There being

Answer

Passage
(221 words)

Perhaps they are the human equivalent of an endangered species. They certainly are the victims of the same encroachment on their land that causes the extinction of many animal species. The last few communities of nomadic people in Asia, Africa and South America have no effective means of defending their traditions and livelihood. Loggers are perhaps the cause of greatest conflict. They illegally enter the lands of these nomadic people, destroy their forests and woods, and hunt their animals. Ranchers may follow, to burn great tracts to clear it for their domesticated animals. Once the land is deprived of trees and plants and the seasonal rains begin, the depleted soil is washed down into the rivers and permanent environmental damage can follow. The loggers and ranchers move on further into the virgin habitat, displacing more nomadic people.

   These are ancient habitats. They have existed for millions of years. But in less than 50 years they, along with the traditional way of hunting and gathering practiced by the peoples of these lands, have all but been lost. Worldwide, only a few thousand people are estimated to still live a truly nomadic life. Most have been forced to abandon their traditional lifestyle practiced for millennia and have had to settle down in villages to a life of hunting combined with subsistence farming.

Q3. Which of the following statements is offered to support the main theme of the passage?

   A.   Loggers and ranchers are destroying the habitat of the world's few remaining nomadic people.
   B.   Worldwide, only a few thousand people remain who lead a nomadic life.
   C.   They are the victims of the same encroachment on their lands that causes the extinction of many animal species.
   D.   Nomadic people take on loggers and ranchers to defend their threatened way of life.
   E.   Perhaps they are the human equivalent of an endangered species.

                                                              Answer [ ]

Q4. The author does which of the following to make his point?

   A.   corrects a misconception
   B.   relies on authority
   C.   uses an analogy   Answer [ ]
   D.   gives examples
   E.   pulls at our heart strings

Q5. The tone of the passage is:

   A.   fatalistic
   B.   sceptical
   C.   cynical   Answer [ ]
   D.   defeatist
   E.   buoyant

GMAT® mini-test 20: verbal

Passage
(279 words)

The printed word, the radio and the television used to be the only sources of information available to a mass audience. Journalists and radio and television presenters were household names. They decided what we saw and heard and their opinions carried great authority. But people no longer passively consume media content. And they are beginning to value their own opinion and offer it alongside that of the supposed experts and authorities. They post online ratings for the restaurants they visit, they share their homemade podcasts and videologs, they contribute entries to collaborative sites offering advice or answers to questions posed on every imaginable subject. They are quickly realizing that the experts and authorities have feet of clay and that all too often a rank amateur offers a more profound contribution to the debate. It is the beginning of an expressive revolution that has only recently become possible and will embrace most people in the future.

Not every review or entry on the internet is correct and sure, some are bizarre. But the same has always been true of the content of our daily newspapers or favorite radio programs. Audiences are receptive to many more versions of truth and are becoming adept editors, deciding for themselves what is worthwhile and credible. The revolution is creating considerable pessimism among the employees of the traditional media corporations as they realize the extent to which the business model they have become accustomed to is threatened. They can barely believe that users might put as much, or more onto the network as they download. They had seen the internet as simply another outlet for their products. How wrong they turned out to be.

Q1. Which of the following statements best expresses the key point made in the passage?

A.   The ongoing media revolution means that to succeed, a media company must let consumers share and configure content.

B.   The newspaper, radio and television journalists and presenters did not deserve the unquestioning trust that we used to place in them.

C.   The era of mass media is giving way to one of personal and participatory media.

D.   The media moguls of yesterday failed to understand what the internet meant for their business.

E.   The internet is liberating audiences from the authoritarian constraints previously imposed by the media moguls.

Answer

Q2. Which of the following statements would the author of the passage most likely agree with?

   A.   People like the certainty provided by a figure from above telling them what's important.
   B.   People are learning to prefer a conversation to a sermon.
   C.   People will become less aware of differing arguments as they become heavier internet users.
   D.   The new media will erode our grammar, our attention spans and dumb down our cognitive abilities.
   E.   Sales of the printed word may be flat or decreasing but there will always be room in our lives for books.

Answer ☐

Q3. Which of the following statements, if true, would most weaken the case made in the passage?

   A.   Future successful media business models will be based on user-created content.
   B.   The future of all successful media business models will be based on a mix of professional and user-generated content.
   C.   The most successful media company of the future will not produce what, traditionally, media companies have always produced, namely, content.
   D.   At some point in the future people may well decide they have had enough of the new media and return to outlets that allow them to listen or watch passively.
   E.   The most successful media company of the future will produce what, traditionally, media companies have always produced, namely, content.

Answer ☐

Q4. A university wrote to the successful business woman offering her an honorary degree.

   A.   A university wrote to the successful business woman offering her an honorary degree.
   B.   An university wrote to the successful business woman offering her an honorary degree.
   C.   A university wrote to the successful business woman offering her a honorary degree.
   D.   An university wrote to the successful business woman offering her a honorary degree.
   E.   In the case of honorary both 'a' and 'an' are correct.

Answer ☐

Q5. The analyst monitored the economy with a set of financial indictors in order <u>to</u>
<u>forecast future exchange rates</u>.

A. to forecast future exchange rates.
B. to forecast a future exchange rates.
C. to forecast the future exchange rate.
D. A and B
E. A and C

Answer

Six timed practice sub-tests

This chapter comprises 234 practice questions organized as three timed quantitative tests and three timed verbal tests; in total, six full-length practice sub-tests. As in the real GMAT®, each quantitative test contain 37 multiple-choice questions and should be completed in 75 minutes. The verbal tests contain 41 questions and should also be completed in 75 minutes.

These timed tests are intended only as practice timed tests, so do not read too much into the results. Use them only as a part of your program of self-study and they will help you develop an effective GMAT® exam technique under realistic conditions and help further identify your strengths and address any weaknesses.

Obviously, these timed tests are not computer adaptive so the levels of difficulty of the questions are not tailored to your particular performance. I have structured the tests so that they serve primarily as an aid to learning and include a good number of questions at the level you might experience if you were to obtain a good, balanced GMAT® score. What I mean by good is a score in the top 25 percent of candidates and so over 600. Setting the level of these timed tests is not a fine science and while they may be appropriate for one candidate I will not have got it right for others. You will find some fiendishly hard questions to help you get used to the idea that you will not get them all right and should not spend too long on any one question.

In keeping with the emphasis of this book you will find many algebraic questions and reading comprehension and critical reasoning questions, so that you can practice at improving your performance in these typically problematic types of question under timed test conditions. It is important you realize, however, that this intentional bias may mean that the tests include a few too many examples of these questions and perhaps too few of the other types. Remember that in a real GMAT®, each question determines the level of the subsequent questions, so double check your answer before you move on to the next question.

To get the most out of these timed tests, take the first one, carefully time yourself, and then grade it. Go over any questions you got wrong and use other GMAT® prep books and educational material to revise the mathematical or verbal principals that you got wrong. Now really try hard to master the gaps in your knowledge, be prepared to spend a whole week, for example, coming to terms with a type of question you have constantly got wrong. Only when you feel you have moved significantly forward in your understanding should you take the next timed test. Then you should find that you get a better score and make fewer errors. Grade this second test and again spend time, if necessary, weeks, addressing any competencies that you have not yet mastered. Finally, take the third test. Set out to prove to yourself that you have improved by working really hard through it. Again, try to beat your best score and if you succeed be justly proud of your achievement.

For the full-on GMAT® experience take a quantitative test followed by a five-minute break and then take a verbal test. This will help you to develop the very high level of stamina and concentration expected of you during a real GMAT CAT®.

A final point to consider is that working very fast is not the most critical factor behind a good GMAT® score, as you have 75 minutes to attempt the questions in each sub-test. However, concentrating and working very hard during the test are critical to a good score, as is a never-give-up approach. So, try your hardest to make every question count in these practice timed tests. It will be an approach that will serve you well in your real GMAT®.

I have not bothered to repeat the instructions for each of the test types, as by now you really should be entirely familiar with the question types and what you have to do, and you can find this information elsewhere in the book.

Sub-test 1: quantitative

To indicate your answer, put a tick alongside the suggested answer of your choice and when you have re-read and checked your answer, fill in the box, then move on to the next question. There is no going back in the real GMAT CAT®, so when you have moved on to the next question, do not be tempted to go back and change your answer as you will not be able to do that in the real test. If you cannot get to the solution of a question then it is worth guessing, but only as a last resort. Remember that to do well in a test you really have to try very hard!

You are allowed 75 minutes in which to attempt the 37 questions that make up this test. Work where you will not be interrupted and complete the test in one continuous period. Do not use a calculator. Do not turn the page until you are really ready to begin.

Sub-test 1

Q1. Are angles A equal?

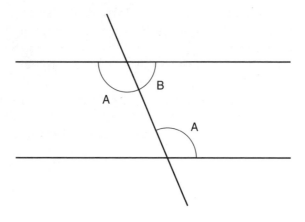

(1)   The horizontal lines are parallel
(2) $A + B = 180°$

A.   1 alone, not 2 alone
B.   2 alone, not 1 alone
C.   1 and 2 together (need both)   Answer
D.   1 alone or 2 alone
E.   1 and 2 together are not sufficient

Q2. What is the probability of getting an odd number if you throw a 6-sided dice?

A.   5/6
B.   2/3
C.   1/3   Answer
D.   1/2
E.   1/6

Q3. A man and a boy together dig 600 kg of earth in an hour (600 kg/hr) working independently but simultaneously. How long would the man take working alone?

(1)   The man moves twice as much earth as the boy
(2)   The boy works 3 hours by himself

A.   1 alone, not 2 alone
B.   2 alone, not 1 alone
C.   1 and 2 together (need both)   Answer
D.   1 alone or 2 alone
E.   1 and 2 together are not sufficient

Q4. What percentage of numbers between 1 and 50 end in either 2 or 8?

    A.   4%
    B.   8%
    C.   10%   Answer
    D.   15%
    E.   20%

Q5. If $2x + 3y = 20$ and $2x + 3z = 20$, then x is:

    A.   4
    B.   5
    C.   2   Answer
    D.   3
    E.   Cannot be determined

Q6. If a man runs 4 miles per hour (mph) for 3 hours but tires and so continues by walking at 2.5 mph, how long will it take him to cover 27 miles?

    A.   7 hours 45 minutes
    B.   8 hours
    C.   9 hours   Answer
    D.   9 hours 15 minutes
    E.   9 hours and 45 minutes

Q7. Which of the following inequalities is the solution to the inequality $3x + 3 < x + 1$?

    A. $x < 0$
    B. $x > 2$
    C. $x < -2$ Answer
    D. $x < -1$
    E.   No solution exists

Q8. Is y negative?

    (1)   x is less than or equal to 0
    (2)   y is less than or equal to x

    A.   1 alone, not 2 alone
    B.   2 alone, not 1 alone
    C.   1 and 2 together (need both)   Answer
    D.   1 alone or 2 alone
    E.   1 and 2 together are not sufficient

Q9. Which of the following inequalities is the solution to the inequality $x + 3 > x + 2$?

    A. $x > 0$
    B. $x < 0$
    C. $x < -\text{infinity}$ Answer
    D. $x > -\text{infinity}$
    E.   Cannot be determined

Q10. What is one month's percentage price change for food?

	18 Apr	9 May	One Month	One Year
Food	127.7	182.4	?	+30.3
All items	172.3	176.1	+3.8	+8.1
Industrials	150.0	169.5	+13.0	+58.9

Commodity Price Index % change

A.   +54.7%
B.   +32.8%
C.   +42.8%   Answer
D.   +18.3%
E.   Cannot be determined

Q11. Is n divisible by 4 with no remainder?

(1) n^2 is divisible by 4 with integer result
(2) $n^2 + 4n$ is divisible by 16 with integer result

A.   1 alone, not 2 alone
B.   2 alone, not 1 alone
C.   1 and 2 together (need both)   Answer
D.   1 alone or 2 alone
E.   1 and 2 together are not sufficient

Q12. How much greater is the volume of the largest of these shapes (work to the nearest full cm³ and treat π as 3.14)?

Radius 3 cm

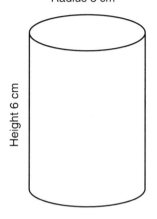

Height 6 cm

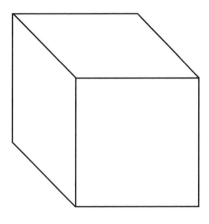

All sides 6 cm

A. 110 cm³
B. 43 cm³
C. 46 cm³   Answer
D. 105 cm³
E. 216 cm³

Q13. If $x + y = x - y$, then $x - 2y$ is:

A. 1
B. 0
C. x   Answer
D. 4
E. Cannot be determined

Q14. What is the sum of all the numbers from 50 through to 70?

A. 1,060
B. 1,100
C. 1,200   Answer
D. 1,260
E. 1,300

Q15. A girl wishing to spend as much of her $5 as possible, i.e., reduce the amount of change, in a shop where she can buy burgers, fries or both. Can she decide what to buy?

(1)   She would get the same change from buying 4 burgers as she would from buying 6 portions of fries

(2)   The burgers are 50% more expensive than the fries

A.   1 alone, not 2 alone
B.   2 alone, not 1 alone
C.   1 and 2 together (need both)   Answer
D.   1 alone or 2 alone
E.   1 and 2 together are not sufficient

Q16. Calculate for day 3 the sales of yellow cloth as a percentage of all sales for that day.

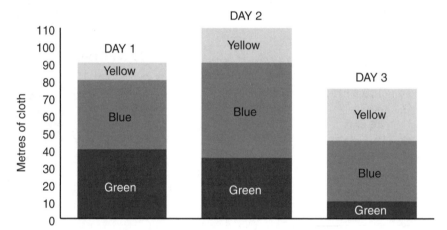

A.   40%
B.   35%
C.   30%   Answer
D.   25%
E.   Cannot be determined

Q17. If x/y = −10, what percentage of x is x − 10y?

A.   10%
B.   200%
C.   50%   Answer
D.   100%
E.   Cannot be determined

Q18. Is x positive or negative?

    (1) $xy > 0$

    (2) $y < 0$

    A.   1 alone, not 2 alone

    B.   2 alone, not 1 alone

    C.   1 and 2 together (need both)   Answer

    D.   1 alone or 2 alone

    E.   1 and 2 together are not sufficient

Q19. If $x/(y + 2) = 3$, $x/(y + 4) = 2$, then $x + y$ is:

    A.   12

    B.   14

    C.   40   Answer

    D.   24

    E.   16

Q20. If two 6-sided dice are thrown, what is the probability that the sum of the faces equals 3?

    A.   1/6

    B.   1/9

    C.   1/18   Answer

    D.   1/24

    E.   1/36

Q21. What is the value of x?

    (1) $1/x + x/y = 5/12$

    (2) $3x/xy - 2x/y = 1/y$

    A.   1 alone, not 2 alone

    B.   2 alone, not 1 alone

    C.   1 and 2 together (need both)   Answer

    D.   1 alone or 2 alone

    E.   1 and 2 together are not sufficient

Q22. What is the area of a quadrant?

    (1) The arc is 4.56 cm

    (2) Its radius is 4 cm

    A.   1 alone, not 2 alone

    B.   2 alone, not 1 alone

    C.   1 and 2 together (need both)   Answer

    D.   1 alone or 2 alone

    E.   1 and 2 together are not sufficient

Q23. If $4x + 4y = x + y + 2$, then $x + y$ is:

A.   2/3
B. $4x + 4y + 2$
C. $(x + y)/4 + 1$ Answer
D.   1/2
E.   Cannot be determined

Q24. If it takes 4 people 3 hours to dig a hole, how long should it take 3 people to complete the same task?

A.   12 hours
B.   6 hours
C.   4 hours   Answer
D.   3 hours
E.   2.5 hours

Q25. Is x positive or negative?

(1) $9/x + 7/x = x$
(2) $x^2 - 2x = 8$

A.   1 alone, not 2 alone
B.   2 alone, not 1 alone
C.   1 and 2 together (need both)   Answer
D.   1 alone or 2 alone
E.   1 and 2 together are not sufficient

Q26. The function &(x) is a clock function; it gives values between 0 and 12. &(13) returns the value 1, for example. What, then, is the result of $\&(10 \times 5) - \&(20)$?

A.   2
B.   4
C.   8   Answer
D.   6
E.   10

Q27. If $x + y = 10$, what percentage of x is $x + 2y$?

A.   10
B.   200
C.   150   Answer
D.   100
E.   Cannot be determined

Q28. Is 81 a prime number? If it is, identify the prime factors of 19; if it is not, identify the prime factors of 21.

    A.   1
    B.   3
    C.   7   Answer
    D.   9
    E.   19

Q29. If $x < -1$ and $y < -2$, then:

    A. $x/y > 1/2$
    B. $x/y > 2$
    C. $x/y > 1$ Answer
    D. $x - y > 0$
    E. $xy > 2$

Q30. What is the value of x?

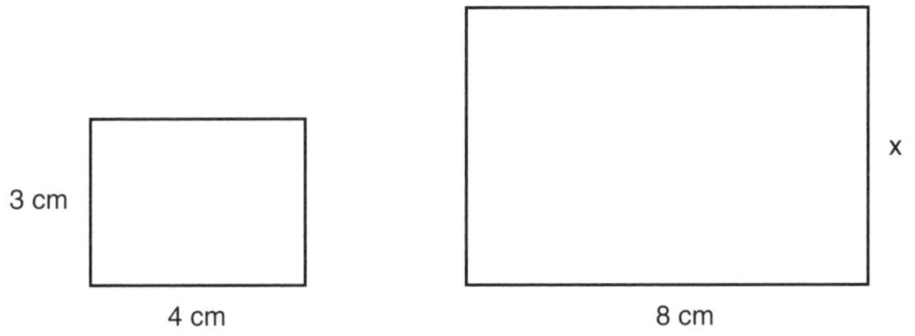

3 cm   x

4 cm   8 cm

(1)   The angles in one shape are equal to corresponding angles in the other
(2)   Pairs of corresponding sides are in the same ratio

    A.   1 alone, not 2 alone
    B.   2 alone, not 1 alone
    C.   1 and 2 together (need both)   Answer
    D.   1 alone or 2 alone
    E.   1 and 2 together are not sufficient

Q31. Is x positive or negative?

(1) $x^3 + x^2 - x - 1 = 0$
(2) $x^3 + 2x^2 - 4x - 8 = 0$

    A.   1 alone, not 2 alone
    B.   2 alone, not 1 alone
    C.   1 and 2 together (need both)   Answer
    D.   1 alone or 2 alone
    E.   1 and 2 together are not sufficient

Q32. If $4(x + 2y) = 8y$, then y is:

A. $4x$
B. $4x + 4y$
C.   1   Answer ☐
D.   0
E.   Cannot be determined

Q33. The function $(x) rounds up to the nearest integer then takes the positive value. For example, $(−3.0) = 3. What, then, is the result of $(2.5) × $(−4)?

A.   12
B.   10
C.   15   Answer ☐
D.   6.5
E.   7

Q34. If potatoes cost 50 cents per lb and you use $\frac{1}{8}$ of all the potatoes in the cupboard to make a meal, what was the value of all the potatoes used if 7 lb of potatoes remain in the cupboard?

A. $6
B. $3
C. $1   Answer ☐
D.   50 cents
E.   Cannot be determined

Q35. Which of the following inequalities is the solution to the inequality $3xy + 3zx <
(y + z)x$?

A. $x < -3$
B. $x < 3$
C. $x < 0$ Answer ☐
D. $x > 0$
E.   Cannot be determined

Q36. There are 200 students in one year, divided into 10 groups. Is it possible to know the average score for all the year?

(1)   The average score is known for groups 1, 2, 3, 4 and 5
(2)   The average score is known for groups 5, 6, 7, 8, 9 and 10

A.   1 alone, not 2 alone
B.   2 alone, not 1 alone
C.   1 and 2 together (need both)   Answer ☐
D.   1 alone or 2 alone
E.   1 and 2 together are not sufficient

Q37. If xy − 3y = 2 and x + y = 6, then x is:

    A.   4 or 5
    B.   3 or 4
    C.   4   Answer
    D.   5
    E.   Cannot be determined

Sub-test 2: verbal

To indicate your answer, put a tick alongside the suggested answer of your choice and when you have re-read and checked your answer, fill in the box, then move on to the next question. There is no going back in the real GMAT CAT®, so when you have moved on to the next question, do not be tempted to go back and change your answer as you will not be able to do that in the real test. If you cannot get to the solution of a question then it is worth guessing, but only as a last resort. Remember that to do well in a test you really have to try very hard!

You are allowed 75 minutes in which to attempt the 41 questions that make up this test. Work where you will not be interrupted and complete the test in one continuous period. Do not turn the page until you are really ready to begin.

Sub-test 2

Q1. <u>I have always disliked cleaning but I've finished it all now</u>.

    A.   I have always disliked cleaning but I've finished it all now.
    B.   I haven't been liking cleaning but I've finished it all now.
    C.   I have always disliked cleaning but I'd finished it all now.
    D.   I have always dislike cleaning but I have finished it all now.
    E.   I have always disliked cleaning but I'd been finishing it all now.

Answer ☐

Q2. You went to the Caribbean for Christmas didn't you? <u>How was the journey like?</u>

    A.   How was the journey like?
    B.   In whose was the journey?
    C.   Which was the journey like?   Answer ☐
    D   What was the journey?
    E.   What was the journey like?

Q3. <u>The countries corporation tax rate was very high so the managing director decided to relocate the company to one more.</u>

    A.   The countries corporation tax rate was very high so the managing director decided to relocate the company to one more.
    B.   The country's corporation tax rate was very high so the managing director decided to relocate the company to another.
    C.   The country's corporation tax rate was very high so the managing director decided to relocate the company to one more.
    D.   The countries corporation tax rate was very high so the managing director decided to relocate the company to another.
    E.   The country's corporation tax rate was very high so the managing director decided to relocate the company to an additional one.

Answer ☐

Q4. <u>The Bank of Australia raised its principal interest rate</u> by a half percentage point to 5.25%, which is expected to cool demand and make future increases less likely.

    A.   The Bank of Australia raised its principal interest rate
    B.   The Bank of Australia's principal interest rate raised
    C.   The Bank of Australia raised its principal interest rates   Answer ☐
    D.   The Bank of Australia raised it principal interest rate
    E.   The Bank of Australia raised it principal interest rates

Q5. <u>The current exchange rate of 115.1 make</u> many Americans less well off than they were a year ago.

    A.   The current exchange rate of 115.1 make
    B.   The current exchange rate of 115.1 seem to make
    C.   The current exchange rate of 115.1 were to make   Answer
    D.   The current exchange rate of 115.1 is making for
    E.   The current exchange rate of 115.1 makes

Q6. I do not think <u>employers should expect people</u> to stay late to get a job finished.

    A.   employers should expect people
    B.   employers ought expect people
    C.   employers had better expect people   Answer
    D.   employers should not expect people
    E.   employers shall expect people

Passage
(207 words)

Widespread help from parents and family members has generally always cast doubt on the value of examinations in which home-completed assignments contribute to the grade awarded. The extent of that contribution is significant, with between 20 and 60 percent of grades coming from such coursework. Most students believe that coursework is a fairer method of assessment when compared with 'all or nothing' exams, however they also admit that it is 'all too easy to cheat'. A review of the extent of cheating found overwhelming evidence of widespread abuse by students, teachers and parents. Incredibly, 1 in 10 parents admitted to doing assignments for their children. Teachers admitted to giving students 'too much help'. But greatest concern arises because of the internet. A whole host of sites now exist, offering for a small fee (or even for free) model essays and examples of coursework awarded top grades. Most of these sites carry requests that the user does not submit the material as their own but there is no attempt to ensure that this request is adhered to, and there is much evidence of a plagiarism free-for-all of internet-obtained material. Many educationalists conclude that the internet has made the policing of coursework impossible.

Q7. In the context of the passage the word plagiarize means:

    A.   the infringement of someone else's copyright
    B.   to borrow or crib the work of someone else
    C.   to take someone else's work and pass it off as your own   Answer
    D.   the illegal use of written material authored by someone else
    E.   to copy someone else's coursework

Q8.   Which of the following would most naturally follow on as the next sentence to the passage?

A.   Coursework is obviously open to cheating and there should be much more emphasis on and more marks for proper invigilated assignments or exams.
B.   Most young people nowadays can get well on the way to a decent pass grade before they even take an exam.
C.   And believe the revelations cast doubt on the continually rising grades.
D.   It will gladden the hearts of traditionalists who have long resented what they have considered the dumbing down of the nation's exams with home assignments.
E.   They have called for it either to be done under controlled conditions or to be dropped altogether.

Answer ☐

Q9.   The author relies on which of the following to make his claims?

A.   examples or analogies
B.   deductive argument
C.   the drawing of comparative assertions   Answer ☐
D.   the findings of an investigative study
E.   the results of an experimental investigation

Q10.   Which of the following statements correctly reflects the point made in the passage?

A.   Between 20 and 60 percent of the total grades obtained result from the help of parents and siblings.
B.   Between 20 and 60 percent of the total grades available come from home-completed assignments.
C.   Between 20 and 60 percent of the total grades awarded in these qualifications comes from the contribution of parents and family.
D.   Between 20 and 60 percent of the grades are allocated to home-completed assignments.
E.   Between 20 and 60 percent of the grades in these exams come from cheating.

Answer ☐

Q11.   The author would agree that:

A.   Widespread help from parents and siblings has led to grade inflation.
B.   Widespread help from parents and siblings has made the policing of home-completed coursework almost impossible.
C.   Widespread help from parents and siblings has made a nonsense of the national exam system.
D.   Widespread help from parents and siblings raises serious questions about the credibility of vocational qualifications.
E.   Widespread help from parents and siblings has resulted in an increased risk of plagiarism.

Answer ☐

Q12. This coming summer <u>Smiths, the transport company, are</u> expecting a turnaround in the market.

    A.   Smiths, the transport company, are
    B.   Smiths, the transport company, is
    C.   the transport company, Smiths, are   Answer
    D.   Smiths, the transport company, was
    E.   Smiths, the transport company, were

Q13. <u>The company director or his legal representatives is to attend the meeting, and almost everyone thinks</u> the news will be bad.

    A.   The company director or his legal representatives is to attend the meeting, and almost everyone thinks
    B.   The company director or his legal representatives are to attend the meeting, and almost everyone think
    C.   The company director or his legal representatives are to attend the meeting, and almost everyone thinks
    D.   The company director or his legal representatives is to attend the meeting, and almost everyone think
    E.   Both the singular and plural form are correct so C and D.

          Answer

Q14. <u>Her success turned out due to her</u> ability to think laterally, and her drive and determination.

    A.   Her success turned out due to her
    B.   Her success seemed to be her
    C.   Her success is to be due to her   Answer
    D.   Her success turned out to be due to her
    E.   Her success appeared to her

Q15. To understand how the rocks formed in the middle Miocene period we have <u>to look forward and backward</u> through the distinctive layered patterns of the sediment.

    A.   to look forward and backward
    B.   to look forward and backwards
    C.   to look forwards and backward   Answer
    D.   to look fore and aft
    E.   to look before and back

Passage
(192 words)

A study of the benefits of a family of cholesterol-lowering drugs used in the treatment of heart attacks has shown that while the greatest benefits are enjoyed by those at greatest risk of a vascular event, every person at risk can gain considerable benefits from the treatment. These findings have led to calls that it should be offered to anybody at risk of a heart attack or stroke. It has long been known that the treatment, if administered daily to the group most at risk of an attack, cuts that risk by a third. At present, doctors prescribe the treatment only once they have considered a number of factors, including cholesterol level, blood pressure, body fat levels and whether the patient smokes. The new evidence suggests that patients with less than very high levels of cholesterol will also experience a significant drop in their cholesterol levels and a consequent lower risk of a vascular event. In fact, it concludes that the benefits of the treatment are directly proportional to the size of the reduction in cholesterol levels that might be achieved and not the level at which the intervention begins.

Q16. Which of the following is a factor that gave rise to the call that the treatment should be offered to anybody at risk of a heart attack or stroke?

A.   the realization that the treatment is literally a life saver
B.   the realization that not every person at risk can gain considerable benefits from the treatment
C.   the realization that in those most at risk the treatment reduces the risk of an attack by as much as a third
D.   the realization that the risk of a heart attack is much higher in people who smoke, are overweight and have high cholesterol levels and blood pressure
E.   the realization that benefits from the treatment were seen in many different patient types

Answer ☐

Q17. The treatment is:

A.   a single drug
B.   a family of related drugs
C.   an unspecified intervention   Answer ☐
D.   a series of painful injections
E.   administered daily

Q18. The best summary of the conclusion to be drawn from the evidence of the study is that:

   A.   The benefits of the treatment are directly proportional to the size of the reduction in cholesterol levels that might be achieved and not the level at which intervention begins.
   B.   This treatment could cut heart attacks by a third.
   C.   The treatment should be prescribed to anyone assessed to be at risk of a heart attack or stroke.
   D.   There is now a much stronger case for the treatment to be prescribed to a much wider group of patients.
   E.   The greatest benefits are enjoyed by those at greatest risk of a vascular event.

   Answer ☐

Q19. Given that the benefits of the treatment are directly proportional to the size of the reduction in cholesterol levels it is correct to say that:

   A.   Doctors should offer this treatment to everybody they believe are at risk of a heart attack regardless of their cholesterol levels.
   B.   Taking the treatment on a daily basis can cut the risk of a heart attack and stroke by a third.
   C.   The treatment may not benefit as wide a range of patients as was originally thought.
   D.   Everyone could gain considerable benefits from the treatment.
   E.   Doctors should look more to the relative drop in cholesterol that may be achieved, rather than prioritizing patients suffering the very highest levels.

   Answer ☐

Q20. Which of the statements, if true, would most weaken the claim that patients with less than very high levels of cholesterol will also experience a significant drop in their cholesterol levels and consequently a much lower risk of a vascular event?

A.   The largest benefits from the treatment are seen among those in greatest risk of a vascular event, and those with less than very high levels of cholesterol are not at greatest risk.

B.   Unfortunately, the best results from the treatment are only obtained when the treatment is customized to the individual patient's cholesterol levels and requires someone with less than very high cholesterol levels to take a smaller daily dose.

C.   Preliminary evidence suggests that the treatment achieves a relatively small reduction in the risk of a heart attack among people with less than very high levels of cholesterol.

D.   Not all the evidence is positive, as people with lower cholesterol levels who take the treatment have been found to develop an increased risk of some cancers.

E.   Originally, it was thought that the treatment worked by lowering the cholesterol level, but it is now believed that this effect alone is not enough to account for all the advantages that the treatment provides.

Answer ☐

Q21. You will find the boy school on the main street next to the shoe shop and clothes shop.

A.   boy school on the main street next to the shoe shop and clothes shop.
B.   boy's school on the main street next to the shoes shop and cloths shop.
C.   boys shop on the main street next to the shoes shop and cloth shop.
D.   boys' school on the main street next to the shoe shop and clothes shop.
E.   boys' school on the main street next to the shoe shop and cloth shop.

Answer ☐

Q22. She greeted them and offered her condolences and goodbyes.

A.   She greeted them and offered her condolences and goodbyes.
B.   She greeting them and offered her condolences and goodbyes.
C.   She greeted them, offered her condolences and said goodbye.
D.   She said hello and offered her condolences and goodbyes.
E.   She said hello to them sorry to hear of your loss and goodbye.

Answer ☐

Q23. We asked the company's management team to explain why there had not been better planning but <u>there was no answers</u>.

    A.   there was no answers.

    B.   there was not any one answer.

    C.   there wasn't none.   Answer

    D.   there were no answer.

    E.   there were no answers.

Q24. My manager must have known that I regularly could not complete all my tasks and would <u>spend many hours after work getting the job done</u>.

    A.   spend many hours after work getting the job done.

    B.   spend lots hours after work getting the job done.

    C.   spend a large number of hours after work getting the job done.

    D.   spent far too much hours after work getting the job done.

    E.   spend large hours after work getting the job done.

                                              Answer

Q25. <u>Almost every day for a month</u> record high metal prices were recorded on all world markets.

    A.   Almost every day for a month

    B.   Almost each day for a month

    C.   Almost all day for a month   Answer

    D.   Not all days for a month

    E.   Not every day for a month

Passage
(223 words)

The projection in the latest quarterly inflation report is for growth to pick up to 2.8 percent. For this forecast to be realized, household spending and domestic consumption would need to increase noticeably from its current lackluster level. The economy has grown below its long-term trend for three out of the last four quarters. Wage growth was under control and the retail and housing markets, while not getting worse, were not getting any better either. Import prices had started to add to inflation after years of deflation in the wake of the $25 jump in the barrel price of crude. But most economists were for ignoring the first-round impact of this rise and waiting for any domestic second effect – higher prices in the shops – before taking action. That action will almost certainly involve interest rate increases, the effect of which would be to squeeze household spending and knock back inflation. The economy would then have to wait for the stable job market and increases in incomes and wage growth to diminish the effect of the rate increase over the medium term. Eventually these factors would give rise to domestic growth on or above the long-term trend. In the meantime, the risk of a full-scale consumer recession or a collapse in house prices are both very unlikely.

Q26. Which of the following is stated as a factor that would give rise to growth on or above the long-term trend?

    A.   pay deal inflation
    B.   consumer confidence
    C.   consumer spending   Answer
    D.   house price increases
    E.   import price deflation

Q27. Which of the following statements would the author of the passage most likely agree with?

    A.   The wider community of economists are split over whether monetary policy should pay heed to the immediate price impact from oil.
    B.   Broadly speaking, economists agree that no immediate action should be taken over inflationary effects of the $25 jump in the price of crude.
    C.   The wider community of economists are against the view that monetary policy should take no action over the immediate price impact from oil.
    D.   The wider community of economists are against taking no action at all over the inflationary effect of the $25 jump in the price of crude.
    E.   Most economists are for ignoring any rise in non-oil inflation.

                            Answer

Q28. For the projection in the latest quarterly inflation report to be realized the author would expect:

    A.   expenditure to get no worse
    B.   spending to pick up
    C.   import inflation to continue   Answer
    D.   interest rates to rise notably
    E.   the economy to grow faster than in the first half

Q29. For the author, the 64 million dollar question is:

    A.   In the short term do interest rates have to rise?
    B.   Will the price of crude continue to increase?
    C.   Must oil price inflation lead to higher wages and shop prices?
    D.   Is labor market inflation sufficiently sustainable to eventually counter any interest rate increase?
    E.   At what rate over the short, medium and long term will the economy grow?

                            Answer

Q30. <u>You didn't need to go</u> to all that trouble, but thank you anyway it was a lovely evening.

    A.   You didn't need to go
    B.   You needed gone
    C.   You needn't have gone   Answer
    D.   You needing to have go
    E.   You need to go

Q31. <u>American workers have less holidays than their European counterparts</u>.

    A.   American workers have less holidays than their European counterparts.
    B.   American workers have little holidays than their European counterparts.
    C.   American workers have fewer holidays than their European counterparts.
    D.   American workers have a bit less holidays than their European counterparts.
    E.   American workers have smaller holidays than their European counterparts.

        Answer

Q32. Many American would-be buyers of foreign technology stock became <u>skeptical when the authorities in America and Europe</u> voiced their concerns.

    A.   became skeptical when the authorities in America and Europe
    B.   became skeptical with the authorities in America and Europe
    C.   became skeptical where the authorities in America and Europe
    D.   became skeptical with the reason why the authorities in America and Europe
    E.   became skeptical whenever the authorities in America and Europe

        Answer

Q33. <u>We drove around to familiarize ourselves with the new surroundings</u>.

    A.   We drove around to familiarize ourselves with the new surroundings.
    B.   We drove around to familiarize ourselves with our new surroundings.
    C.   We drove around to familiarize ourself with the new surroundings.
    D.   We drove around to familiarize ourselves with their new surroundings.
    E.   We drove around to familiarize oneself with the new surroundings.

        Answer

Q34. We went to the shops but only went into the one that were advertising special offers.

- A.   We went to the shops but only went into the one that were advertising special offers.
- B.   We went to the shops but only went into the shop that were advertising special offers.
- C.   We went to the shops but only went into ones that were advertising special offers.
- D.   We went to the shops but only went into won that was offering special offers.
- E.   We went to the shops but only went into everyone that was offering special offers.

Answer

Q35. We didn't need to work all hours on the presentation as the meeting was cancelled at the last minute.

- A.   We didn't need to work
- B.   We needn't have worked
- C.   We don't have to work   Answer
- D.   We mustn't have worked
- E.   We don't need to work

Passage
(171 words)

Road congestion has grown by 37 percent, and as people switch from private cars to public transport, the total distance traveled by rail is expected to increase 60 percent. Despite the obvious increase in demand for space on our roads and trains, governments are failing to match forecast growth with investment in either mode of transport. In the 10 worst areas, the problems are already chronic, with immediate investment needed if sufficient capacity is to be created to cope with future demand. In these areas, new roads and tracks and longer platforms that can handle longer trains are already needed to relieve bottlenecks, congestion and severe overcrowding during peak hours. Despite demand, there are no plans to expand road and rail networks significantly and, indeed, closures and cuts in funding are on the agenda. The paucity of public investment raises considerable doubts that those few projects that are currently supported by government will ever be completed because ministers are refusing to say how much public money they will receive.

Q36. Which of the following statements can you infer to be true?

A. People are giving up their cars to undertake journeys by train.
B. Rail passengers face a bleak future of overcrowding and more expensive journeys.
C. Road use has grown by 37 percent and rail use by 60 percent.
D. Despite increased demand there are no plans to increase road and rail networks significantly.
E. As road congestion has grown, the total distance traveled by rail has increased.

Answer ☐

Q37. It is hard to arrive at any other conclusion than travelers face a bleak future of:

A. overcrowded networks, slower journey times and higher fares
B. congestion, bottlenecks and overcrowding
C. congestion, overcrowded networks and higher fares
D. overcrowding, congestion and even slower journey times
E. slower journey times and higher fares

Answer ☐

Q38. In the context of the passage, the word paucity means:

A. the small amount of rail investment
B. the diminutive public investment in the expansion of the railway
C. the presence of something in only immense quantities
D. the low level of public investment
E. the presence of something in only diminutive quantities

Answer ☐

Q39. In the worst 10 areas, immediate investment is already needed:

A. because the problem there is already chronic
B. because during peak periods they suffer bottlenecks, congestion and severe overcrowding
C. if the infrastructure is to cope with future demand
D. if they are to build the extra rail tracks, roads and longer train platforms
E. before people can switch from private to public transport

Answer ☐

Q40. It can be inferred from the passage that:

 A.   There was a greater demand for rail travel than travel by private car.
 B.   Governments were in favor of people switching from cars to public transport.
 C.   There is every indication that governments were against people switching modes of transport.
 D.   Governments were undermining the switch from private to public transport by failing to invest in transport networks.
 E.   Governments were doing little in practical terms to encourage people to switch from cars to public transport.

Answer

Q41. The CEO was convinced that the legal advice was wrong, and he made sure that everyone knew that he did not think so.

 A.   everyone knew that he did not think so.
 B.   everyone knew that he thought not.
 C.   everyone knew that he doubt it.   Answer
 D.   everyone knew that he did think so.
 E.   everyone knew that he thought so.

Sub-test 3: quantitative

To indicate your answer, put a tick alongside the suggested answer of your choice and when you have reread and checked your answer, fill in the box, then move on to the next question. There is no going back in the real GMAT CAT® so when you have moved on to the next question, do not be tempted to go back and change your answer as you will not be able to do that in the real test. If you cannot get to the solution of a question then it is worth guessing, but only as a last resort. Remember that to do well in a test you really have to try very hard!

You are allowed 75 minutes in which to attempt the 37 questions that make up this test. Work where you will not be interrupted and complete the test in one continuous period. Do not use a calculator. Do not turn the page until you are really ready to begin.

Sub-test 3

Q1. Are all the angles equal?

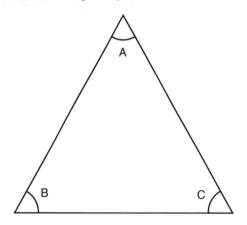

(1) Angle A = 60° and the sum of angles B + C = 120°
(2) It is an equilateral triangle

A.   1 alone, not 2 alone
B.   2 alone, not 1 alone
C.   1 and 2 together (need both)   Answer
D.   1 alone or 2 alone
E.   1 and 2 together are not sufficient

Q2. A lottery syndicate wins $399,000, which is to be split by the ratio 7:3:9. How much more is the highest payout than the lowest?

A. $126,000
B. $189,000
C. $149,000   Answer
D. $63,000
E. $21,000

Q3. Is x positive?

(1) x is greater than or equal to y
(2) y is greater than 0

A.   1 alone, not 2 alone
B.   2 alone, not 1 alone
C.   1 and 2 together (need both)   Answer
D.   1 alone or 2 alone
E.   1 and 2 together are not sufficient

Q4. For which values of x is $x^2 - x$ negative?

    A. $-1 < x < 1$
    B. $x < 1$
    C. $0 < x < 1$ Answer ☐
    D. $1 > x > -1$
    E. $x > 1$

Q5. If $4x + 6y = 20$, then $10x + 15y$ is:

    A.   40
    B.   50
    C.   20   Answer ☐
    D.   30
    E.   Cannot be determined

Q6. If this pie chart was drawn so that each sector was represented proportionately, what should angle A be?

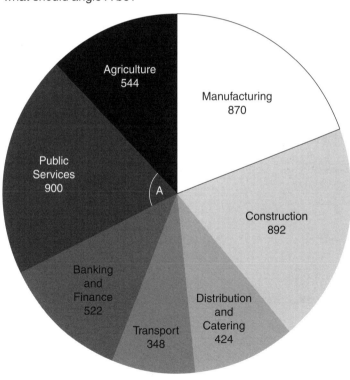

Employment by Industrial Sector (NOT to scale)

    A.   26°
    B.   28°
    C.   30°   Answer ☐
    D.   32°
    E.   72°

Q7.   The function $(x) rounds up to the nearest integer then takes the positive value. For example, $(−3.0) = 3. What, then, is the result of $(−2.5) divided by $(2.5)?

A.   1
B.   2/3
C.   2.5   Answer
D.   6.25
E.   3/3

Q8.   If the sum of three consecutive numbers (integers) is 93, then the sum of the two largest of that series is:

A.   63
B.   64
C.   65   Answer
D.   66
E.   67

Q9.   Is n divisible by 11 with no remainder?

(1)   n is divisible by m with integer result
(2)   m is divisible by 5.5 with integer result

A.   1 alone, not 2 alone
B.   2 alone, not 1 alone
C.   1 and 2 together (need both)   Answer
D.   1 alone or 2 alone
E.   1 and 2 together are not sufficient

Q10.   What is the probability of getting tails 6 consecutive times when you toss a coin (assume the coin has no bias)?

A.   1/4
B.   1/8
C.   1/16   Answer
D.   1/32
E.   1/64

Q11.   If $2y − x < 0$ and both x and y are positive then:

A. $x < y$
B. $x > y/2$
C. $x > 2y$ Answer
D. $2x > y$
E.   None of the above

Q12. What speed must a driver maintain for the 25 miles that remain of a trip if he wants to average 50 mph for the entire journey and he has taken 36 minutes to complete the first 55 miles?

    A.   20 mph
    B.   25 mph
    C.   30 mph   Answer
    D.   35 mph
    E.   40 mph

Q13. If $5a + 4b = 20$ and $4a + 5b = 30$, what is $9a + 9b$?

    A.   50
    B.   40
    C.   90/5   Answer
    D.   90/4
    E.   220/9

Q14. Which of these two is the greater, x or y?

    (1) $x/3 > y$
    (2)   Both are positive

    A.   1 alone, not 2 alone
    B.   2 alone, not 1 alone
    C.   1 and 2 together (need both)   Answer
    D.   1 alone or 2 alone
    E.   1 and 2 together are not sufficient

Q15. If $a - b = -3$ and $a + b = 11$, then:

    A. $ab = 8$
    B. $a/b = 7/3$
    C. $ab = 21$ Answer
    D. $a/b = 7/4$
    E. $ab = 28$

Q16. For which values of x is $-x^2 + 4x - 3$ positive?

    A. $1 > x > 3$
    B. $x < -3$
    C. $-4 < x < 3$ Answer
    D. $1 < x < 3$
    E. $x > 1$

Q17.

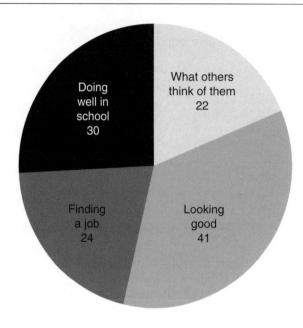

What others
think of them
22

Doing
well in
school
30

Finding
a job
24

Looking
good
41

What interests 117 young people most

What is the ratio of young people most interested in looking good and what others think of them compared to the young people most interested in doing well at school and finding a job (express the ratio in it simplest form)?

A.   6:5
B.   5:4
C.   7:6   Answer ☐
D.   8:6
E.   9:7

Q18. Is x is positive or negative?

(1) $x = y^2$
(2) $x^2 = 2$

A.   1 alone, not 2 alone
B.   2 alone, not 1 alone
C.   1 and 2 together (need both)   Answer ☐
D.   1 alone or 2 alone
E.   1 and 2 together are not sufficient

Q19. If $3y + x < 0$:

A. $y < -x/3$
B. $-y > x/3$
C. $y < -x/3$ and $-y > x/3$ Answer ☐
D. $2x > y/6$
E.   None of the above

Q20. If a/b = −3 and ab = −12, then:

    A.   a − b = 8
    B.   a − b = −8
    C.   a − b = 8 or −8   Answer ☐
    D.   a − b = 9
    E.   a − b = 4 or −4

Q21. How much smaller is the volume of the hemisphere than that of the triangular prism (work to the nearest full cm³, treat π as 3.14)?

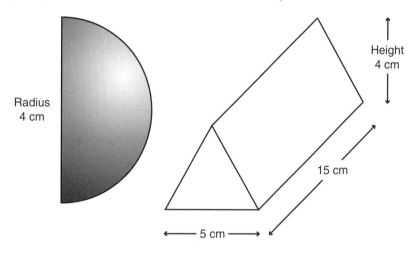

Hemisphere　　　　　　　**A prism**

    A.   118 cm³
    B.   76 cm³
    C.   23 cm³   Answer ☐
    D.   18 cm³
    E.   16 cm³

Q22. If $x = y^2$, $y = 4z$ and $xyz = 16$, x is:

    A.   16
    B.   4
    C.   8   Answer ☐
    D.   6
    E.   2

Q23. If two 6-sided dice are thrown, what is the probability of the sum of the two faces totaling 5?

A.   1/9
B.   1/6
C.   1/12   Answer
D.   1/18
E.   5/36

Q24. A sequence of numbers a_1, a_2, a_3 etc. is generated using the following algorithm: $a_{n+1} = 1/a_n$. Does the number 1 appear in the sequence if:

(1) 2 appears in the sequence
(2) $a_{n+1} - a_n = 2$ at some point

A.   1 alone, not 2 alone
B.   2 alone, not 1 alone
C.   1 and 2 together (need both)   Answer
D.   1 alone or 2 alone
E.   1 and 2 together are not sufficient

Q25. If $1/y = 1/x + 2/x$ and $x = 10$, then y is:

A.   10/9
B.   10/3
C.   20/9   Answer
D.   8/9
E.   None of the above

Q26. If $y = x/3 + 3/x$ and $3x = 1$, then y is:

A.   10/9
B.   18/3
C.   82/9   Answer
D.   8/9
E.   None of the above

Q27. What is the sum of all the numbers from 20 through to 48?

A.   986
B.   999
C.   852   Answer
D.   851
E.   850

Q28. Is $1/\sqrt{x} > 1\sqrt{y}$, if both x and y are positive?

    (1)   x − y > 0
    (2)   x > y

    A.   1 alone, not 2 alone
    B.   2 alone, not 1 alone
    C.   1 and 2 together (need both)   Answer
    D.   1 alone or 2 alone
    E.   1 and 2 together are not sufficient

Q29. If $3x + y = 2x − y$, then $x + y$ is:

    A.   −y
    B.   −x
    C.   (2x − y)/3   Answer
    D.   x/2 − y/3
    E.   Cannot be determined

Q30. For which values of x is $x^2 − 2x + 3$ greater than 3?

    A.   1 > x > 3
    B.   None
    C.   −4 < x < 3   Answer
    D.   0 < x < 2
    E.   0 > x > 2

Q31. What are the values of x and y?

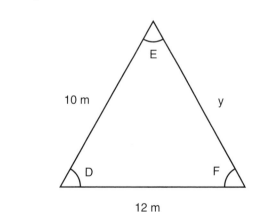

    (1)   Angles A + D and angles C + F are equal
    (2)   x = 7.5 cm

    A.   1 alone, not 2 alone
    B.   2 alone, not 1 alone
    C.   1 and 2 together (need both)   Answer
    D.   1 alone or 2 alone
    E.   1 and 2 together are not sufficient

Q32. Is $y < x^2$?

    (1) $y = x$
    (2) $0 > x > 1$

    A.   1 alone, not 2 alone
    B.   2 alone, not 1 alone
    C.   1 and 2 together (need both)   Answer
    D.   1 alone or 2 alone
    E.   1 and 2 together are not sufficient

Q33. If $x/2$ divided by $y/4 = 10$, what percentage of x is $x - y$?

    A.   40
    B.   20
    C.   80   Answer
    D.   60
    E.   Cannot be determined

Q34. What is the value of xy?

    (1) $3x + 4y = 10$
    (2) $7.5x + 10y = 25$

    A.   1 alone, not 2 alone
    B.   2 alone, not 1 alone
    C.   1 and 2 together (need both)   Answer
    D.   1 alone or 2 alone
    E.   1 and 2 together are not sufficient

Q35. If $x + y > 0$, then:

    A. $x/y > 0$
    B. $xy > 0$
    C. $x - y > 0$ Answer
    D. $xy > -1$
    E. $y + x > -1$

Q36. If $5a + 4b = 40 - 2a$ and $a + 5b = 30 + 2b$, what is ab?

    A.   10
    B.   0
    C.   30   Answer
    D.   40
    E.   45

Q37. What is the value of x?

(1) $x^3 - 6x^2 + 11x = 6$

(2) $x > 2$

A. 1 alone, not 2 alone
B. 2 alone, not 1 alone
C. 1 and 2 together (need both)
D. 1 alone or 2 alone
E. 1 and 2 together are not sufficient

Answer

Sub-test 4: verbal

To indicate your answer, put a tick alongside the suggested answer of your choice and when you have re-read and checked your answer, fill in the box, then move on to the next question. There is no going back in the real GMAT CAT® so when you have moved on to the next question, do not be tempted to go back and change your answer as you will not be able to do that in the real test. If you cannot get to the solution of a question then it is worth guessing, but only as a last resort. Remember that to do well in a test you really have to try very hard!

You are allowed 75 minutes in which to attempt the 41 questions that make up this test. Work where you will not be interrupted and complete the test in one continuous period. Do not turn the page until you are really ready to begin.

Sub-test 4

Q1. Until I read the magazine article, I was not well informed and did not know <u>of</u> the important role heredity plays in behavior.

    A.   of
    B.   after
    C.   for   Answer
    D.   on
    E.   that

Q2. The carrier arrived <u>at the city of New York with the document by 12 noon.</u>

    A.   at the city of New York with the document by 12 noon.
    B.   in the city of New York with the document by 12 noon.
    C.   to the city of New York with the document by 12 noon.   Answer
    D.   at the city of New York with the document at 12 noon.
    E.   by the city of New York with the document by 12 noon.

Q3. No wonder he is reluctant to continue the treatment. The doctor told him that there is <u>a likelihood of life-threatening complications</u>.

    A.   a likelihood of life-threatening complications.
    B.   a likelihood of threaten life complications.
    C.   a likelihood with life-threatening complications.   Answer
    D.   a likelihood for life-threatening complications.
    E.   a likelihood about threatening life complications.

Q4. Their son had become absorbed <u>in his study and his parents were becoming accustomed with the fact</u>.

    A.   in his study and his parents were becoming accustomed with the fact.
    B.   at his study and his parents were becoming accustomed with the fact.
    C.   to his study and his parents were becoming accustomed with the fact.
    D.   in his study and his parents were becoming accustomed in the fact.
    E.   in his study and his parents were becoming accustomed to the fact.

                                          Answer

Passage
(247 words)

The Agency for Crude Oil estimates that China's imports of crude will increase 8 percent a year, a figure more than twice the predicted rate of growth in global demand. To protect Chinese farmers, the group that has gained least from the economic reforms, and for fear of social unrest, the People's Congress has held the price of diesel at the pumps artificially low. These price controls mean that Chinese state-owned refineries are losing vast sums of money supplying domestic markets. To offset these losses, the refinery managers must export fuel and, as a consequence, create the single most important cause of the chronic fuel shortages facing the domestic market of China.

China's energy companies are desperately trying to resolve the issue by securing more suppliers of crude. Their greatest hope lies with Russia, which currently only supplies a small fraction of China's annual consumption. Chinese officials would dearly love a pipeline from the Siberian oilfields. But Russia is anxious to keep control of its export market and is understandably reluctant to provide its neighbor's refineries with oil, only to see it sold on to a third party in order to cross-subsidize the artificially low cost of fuel in China's domestic markets.

Perhaps a more viable solution lies with a price increase in the cost of diesel in Chinese domestic markets. This might well mean that the current runaway demand will be curtailed and Chinese refineries will be better able to supply their home markets.

Q5. Which of the following statements best captures the general theme of the passage?

    A.   the solution to China's fuel problems
    B.   China's fuel crisis and potential solutions to it
    C.   how China can solve its fuel troubles   Answer
    D.   the nature of China's fuel predicament
    E.   China's fuel catastrophe and its explanation

Q6. Which of the following is mentioned as a solution to fuel shortages?

    A.   securing more suppliers of crude
    B.   a pipeline from the Siberian oilfields
    C.   an end to refineries selling overseas
    D.   an end to the artificially low cost of fuel on China's domestic markets
    E.   curtailment of the current runaway demand

Answer

Q7. Which topic is not touched upon in the passage?

    A.   fiscal policy
    B.   international relations
    C.   fuel exports   Answer
    D.   retail price
    E.   rationing

Q8. The author would agree least with which of the following statements?

    A.   The Chinese government was not ready to raise the price of oil products.
    B.   The artificially low price of oil products gives Chinese manufacturers an unfair advantage in foreign markets.
    C.   Russia holds the solution to its neighbor's shortage.
    D.   Chinese officials express frustration with Russian reluctance to increase supplies.
    E.   The supply crunch comes as the country's refineries continue to supply overseas markets.

Answer

Q9.   Which of the following reasons were not given for China keeping a lid on prices at the pumps?

A.   To prevent social unrest over the price of gasoline.
B.   To protect farmers.
C.   To protect the group that has gained least from the economic reforms.
D.   A fear of social unrest.
E.   Fearing social unrest, China has kept the price of diesel artificially low.

Answer

Q10.   The reader was really angry at the inaccuracy of the article.

A.   The reader was really angry at the inaccuracy of the article.
B.   The reader was really angry with the inaccuracy of the article.
C.   The reader was really angry for the inaccuracy of the article.
D.   The reader was really angry in the inaccuracy of the article.
E.   The reader was really angry of the inaccuracy of the article.

Answer

Q11.   Few families in extreme poverty have the resources to care after their children properly.

A.   Few families in extreme poverty have the resources to care after their children properly.
B.   Few families in extreme poverty have the resources to care of their children properly.
C.   Few families in extreme poverty have the resources to care about their children properly.
D.   Few families in extreme poverty have the resources to care with their children properly.
E.   Few families in extreme poverty have the resources to care for their children properly.

Answer

Q12.   Has she not already asked the languages what I speak?

A.   Has she not already asked the languages what I speak?
B.   Hasn't she already asked what languages I speak?
C.   Hasn't she already asked the languages what I speak?   Answer
D.   Has she already asked the languages I speak?
E.   Hasn't she not already asked what languages I speak?

Q13. I was fascinated to learn <u>for</u> some of the mechanisms at work.

 A. for
 B. with
 C. before   Answer
 D. about
 E. after

Passage
(229 words)

We may not much like the fact, but we are 99.9 percent identical. This is because 99.9 percent of our DNA is common to every person, and the Human Genome Project is rightly celebrated for sequencing it. But what of the remaining 0.1 percent? It is far more significant than one might assume, because if it was not for this minute percentage there would be no individual differences. We would be clones. These variations in the human code account for all individual idiosyncrasies. They are responsible for the differences between ethnic and racial groups. Perhaps most interesting of all, they also explain why some of us enjoy good health while others are more susceptible to many common diseases. It is thought that the mapping of the remaining 0.1 percent of human DNA will hasten the identification of new ways to treat common ailments such as obesity, cancer and heart disease. The work will prove particularly useful in the search for new diagnostic tests, the customizing of treatments to best suit an individual's genetic code and ultimately the development of new drugs that target the DNA linked to a particular disease. The task of charting the inherited differences in the human genome has fallen to 200 scientists drawn from nine countries across every (populated) continent. They will screen people drawn from all the major human populations.

Q14. In the context of the passage the word sequencing refers to:

 A. the human genetic code
 B. the order in which things are repeated
 C. a chart or map of the genetic differences between people Answer
 D. the work of the Human Genome Project
 E. the order in which amino acids are arranged in DNA

Q15. Which of the following topics is not touched upon in the passage?

 A. genetic research
 B. human biology
 C. susceptibility to common diseases   Answer
 D. preventative treatments
 E. populations that share a genetic inheritance

Q16. It can be inferred that the work will:

- A.   accelerate the search for genes involved in common diseases
- B.   chart the inherited differences in the human genome
- C.   speed up the development of new treatments   Answer
- D.   map the DNA that is shared by every person
- E.   be made freely available on the internet

Q17. In reaching the conclusion that some of us enjoy good health while others are more susceptible to many common diseases, the author relies on which premise?

- A.   Humans are 99.9 percent genetically identical.
- B.   The genetic differences between people hold the key to our predisposition to many common diseases.
- C.   0.1 percent of the human genetic code accounts for all the genetic differences between human beings.
- D.   The human genome sequence provides us with a blueprint of all the DNA shared by every human being.
- E.   The sequencing of the genetic differences allows scientists to identify genes that influence common diseases.

Answer

Q18. Which of the following questions are not answered in the passage?

- A.   Will new ways to treat common ailments such as obesity, cancer and heart disease be made possible by the gene map?
- B.   Who will map the genetic differences?
- C.   What would be the consequences if 100 percent of our DNA were common to every person?
- D.   Why is the minute percentage of inherited differences significant?
- E.   How can mapping of the remaining 0.1 percent of human DNA help in the search for new diagnostic tests, customized treatments and new drugs?

Answer

Q19. The organizers of the march issued a statement claiming that <u>thousands of persons were present, but the police estimated the number to be nine hundreds</u>.

    A.   thousands of persons were present, but the police estimated the number to be nine hundreds.

    B.   thousand of people to be present, but the police estimated the number to be nine hundred.

    C.   thousands of people were present, but the police estimated the number to be nine hundreds.

    D.   thousands of people were present, but the police estimated the number to be nine hundred.

    E.   thousands of persons were present, but the police estimated the number to be nine hundred.

Answer ☐

Q20. The gold price is the highest for 10 years, <u>except</u> May 2000, when the South African gold miners went on strike.

    A.   except

    B.   but for

    C.   apart from   Answer ☐

    D.   besides

    E.   aside from

Q21. I have been working <u>when 7am when</u> the shift started at 5pm.

    A.   when 7am when

    B.   since 7am while

    C.   when 7am since   Answer ☐

    D.   since 7am since

    E.   since 7am when

Q22. <u>During the worst quarters of</u> the economic recession, corporate investors look for bargains. This is called 'bottom-fishing' by venture capitalists.

    A.   During the worst quarters of

    B.   Between the worst quarters of

    C.   Among the worst quarters of   Answer ☐

    D.   Until the worst quarters of

    E.   Up to the worst quarters of

Passage
(239 words)

Colorectal cancer occurs in the colon or rectum. It is more common among men than women and the majority of cases occur in the over-50s. Triggers are thought to be little or no exercise and excessive weight. A propensity for the disease is also known to be inherited, and therefore when it occurs, a family history of the disease may be found. Diet is believed to play an important role in both the risk of developing the disease and in its prevention. It used to be thought that a diet high in fiber greatly reduced the risk of colorectal cancer, however, it is now thought that eating too much red meat and milk products has a much stronger, unfortunately negative, association and increases the risk of the disease significantly. It so happens that people with high fiber diets eat less red meat and milk products than people with low fiber diets. People who eat lots of fiber also tend to enjoy a lifestyle with many other factors that may confer a lower risk of contracting colorectal cancer. If there is any accepted truism regarding diet, lifestyle and the risk of contacting colorectal cancer then it is no longer the view that eating lots of fiber has an inverse association. Today, dieticians are likely to stress the factors that give rise to greater risk, and at the top of the list of factors will be the consumption of too much alcohol.

Q23. The author would agree that:

    A. Eating lots of fiber may protect against colon cancer.
    B. There is a linear inverse association between fiber intake and colorectal cancer.
    C. There is no longer an accepted truism about lifestyle and the risk of contracting colorectal cancer.
    D. There is no adverse association between colorectal cancer and a diet rich in fibre.
    E. A diet of cereals, vegetables and fruit does protect against diseases such as heart disease.

Answer

Q24. It can be inferred from the passage that:

A.   There may appear a link between fiber intake and the risk of colorectal cancer, but when other dietary factors are taken into account any link between fiber and cancer becomes insignificant.

B.   It is largely coincidental that people who eat a diet rich in fiber such as whole grains, fruit and vegetables are less likely to get colorectal cancer than people with a diet poor in fiber.

C.   It is impossible to be certain that there is no causal link between a high dietary fiber intake and the risk of colorectal cancer.

D.   People who enjoy a diet high in fiber also have a lot of other traits that account for the benefits they gain in terms of a reduced risk of colorectal cancer.

E.   A comprehensive study challenges the once accepted truism that a high fiber intake reduces the risk of cancer of the colon.

Answer [   ]

Q25. Which of the following facts about colorectal cancer can be disproved by the passage?

A.   It is the fourth most common cancer among men and the third most common among women.

B.   Risk factors are a family history of the disease, smoking heavily, a diet low in vegetables and drinking too much alcohol.

C.   Each year 5,000 men and 4,000 women contract the disease and 4,000 of these patients are aged over 50.

D.   Each year 3,000 men and 4,000 women are treated for the disease.

E.   Colorectal cancer is sometimes called bowel cancer and eating fruit and cereal does little to reduce the risk of contracting this life-threatening disease.

Answer [   ]

Q26. According to the terms of your contract of employment <u>you are expecting to work</u> 40 hours a week.

A.   you are expecting to work
B.   you expect to work
C.   it is hoped that you will work   Answer [   ]
D.   you are hoping to work
E.   your employer is looking forward to you working

Q27. The relationship <u>among</u> the three friends went from bad to worse.

    A.   among
    B.   among other things
    C.   between   Answer
    D.   amongst
    E.   between them

Q28. I thought they would make an offer and was not surprised <u>when they did that</u>.

    A.   when they did that.
    B.   when they had done so.
    C.   when they did it.   Answer
    D.   when they did so.
    E.   when they did.

Q29. The city is located <u>over London, underneath Birmingham</u> along the new motorway.

    A.   over London, underneath Birmingham
    B.   above London, under Birmingham
    C.   over London, below Birmingham   Answer
    D.   above London, below Birmingham
    E.   across London, beneath Birmingham

Passage
(226 words)

We all know that our criminal system is failing, but how many of us know the extent of the failure? Do you know, for example, that 9 out of 10 offenders re-offend within two years of completing their punishment? No wonder that our prisons are so overcrowded that programs of education and rehabilitation have been abandoned. Staff simply do not have the time or resources to run them any longer. An offender rarely gets a prison sentence on the occasion of their first conviction. They are far more likely to be sentenced to a curfew monitored by an electronic tag and police surveillance. But by the time they have appeared before the judge on the third or fourth occasion, all hope that community-based punishments will work are abandoned and the persistent offender is sentenced to a period of imprisonment. Many don't even wait for the end of their period of curfew before re-offending. Large numbers breach their curfew repeatedly and even remove their electronic tags. Under the current system, even the fear of being caught and punished again is failing to deter. As already mentioned, rehabilitation programs have been abandoned due to the sheer overcrowding in the system, with thousands of offenders waiting six months or more to be offered a place on one of the few schemes still operating. No wonder crime rates are soaring.

Q30. Which of the following statements serves as a premise to the author's main claim?

    A.   that rehabilitation programs reduce offending rates
    B.   that today's punishments fail to deter re-offending
    C.   that the objective of punishment is to deter re-offending   Answer
    D.   that the frequency of re-offending is increasing
    E.   that crime rates are soaring

Q31. A reason given for the abandonment of rehabilitation programs is best captured by which of the following statements?

    A.   Prisons are so overcrowded that prisoners must forgo education and rehabilitation programs so that staff may concentrate on issues of security.
    B.   The criminal system is slow or unwilling to provide the resources required for rehabilitation provision.
    C.   Prisons are so overcrowded that staff must forgo education and rehabilitation programs, as they simply do not have the time or resources.
    D.   Overcrowding in the criminal system means that thousands of offenders are waiting six months or more to be offered a place on one of the few rehabilitation schemes still operating.
    E.   The time or wherewithal to run rehabilitation programs is no longer available, as it is taken up by the need to cope with overcrowding.

Answer

Q32. Which of the following sentences would most likely follow as the next in the passage?

    A.   It is abundantly clear that we need to find alternative workable solutions to tackle this very real challenge to society.
    B.   Perhaps we need to find other ways to punish those in society who refuse to stop offending.
    C.   Persistent offenders need longer sentences that might change their attitude towards rehabilitation programs and encourage them to reform their criminal behavior.
    D.   It seems beyond the wit of everyone involved to find a workable way of curbing the rate of offending by persistent young offenders.
    E.   Recidivism will decline as long as our community- and prison-based punishments fail to deter the persistent offender.

Answer

Q33. <u>Almost each of them had finished teaching in farther education</u>.

   A.   Almost each of them had finished teaching in farther education.
   B.   Almost all of them had finished teaching in further education.
   C.   Each of them had finished teaching in farther education.
   D.   Almost each of them had ended teaching in further education.
   E.   Each of them had ended teaching in further education.

Answer [ ]

Q34. Always prepare for the worst; <u>moreover, when</u> all the hard work has been done and the potential problems anticipated you can celebrate the inevitable success.

   A.   moreover, when
   B.   although, when
   C.   after all, when   Answer [ ]
   D.   until
   E.   above all, when

Q35. You can't open a bank account <u>if you have</u> money to deposit.

   A.   if you have
   B.   if you have not
   C.   whether or not you have   Answer [ ]
   D.   unless you have
   E.   whether you have

Q36. I would be surprised <u>if it turns out as</u> you predicted.

   A.   if it turns out as
   B.   as if it turns out as
   C.   if it will turn out as   Answer [ ]
   D.   if it should happen to be
   E.   as though it turns out as

Passage
(231 words)

Documents dating from centuries ago record sighting of the giant squid washed up dead on beaches or found in the stomachs of sperm whales. Since those times, occasional sightings and even reported attacks on boats have ensured that the species remains to this day a part of the lore told by sailors about the ocean and its unknown depths. The largest specimens are believed to reach almost 18 m and normally to live at depths of 1,000 m. A Japanese team decided to use sperm whale migration patterns to try to locate and film these enigmatic creatures. They made up a fishing line and baited it with hooks and fish. On the line they also hung lights and a camera and they lowered it more than a kilometer into the ocean at a location well known for sightings of sperm whales. The plan paid off. When they eventually recovered their line and examined the film they watched a giant squid shoot out from the dark with tentacles outstretched and a snapping beak to attack one of the baited hooks. It became caught and struggled furiously until it was able to free itself. The team believe their film is the first ever of a giant squid alive in its deep water habitat. They hope that careful study of the footage will reveal much new information about the behavior of this elusive creature.

Q37. The researchers reasoned that where the whales congregate might be a good place to film the squid because:

  A. The whales too dive to a depth of 1,000 m and also live in open ocean.
  B. The whales are known to feed on the creatures.
  C. Sperm whales are well known to sport tentacle-inflicted wounds.
  D. There have been reported sightings of the giant squid when it nears the surface.
  E. The giant creature has been caught on their camera.

  Answer

Q38. The researchers will be able to conjecture that the giant squid:

  A. attacks its prey head-on
  B. is a vigorous predator
  C. approaches its food cautiously
  D. approaches its food with tentacles extended
  E. attacks its prey from the deep

  Answer

Q39. Enigmatic means:

  A. mystifying
  B. hard to interpret
  C. difficult
  D. confusing
  E. mysterious

  Answer

Q40. If it had not been for what I know now I would have chosen a full-time rather than a part-time MBA course.

  A. If it had not been for
  B. Had it not been for
  C. If I knew then
  D. If it were not for
  E. If I were to know then

  Answer

Q41. I like nothing better than to get my teeth into a challenge, while I tend to get stressed if things do not go to plan.

  A. while I tend
  B. if I tend
  C. whether or not I tend
  D. whereas I tend
  E. despite the fact that I tend

  Answer

Sub-test 5: quantitative

To indicate your answer, put a tick alongside the suggested answer of your choice and when you have reread and checked your answer, fill in the box, then move on to the next question. There is no going back in the real GMAT CAT® so when you have moved on to the next question, do not be tempted to go back and change your answer as you will not be able to do that in the real test. If you cannot get to the solution of a question then it is worth guessing, but only as a last resort. Remember that to do well in a test you really have to try very hard!

You are allowed 75 minutes in which to attempt the 37 questions that make up this test. Work where you will not be interrupted and complete the test in one continuous period. Do not use a calculator. Do not turn the page until you are really ready to begin.

Sub-test 5

Q1. What is the area of the rectangle ABCD?

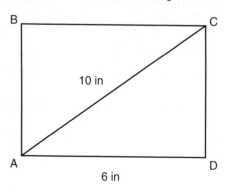

A.   64 in²
B.   48 in²
C.   24 in²
D.   8 in²
E.   6 in²

Answer

Q2. If 2x + 3y = 20 and 6x + 9y = 60, then x is:

A.   4
B.   5
C.   2
D.   3
E.   Cannot be determined

Answer

Q3. Is x > 0?

(1) $x^2 - x = 0$
(2) $2x^2 - 2x = 0$

A.   1 alone, not 2 alone
B.   2 alone, not 1 alone
C.   1 and 2 together. (need both)
D.   1 alone or 2 alone
E.   1 and 2 together are not sufficient

Answer

Q4. How many 3-digit numbers can you form with the numbers 345 if you can use each number just once in each of the 3-digit numbers you create?

A.   27
B.   12
C.   9
D.   6
E.   3

Answer

Q5. Which of the following inequalities is the solution to the inequality $2x^2 + 1 < x + 1$?

    A. $1/2 > x > 0$
    B. $-1 < x < 0$
    C. $x < 1/2$ Answer
    D. $x < 0$
    E.   Cannot be determined

Q6. Is n divisible by 6 with remainder 1?

    (1) $n - 7$ is divisible by 6 with integer result
    (2) $n - 1$ is divisible by 6 with integer result

    A.   1 alone, not 2 alone
    B.   2 alone, not 1 alone
    C.   1 and 2 together (need both)   Answer
    D.   1 alone or 2 alone
    E.   1 and 2 together are not sufficient

Q7. What is the probability of drawing two queens consecutively from a pack of 52 cards if the first card is not replaced and then the second card is drawn (assume that there are 4 queens in the pack before the first card was drawn)?

    A.   1/169
    B.   3/52
    C.   9/103   Answer
    D.   1/13
    E.   1/221

Q8. If $2x + 4y = 10$, what percentage of x is $5 - 2y$?

    A.   10%
    B.   200%
    C.   150%   Answer
    D.   100%
    E.   Cannot be determined

Q9. Which of these two is the greater, x or y?

    (1) $xy < 0$
    (2) $x/2y < 0$

    A.   1 alone, not 2 alone
    B.   2 alone, not 1 alone
    C.   1 and 2 together (need both)   Answer
    D.   1 alone or 2 alone
    E.   1 and 2 together are not sufficient

Q10. If 79 is a prime number, then identify the prime factors of 44; if it is not a prime number then identify the prime factors of 18.

A.   2
B.   3
C.   5   Answer ☐
D.   7
E.   11

Q11. If $x > 2$ and $y < -2$, then:

A. $x/y > 1$
B. $x/y < -1$
C. $x/y < 0$ Answer ☐
D. $x + y > 0$
E. $xy > 0$

Q12. A sequence of numbers a_1, a_2, a_3 etc. is generated using the following algorithm: $a_{n+1} = (-1)a_n$. Does the number 1 appear in the sequence if:

(1) a_3 is negative
(2) a_1 is negative

A.   1 alone, not 2 alone
B.   2 alone, not 1 alone
C.   1 and 2 together (need both)   Answer ☐
D.   1 alone or 2 alone
E.   1 and 2 together are not sufficient

Q13. What is the difference between the volumes of these two shapes (the radius of both is 3 cm, treat π as 3.14, and work to the nearest whole cm^3)?

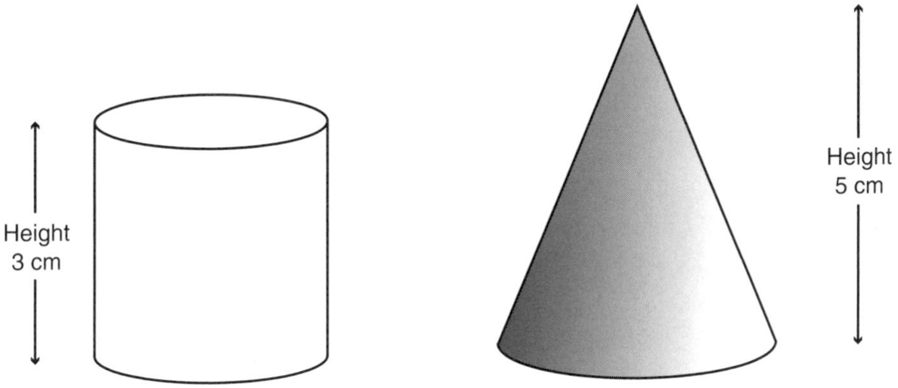

Height
3 cm

Cylinder

Height
5 cm

Cone

   A.   85 cm^3
   B.   47 cm^3
   C.   38 cm^3 Answer
   D.   32 cm^3
   E.   28 cm^3

Q14. If $5x + 4y = 22$ and $3x + 5y = 21$, then x is:

   A.   2.1
   B.   2.2
   C.   2.5   Answer
   D.   2.0
   E.   2.8

Q15. Is $(x/y)^2 > 1$?

   (1) $yx < x^2$
   (2)   Both x and y have the same sign

   A.   1 alone, not 2 alone
   B.   2 alone, not 1 alone
   C.   1 and 2 together (need both)   Answer
   D.   1 alone or 2 alone
   E.   1 and 2 together are not sufficient

Q16. If $5a + 4b = 20$ and $4a + 5b = 30$, what is $a + b$?

   A.   50/9
   B.   40/9
   C.   90/5   Answer
   D.   90/4
   E.   220/9

Q17. If x = z/y, y = z/x and x/(y/z) = 64, x is:

    A.   2
    B.   4
    C.   8   Answer
    D.   1
    E.   16

Q18. Is 2x/5 – 3y/4 > 0?

    (1)   x > 2y
    (2)   x > 1⁷/₈ y

    A.   1 alone, not 2 alone
    B.   2 alone, not 1 alone
    C.   1 and 2 together (need both)   Answer
    D.   1 alone or 2 alone
    E.   1 and 2 together are not sufficient

Q19.

	Ranked Position 2005	(Change from 2004)
Singapore	1	(+1)
USA	2	(−1)
South Korea	4	(−1)
Canada	6	(+2)
Mexico	8	(−2)
China	41	(+9)
France	20	(−3)

Information technology ranking index

Which statement(s) can you infer as true?

    A.   France in 2004 was ranked 23rd (23 – 3 = 20).
    B.   In 2004 Mexico occupied Canada's position.
    C.   The United States and South Korea have both slipped down the index.
    D.   In 2004 China was ranked 50th.
    E.   Singapore has returned to the top of the index.

Answer

Q20. If $2a - 6b = 2$ and $3b - 3a = 9$, what is ab?

   A. -4
   B.   10
   C. -2 Answer
   D. $-1/2$
   E. -10

Q21. What is the value of xy?

   (1) $x = 3y$
   (2) $y^2 = 6$

   A.   1 alone, not 2 alone
   B.   2 alone, not 1 alone
   C.   1 and 2 together (need both)   Answer
   D.   1 alone or 2 alone
   E.   1 and 2 together are not sufficient

Q22. What is the probability of drawing the letters G, then M, then A and finally, T
      (in the order it spells GMAT®) from a set of alphabetical cards (one card for each
      letter of the alphabet) if each card is replaced before the next card is drawn?

   A. $1/26$
   B. $1/104^4$
   C. $1/676$ Answer
   D. $1/676^4$
   E. $1/26^4$

Q23. For which values of x is $2x^2 - 3x$ greater than x?

   A. $1 > x > 3$
   B. $0 > x > 2$
   C. $-4 < x < 3$ Answer
   D. $0 < x < 2$
   E.   None

Q24. What is the value of x?

   (1) $1/x + 1/y = 5/12$
   (2) $y = 0$

   A.   1 alone, not 2 alone
   B.   2 alone, not 1 alone
   C.   1 and 2 together (need both)   Answer
   D.   1 alone or 2 alone
   E.   1 and 2 together are not sufficient

Q25. If the sum of three consecutive numbers is 177, then the sum of the two lowest values in the series is:

    A.　115
    B.　116
    C.　117   Answer ☐
    D.　118
    E.　119

Q26. If $1/(a + b) = 6$ and $1/(a - b) = 12$, then $1/2a$ is:

    A.　8
    B.　4
    C.　6   Answer ☐
    D.　18
    E.　12

Q27. Is x is positive or negative?

    (1)　$x^2 - 5x = -6$
    (2)　$4/x = x$

    A.　1 alone, not 2 alone
    B.　2 alone, not 1 alone
    C.　1 and 2 together (need both)   Answer ☐
    D.　1 alone or 2 alone
    E.　1 and 2 together are not sufficient

Q28. If $105,000 is spent on land and building a house, how much did the land cost if the cost of building the house was 25% less than the cost of the land?

    A.　$45,000
    B.　$50,000
    C.　$55,000   Answer ☐
    D.　$60,000
    E.　$65,000

Q29. If $1/y + 1/x < 1/2$:

    A.　$xy < x + y$
    B.　$2xy < x + y$
    C.　$xy < 2x - 2y$ Answer ☐
    D.　$xy < 2x + 2y$
    E.　None of the above

Q30. A man, a woman and a girl take 5 hours to label 1,000 packages. How long would the woman take to label 100?

    (1)   The woman works 10% faster than the man who works 15% faster than the girl

    (2)   The man and the girl together label 10 in 5 minutes

    A.   1 alone, not 2 alone
    B.   2 alone, not 1 alone
    C.   1 and 2 together (need both)   Answer
    D.   1 alone or 2 alone
    E.   1 and 2 together are not sufficient

Q31. If $(x + y)/(x - y) = 1/2$ and $(x + y)/(y + 1) = 2$, then y is:

    A   −1/2
    B.   1/2
    C.   −4   Answer
    D.   2
    E.   −1

Q32. If $xy = 1 + 2x$ and $2x = 1$, then y is:

    A.   4
    B.   2
    C.   1   Answer
    D.   8/3
    E.   None of the above

Q33. Is $y > x^2$?

    (1) $y > x^3$
    (2) $x > 0$

    A.   1 alone, not 2 alone
    B.   2 alone, not 1 alone
    C.   1 and 2 together (need both)   Answer
    D.   1 alone or 2 alone
    E.   1 and 2 together are not sufficient

Q34. Which of the following inequalities is the solution to the inequality $(x/2) + 3 < (x/3) + 2$?

    A. $x < -2$
    B. $x < -3$
    C. $x < -6$ Answer
    D. $x > -12$
    E. $x < 0$

Q35. A sequence of numbers a_1, a_2, a_3 etc. is generated using the following algorithm: $a_{n+1} = 3a_n$. Does the number 1 appear in the sequence if:

(1) a_1 is positive
(2) $a_5 - a_4 = 2$

A. 1 alone, not 2 alone
B. 2 alone, not 1 alone
C. 1 and 2 together (need both)   Answer
D. 1 alone or 2 alone
E. 1 and 2 together are not sufficient

Q36. If $57x + 29y = 105$ and $4x + 58y = 100$, then the value of y is nearest:

A. 2
B. 52/29
C. 1.655   Answer
D. 31
E. Cannot be determined

Q37. Is $(x - y)(x + y) > 0$?

(1) Both x and y are positive
(2) $x > y$

A. 1 alone, not 2 alone
B. 2 alone, not 1 alone
C. 1 and 2 together (need both)   Answer
D. 1 alone or 2 alone
E. 1 and 2 together are not sufficient

Sub-test 6: verbal

To indicate your answer, put a tick alongside the suggested answer of your choice and when you have reread and checked your answer, fill in the box, then move on to the next question. There is no going back in the real GMAT CAT®, so when you have moved on to the next question, do not be tempted to go back and change your answer as you will not be able to do that in the real test. If you really cannot get to the solution of a question then it is worth guessing, but only as a last resort. Remember that to do well in a test you really have to try very hard!

You are allowed 75 minutes in which to attempt the 41 questions that make up this test. Work where you will not be interrupted and complete the test in one continuous period. Do not turn the page until you are really ready to begin.

Sub-test 6

Passage
(262 words)

Postage stamps have followers in every strand of society all over the world. As an alternative investment to more traditional markets, stamps have performed well, with high-quality examples beating the return on most of the rest of the economy during low interest rate periods. Stamps as an asset help a portfolio achieve diversification, so maximizing opportunity while minimizing risk. The market-makers are sometimes reported in the national press when they pay vast sums of money for examples of the world's most expensive stamps. Particularly valuable are stamps that were misprinted, the most famous (and valuable) of which is perhaps the 1920s' 24-cent American stamp with an upside-down biplane. Equally high prices are paid for examples of otherwise common stamps that carry unique differences. These variations may have been unintentional but their rarity sets them apart. In many instances, these differences are minuscule and what appears to the casual observer as an unremarkable example of an everyday stamp, is to the rich fanatic with a magnifying glass a highly valuable prize. For the vast majority of dealers and their customers, the celebrated super expensive stamps are the subject only of catalogues and magazine articles. Their domain is more likely to be the newly issued colorful commemorative stamps printed in the millions by national post offices. Thousands buy sheets of these stamps in the expectation that they will rise in value. All too often however, when the time comes to sell the collection they discover that the stamps are worth less than they were originally worth in terms of their posting value.

Q1. The primary objective of this passage is to:

    A. promote stamps as an alternative investment to more usual investments such as the bond markets

    B. describe philately, the hobby of collecting postage stamps

    C. describe investing in stamps

    D. describe the two worlds of philately: the small-time collector of decorative stamps with little real value and the international market of high-value, rare stamps

    E. describe the two worlds of philately: the investor and the collector

Answer [ ]

Q2. In the context of the passage the word portfolio means:

    A. a range of investments

    B. a flat case for the safe transportation of stamps or other paper valuables

    C. the duties of a minister of state

    D. a sample of the items in a collection that demonstrate its extent

    E. a set of stamps that collectively are worth more than they can command individually

Answer [ ]

Q3. Criminals sometimes use stamps to transport and launder large sums of money. Which of the features that make stamps attractive to criminals is not mentioned in the passage?

    A.   The casual observer is unlikely to realize the high value of some stamps.

    B   There is a ready market for stamps in most countries.

    C.   There are stamp dealers all over the world.

    D.   A few stamps can be worth a large sum of money.

    E.   Their size and value makes them highly portable.

Answer ☐

Q4. Which of the following statements, if true, would prove the case that the vast majority of collectors find their collections worth less than they originally paid for them?

    A.   The world's most expensive stamps have doubled in value in the last 12 years.

    B.   Over the years, high-quality stamps have risen in value at a rate equal to the growth rate of the rest of the economy.

    C.   The collecting price for a stamp is determined more by rarity than original posting value.

    D.   Commemorative stamps from the 1940s command the best prices.

    E.   After decades, some new issues command higher prices for collecting than their original posting.

Answer ☐

Q5. Which of the following motives is not mentioned in the passage?

    A.   obsessive enthusiasm

    B.   a means to diversify investments

    C.   the expectation that they will rise in value

    D.   to beat the return of other markets at a time of low interest rates

    E.   to collect them

Answer ☐

Q6. The perfectly low rate of taxation in America means that working Americans have relatively high spending power, yet their typical monthly salary remains internationally competitive.

    A.   The perfectly low rate

    B.   The a bit low rate

    C.   The excessively low rate

    D.   The totally low rate

    E.   The really low rate

Answer ☐

Q7. Her success was due to her ability to think strategically while overseeing day-to-day activities, <u>and such an ability is</u> rare indeed.

  A.   and such an ability is
  B.   and to do so is
  C.   and to think strategically while overseeing day-to-day activities is
  D.   and as such an approach is
  E.   and her successful ability is

  Answer ☐

Q8. We have <u>no reasons to be optimistic and do not expect any changes</u> in the foreseeable future.

  A.   no reasons to be optimistic and do not expect any changes
  B.   few reasons to be optimistic and do not expect much changes
  C.   no reason to be optimistic and do not expect much changes
  D.   little reason to be optimistic and do not expect much to change
  E.   much reasons to be optimistic and do not expect much change

  Answer ☐

Q9. <u>Only the children interested went to the natural history museum to see the dinosaur exhibition. All but one of them was well behaved</u>.

  A.   Only the children interested went to the natural history museum to see the dinosaur exhibition. All but one of them was well behaved.
  B.   Only the interested children went to the natural history museum to see the dinosaur exhibition. All but one of them was behaved well.
  C.   Only the children interested went to the natural history museum to see the dinosaur exhibition. All but one of them was behaved.
  D.   Only the interested children went to the natural history museum to see the dinosaur exhibition. All but one of them was behaved.
  E.   Only the children interested went to the natural history museum to see the dinosaur exhibition. All but one of them was behaved well.

  Answer ☐

Passage
(205 words)

There is hardly a corporation that does not have a PR (public relations) budget that runs into the tens of millions. It is all about positive image building. Most of the millions are spent with advertising agencies for slick multimedia campaigns that seek to improve the profile of the business or its brands. But it also includes the placement of positive stories that purport to be news or items of public interest. There are many examples of fabulously successful campaigns. But when things go wrong they can go spectacularly wrong. The biggest and one of the most high-profile blunders occurred when one of the world's largest public utilities ran a campaign promoting its size as a virtue in the modern world. All may have gone well had it not been for the timing of the campaign, for it coincided with an announcement to lay off thousands and to close a large number of outlets. The protests were heard from customers in isolated villages through to the national legislative body. Another infamous case occurred when a candy manufacture announced that it was improving the taste of its traditional product. The reaction of millions of loyal customers caused utter pandemonium. Spontaneous protests and boycotts erupted worldwide.

Q10. The author holds that PR is all about positive image built through:

A. a series of TV advertisements
B. news or items of public interest
C. fabulously expensive campaigns   Answer
D. publicity
E. the services of advertising agencies

Q11. The audience that the author had in mind when he wrote the passage was:

A. someone conversant with the subject
B. his peers in public relations
C. prospective purchasers of the services of his advertising agency
D. someone with only a passing acquaintance with the subject
E. graduate students of business studies

Answer

Q12. According to the passage, PR can go wrong when corporations:

A. are caught lying
B. fail to consider environmental issues
C. promote their size   Answer
D. tamper with tradition
E. misjudge their customers' attachments

Q13. The author of the passage would agree that when things go wrong and a negative image results, the effect is:

A. exactly opposite to the one intended
B. parallel to the one intended
C. contrary to the one intended
D. comparable to the one intended
E. dissimilar to the one intended

Answer [ ]

Q14. Which of the following would most logically follow as the next sentence?

A. The company stood its ground and persisted with the change, hoping that its customers would come around to its way of thinking.
B. The old formula was quickly reintroduced and a solemn promise made that it would never be tampered with again.
C. Public relations blunders come no bigger.
D. PR campaigns are intended to improve a company's profile and sometimes they have the opposite effect.
E. The company had no choice but to expedite the plan.

Answer [ ]

Q15. I was a professional in the same department as Dr James, but I found his paper nearly technical and practically academic.

A. I was a professional in the same department as Dr James, but I found his paper nearly technical and practically academic.
B. I was highly professional in the same department as Dr James, but I found his paper highly technical and extremely academic.
C. I was totally professional in the same department as Dr James, but I found his paper intensely technical and entirely academic.
D. I was a professional in the same department as Dr James, but I found his paper extremely technical and fairly academic.
E. I was a professional in the same department as Dr James, but I found his paper perfectly technical and largely academic.

Answer [ ]

Q16. The assignment was not very impossible.

A. The assignment was not very impossible.
B. The assignment is not very impossible.
C. The assignment was very impossible.
D. The assignment is fairly impossible.
E. The assignment was quite impossible.

Answer [ ]

Q17. The advertised position received 1,200 applicants but <u>none of the applying candidates</u> were suitable.

    A.   none of the applying candidates
    B.   none of the affected candidates
    C.   none of the candidates affected   Answer
    D.   none of the candidates applying
    E.   none of these

Q18. <u>No one seems certain of why</u> the government took so long to recognize the benefits of a managed, skills-based immigration policy.

    A.   No one seems certain of why
    B.   No one seems certain about why
    C.   No one seems certain why   Answer
    D.   He became certain why
    E.   It is easy to be certain why

Passage
(280 words)

We face a pensions crisis because more than half of working people will rely solely on the state to provide a pension in their old age. These people have paid into a state pension scheme all their working lives. In return they expected to be provided with a state pension to live on during their old age. Why then the crisis? In the 1960s there was one pensioner for every five workers. This ratio dropped to one pensioner for every three workers and is forecast to go as low as one pensioner to every two workers within the next 20 years. The government will simply not be able to afford to provide pensions to the millions of dependent pensioners. To make ends meet it is estimated that the government will have to cut pensions by 30 percent of the current already low pension rate. This means that if you rely solely on the state for your pension you may well find yourself retiring to utter poverty. No wonder people are talking about a crisis, and it will directly affect around 12 million people. A large slice of the other half of working people is also at risk of retiring to poverty. These workers have, as well as their state pension, a private scheme to which they contribute and intend to use it to top up their state pension in retirement. However, most are contributing only a pittance towards these schemes and have funds currently valued at less than $10,000. On their retirement the majority of this group of people will find that their private schemes are insufficient to buy them a meaningful second source of income.

Q19. Which of the following would most likely follow on as the next sentence in the passage?

A.   The government faces an $800 billion bill for public sector pensions.
B.   They too will not be able to enjoy a decent quality of life in their retirement.
C.   Long-awaited proposals to tackle the looming crisis were rejected out of hand by the government yesterday.
D.   They too eagerly await proposals as to how the crisis might be avoided.
E.   Long-awaited proposals as to how workers can be encouraged to save more for their retirement were announced recently.

Answer ☐

Q20. In making his case the author relies on which of the following assumptions?

A.   that the government has not been putting aside workers' contributions in order to meet its future pension commitments
B.   that a net influx of migrants could help improve the future pensioner–worker ratio
C.   that the government has been putting aside workers' contributions so that it can afford future pension commitments
D.   that a net outflow of migrants could serve to improve the future pensioner–worker ratio
E.   that the government is unlikely to accept future recommendations to increase the rate of the basic state pension

Answer ☐

Q21. Which of the following is answered in the passage?

A.   the extent to which the number of pensioners will increase and the number of workers will fall over the next 20 years
B.   the extent to which the ratio between pensioners and workers is likely to fall ultimately
C.   how relatively uncomfortable retirement will become given the fall in the ratio between pensioners and workers
D.   how many millions of people are at risk of retiring in poverty
E.   to what extent future increases in life expectancy will exacerbate the problem

Answer ☐

Q22. <u>He slowly realize that it was his elderly relative who had supposedly</u> won the lottery.

    A.   He slowly realize that it was his elderly relative who had supposedly
    B.   He was slow to realize that it was his elder relative who had supposedly
    C.   He was slowly to realize that it was his elderly relative who had supposed to
    D.   He was slow to realize that it was his elderly relative who had supposedly
    E.   He slowly realized that it was his elderly relative who suppose to

Answer [ ]

Q23. In February Japan's manufacturing output expanded <u>by as many as 1 percent,</u> making it 3 percent high than a year earlier.

    A.   by as many as 1 percent,
    B.   by as few as 1 percent,
    C.   by as many than 1 percent,
    D.   by so much as 1 percent,
    E.   by as much as 1 percent,

Answer [ ]

Q24. <u>They in September consulted on the issue extensively and began immediately implementing the new strategy</u>.

    A.   They in September consulted on the issue extensively and began immediately implementing the new strategy.
    B.   They consulted in September on the issue extensively and immediately began implementing the new strategy.
    C.   In September they consulted extensively on the issue and immediately began implementing the new strategy.
    D.   They consulted on the issue extensively in September and immediately began implementing the new strategy.
    E.   They consulted on the issue extensively in September and began immediately implementing the new strategy.

Answer [ ]

Q25. <u>The price of gold is nearly at a historic high. I, when trading resumes tomorrow,</u> <u>expect the price to rise further</u>.

   A.   The price of gold is nearly at a historic high. I, when trading resumes tomorrow, expect the price to rise further.

   B.   Nearly the price of gold is at a historic high. When trading resumes tomorrow, I expect the price to rise further.

   C.   The price of gold is nearly at a historic high. Tomorrow I expect, when trading resumes, the price to rise further.

   D.   The price of gold is at a historic high nearly. I expect tomorrow, when trading resumes, the price to rise further.

   E.   The price of gold is nearly at a historic high. Tomorrow, when trading resumes, I expect the price to rise further.

Answer ☐

Passage
(223 words)

A paper plane should be made by folding a single sheet of A4 (8½ in × 11 in) paper and not involve any cuts or the addition of anything such as sticky tape, glue or weights. The indoor flight record for such a plane is over 60 m. The aerodynamics involved are as complex as the principles behind any plane, but the secret to one built from paper is ease of construction, folds that impart strength, the correct location of the center of balance, minimum drag and maximum lift. Key to a successful design is the nose and wing shape. The best designs seem to involve a blunt nose made from multiple folds. This makes the craft strongest at the point of impact in the (hopefully) many crash landings. It also sets the center of gravity further back than on a pointed nose design and so affords more stable flight. The wing shape that affords the longest flights is delta, which is cambered upwards to increase lift by forcing the air as it passes over the wing through a greater angle. A plane with such wings is capable of flight in excess of 20 seconds when launched from a height of 2 m in still air. Outside, where wind conditions and thermal lifts may be harnessed, flights may last considerably longer and go much further than 60 m.

Q26. The secret to the ultimate paper plane is best summed up as:

   A.   a plane with delta-shaped wings

   B.   getting the balance and shape right

   C.   the design of the nose and wing

   D.   using sticky tape, glue and weights

   E.   complex aerodynamic principles captured by simplicity of design

Answer ☐

Q27. Which of the following points is made in the passage?

    A.   The nose should be heavy so as to realize stable flight.

    B.   The center of gravity should be towards the back to prevent stalling.

    C.   Viewed from the front the wings should give the plane a 'v' shape.

    D.   Wings should be slightly convex so that they increase lift.

    E.   The plane should have a pointed nose design.

Answer ☐

Q28. Which of the following statements, if true, would most weaken the case made in the passage?

    A.   A paper plane should be made using cuts, glue and weights.

    B.   A flight of over 30 seconds has been achieved by a plane without delta wings made from a single sheet of paper only, in an indoor test where the air was still.

    C.   A paper plane made using cuts, glue and sticky tape would fly further than 60 m if launched indoors in still air.

    D.   A flight of over 60 m has been achieved by a plane made only from a single sheet of paper but with a pointed nose.

    E.   A flight of over 30 seconds has been achieved by a plane made from only a single sheet of paper with a pointed nose.

Answer ☐

Q29. The respondents to the <u>survey much agree with</u> the statement that the election campaign is boring.

    A.   survey much agree with

    B.   survey very much agree with

    C.   survey too much agree with   Answer ☐

    D.   survey very agree with

    E.   survey extremely agree with

Q30. <u>If a customer was unhappy with the service they had received I would personally listen to their complaint, tell them what I was going to do about it and let them know when I had done what I said I would do.</u>

A.   If a customer was unhappy with the service they had received I would personally listen to their complaint, tell them what I was going to do about it and let them know when I had done what I said I would do.
B.   Interestingly, if a customer was unhappy with the service they had received I would listen to their complaint, tell them what I was going to do about it and let them know when I had done what I said I would do.
C.   If a customer was unhappy with the service they had received I would listen to their complaint, tell them what I was going to do about it and let them know when I had done what I said I would do personally.
D.   I would wisely, if a customer was unhappy with the service they had received I would personally listen to their complaint, tell them what I was going to do about it and let them know when I had done what I said I would do.
E.   Personally, if a customer was unhappy with the service they had received I would listen to their complaint, tell them what I was going to do about it and let them know when I had done what I said I would do.

Answer ☐

Q31. The candidate's success in the race to win the endorsement of the Democratic Party <u>is owing to</u> his support for citizenship rights for illegal immigrants.

A.   is owing to
B.   is because
C.   is due to   Answer ☐
D.   seeing that
E.   as a result of

Passage
(256 words)

Recruitment to most courses opens to applicants in October when all the places are available and is closed in April when the course administrator hopes there are no places left. Between these two dates the number of places steadily decreases. By the end of February it is a fair assumption that the popular courses have only a few places left to fill. The likelihood is that in October places are offered purely on the basis of merit, however, as the course fills, those responsible increasingly turn to the issue of ensuring the correct balance of the class. In deciding to whom to make an offer they will look to ensure, for example, a good balance of backgrounds in the hope of ensuring a well-balanced class that can bring a broad church of experiences to discussions and seminars. On many courses, quotas are set as to the preferred mix of candidates to be offered a place. Schools will want the genders to be equally represented. They will wish the intake to be representative of the ethnicity of the community that they serve. They will seek to recruit a representative sample of students who declare a disability. It is a distinct possibility that the last few places are effectively reserved for applicants who offer a profile that remains under-represented in the class. By this stage the school may not be looking to recruit the best in terms of merit and it is possible that an offer will be made to less well-qualified candidates because they fill the under-represented profile.

Q32. It can be inferred from the passage that:
    A.   Less-than-popular courses do not have the same opportunity to achieve a preferred mix of students.
    B.   A candidate with less-than-perfect academic credentials stands a better chance of success if they apply in the latter part of the period of recruitment.
    C.   A candidate who declares a disability is more likely to be offered a place than an able-bodied applicant with identical qualifications.
    D.   Academically strong candidates should submit their applications as soon as the recruitment process opens.
    E.   The last few places of a course are effectively reserved for applicants who conform to under-represented profiles.

Answer ☐

Q33. Which of the following statements is the author most likely to disagree with?
    A.   Most schools set a series of deadlines, and as each is passed, in effect another mini-recruitment campaign begins.
    B.   The first mini-round is the most straightforward in terms of the candidates being offered places purely on the basis of merit.
    C.   The second of these mini-recruitment rounds is when the course administrator turns to the issue of balancing applicants with the candidates who have already accepted a place in order to ensure a representative mix of students.
    D.   Once the second half of the recruitment campaign is reached, schools will have received most serious applications.
    E.   Towards the end of the recruitment cycle, popular courses will only have a few places left and the administrator is as much concerned with ensuring a representative and well-balanced class as selection on the basis of merit.

Answer ☐

Q34. In the context of the passage the term 'broad church' refers to:

A.   students who are broad-minded
B.   a course of study on the subject of a religious sect that favors a liberal interpretation of doctrine
C.   a policy that promotes diversity in education
D.   a wide set of criteria adopted so as to ensure a fair and equitable recruitment policy
E.   a group that encompasses a wide range of views

Answer ☐

Q35. The core banking system was designed <u>in order to</u> improvements in customer service, management information and product development were realized.

A.   in order to
B.   so as to
C.   in such a way
D.   in such a way as to
E.   such that

Answer ☐

Q36. My current job is 24/7 and I can't help but feel resentment when my working life starts to impinge on <u>my home life though</u>.

A.   my home life though.
B.   my home life although.
C.   my home life even though.
D.   my home life.
E.   my home life even although.

Answer ☐

Q37. <u>I get an e-mail from the auction house about our painting. Apparently it got painted in 1905 and they are having lots of interest in it from bidders</u>.

A.   I get an e-mail from the auction house about our painting. Apparently it got painted in 1905 and they are having lots of interest in it from bidders.
B.   I got an e-mail from the auction house about our painting. Apparently it got painted in 1905 and there're getting lots of interest in it from bidders.
C.   I get an e-mail from the auction house about our painting. Apparently it was painted in 1905 and they get a lot of interest in it from bidders.
D.   I got an e-mail from the auction house about our painting. Apparently it got painted in 1905 and they have got a lot of interest from bidders.
E.   I got an e-mail from the auction house about our painting. Apparently it was painted in 1905 and they are getting lots of interest in it from bidders.

Answer ☐

Q38. The new job <u>complemented her very much</u>.

    A.   complemented her very much.
    B.   suited her very well.
    C.   fitted her very well.   Answer
    D.   harmonized with her much.
    E.   fit her well.

Q39. <u>Was it to rain</u> then the gardener could go home early as he would not have to water the plants.

    A.   Was it to rain
    B.   Were it not to rain
    C.   Supposing it was to rain   Answer
    D.   As it was to rain
    E.   If it were to rain

Q40. They have turned the old steel <u>work into a library and you can see all the author's works there</u>.

    A.   work into a library and you can see all the author's works there.
    B.   works into a library and you can see all the author's works.
    C.   works into a library and you can see all the author's work.
    D.   work into a library and you can see all the author's work.
    E.   foundry into a library and you can see all the author work.

    Answer

Q41. <u>I'mn't too much interested in the film</u>.

    A.   I'mn't too much interested in the film.
    B.   I am not interested much in the film.
    C.   I'm not very interested in the film.   Answer
    D.   I am not too much interested in the film.
    E.   I'mn't too interested in the film.

Answers and explanations

Chapter 3   Warm up questions for the quantitative and verbal sub-tests

Warm up for the quantitative sub-test

Problem-solving questions

1. Answer: C

    Explanation: It is not necessary to know the values of x and y, simply to multiply the sum of x + y from the first equation by 2.

2. Answer: 14, 28, 42, 56

3. Answer: B

    Explanation: Rearrange the first equation to give y = 4x. Substitute this into the second equation to replace y and to give x + 4x = 5. Therefore, 5x = 5 and x = 1. It is possible to double check by putting the values obtained into the original equations.

4. Answer: 2 and 3

    Explanation: All numbers can be written as a product of their prime factors. Find a number's prime factors by dividing by the prime numbers in increasing order.

5. Answer: A

    Explanation: Subtract x + 3y from both sides to give 0 = x − 2y.

6. Answer: 1, 7, 5, 35

    Explanation: This is another way of asking for the factors of a number, the numbers that divide exactly without remainder.

7. Answer: B
    Explanation: Subtract x + y from both sides to give 0 = x + y. 4 times x + y, 4x + 4y, must therefore also be equal to 0.

8. Answer: 24
    Explanation: The lowest common multiple (LCM) is the lowest multiple common to both. In this case it is 3 × 8 = 24 and 6 × 4 = 24. Find the factors for each number, then identify the lowest common multiple.

9. Answer: C
    Explanation: Rearrange the equation to give y = x/2. Substitute for y into the equation x – y to give x – x/2. This, then, resolves to x/2, which is 50% of x.

10. Answer: No
    Explanation: To test if a number is prime, find its square root, then divide by the prime numbers up to the value of its square root. If none divide exactly, then it is prime. $\sqrt{49} = 7$, divide 49 by the primes 2, 3, 5, 7. You will find that 49 ÷ 7 = 7, so 49 is not a prime number.

11. Answer: B
    Explanation: Rearrange the equation to give y = x/199. Substitute for y into the equation x – y to give x – x/199. This then resolves to 198x/199, which is just over 99.5% of x and hence nearest 100%.

12. Answer: 8
    Explanation: 8 × 5 = 40, 40 ÷ 4 = 10, ½ of 10 = 5.

13. Answer: 4
    Explanation: All 3 are prime numbers so they each have 2 divisors. Without repeating the same divisor there are 4: 1, 23, 41 and 79.

14. Answer: B
    Explanation: Rearrange the equation to give y = 40 – x. 80 – 2y is therefore 80 – (80 – 2x) = 2x. This is 200% of x.

15. Answer: D
    Explanation: 4^3 and 8^2. Both = 64.

16. Answer: D
    Explanation: Solution A is not always true. For example, a negative number multiplied by a large positive number would give a large negative number, i.e., less than –1. Similarly for B. E is obviously not true. If x > 1, then –x must be less than –1. Therefore, – x < –1 < y, so –x < y and D must be true, so C cannot be true.

17. Answer: 169
    Explanation: 13^2 or 13 × 13 = 169. For the GMAT® you should know the value of the sequence of squared numbers: 4, 9, 16, 25, 36, 49, 64, 81, 100, 121, 144, 169, 196, 225.

18. Answer: E

    Explanation: No reason why x should be greater than y, so both A and D are false. Y can be less than 1, so B is not true. The relative values of x and y are not known, so C is not necessarily true. Both are positive, so E must be true.

19. Answer: 17, 31, 53 and 79.

    Explanation: For the GMAT® you should learn the low value prime numbers off by heart: 2, 3, 5, 7, 11, 13, 17, 19, 23, 29, 31, 37, 41 etc.

20. Answer: C

    Explanation: If y is much larger than x, A is not true and nor are B or D. Similarly, if the opposite is the case, then E is not true. Positive divided by positive is positive, so C is always true.

21. Answer: 1,500

    Explanation: Be fully up to speed in fractions, decimals and percentages before you take the GMAT®. $1/5$ of 45% = 9%, so 9% = 135; 100% = 135/9 × 100 = 15 × 100 = 1,500.

22. Answer: C

    Explanation: If y is negative and x positive, then A is not true, nor B or D. E is obviously wrong and C is always true.

23. Answer: 600

    Explanation: $1/4$ of 25% = 6.25%, so 37.5 = 6.25%; 100% = 37.5/6.25 × 100 = 6 × 100 = 600.

24. Answer: A

    Explanation: Subtract x from both sides to give 2x – 3 < 2. Add 3 to both sides to give 2x < 5 and x < 5/2 or 2.5.

25. Answer: 1,122

    Explanation: 999 + 1,245 = 2,244 ÷ 2 = 1,122.

26. Answer: A

    Explanation: Rearrange to give –6x > 4, therefore x < –2/3. Careful of negatives!

27. Answer: 33

    Explanation: 99 – 67 + 1 (we add the 1 otherwise we fail to count 67) = 33.

28. Answer: C

    Explanation: Subtract the second equation from the first to give 5y = 6, y = 6/5. Substitute this value into either equation to obtain x = 2.2.

29. Answer: 667

    Explanation: Find the average to calculate the sum. There are 40 – 18 + 1 numbers in the range (you have to add the 1 otherwise you are a number short) = 23 numbers. The average is 18 + 40 = 58 ÷ 2 = 29. The sum = 29 × 23 = 667.

30. Answer: E
    Explanation: Multiply the first equation by 4 to give $2x + 4/3y = 8$. Subtract the first from the second, giving $5y/3 = 5$. $y = 3$.

31. Answer: 38, 39, 40
    Explanation: Make x the first number, $x + (x + 1) + (x + 2) = 117$, so $3x + 3 = 117$, so $3x = 114$, $114 \div 3 = x$, $x = 38$. The numbers are 38, 39, 40.

32. Answer: A
    Explanation: These equations are identical, as $x = 2y$, so there is not enough information to solve the problem.

33. Answer: 7 and 21
    Explanation: The first number $= 3 \times$ the second, so first number $= 3x$ and $3x + x = 28$, so $4x = 28$; $x = 7$. The numbers are 7 and (3×7) 21.

34. Answer: C
    Explanation: *4 is 3, as 3 is the largest integer less than 4 and *2.5 is 2. 3 times 2 is 6.

35. Answer: 12
    Explanation: $4x - 8 = 40$, $4x = 48$, $4 \times 12 = 48$, so $x = 12$.

36. Answer: D
    Explanation: *(13.5 − 0.51) is *(12.99) and therefore 12. *(2.5 + 2.49) is *(4.99), i.e., 4. 12 divided by 4 = 3.

37. Answer: 400
    Explanation: $1/2$ of 5% = 2.5%, so $10 = 2.5$; $10/2.5 = 4 \times 100 = 400$.

38. Answer: C
    Explanation: &(15) corresponds to 3 and &(16) corresponds to 4. $3 - 4 = -1$, but starting at 0 (or 12 on the clock) and moving one backwards, this gives 11, minus 1 not being a valid number on the clock.

39. Answer: 20
    Explanation: $5x - 99 = 1$, $5x = 100$, $5 \times 20 = 100$, so $x = 20$.

40. Answer: E
    Explanation: &(36) is 12. &(12) corresponds to 12. $12/12 = 1$.

41. Answer: A
    Explanation: The two people can fill the truck twice in 8 hours so they will take 4 hours to fill it and 2 hours to half fill it.

42. Answer: E
    Explanation: Using the first equation and substituting for y and z into the second equation gives $(x)(2x)(4x) = 8x^3 = 128$. Therefore, x is the cube root of $64/8 = 2$.

43. Answer: 600

    Explanation: 492 gallons represent 82% of the original amount of fuel you must find (100%), 1% = 492 ÷ 82 = 6, so 100% = 600.

44. Answer: C

    Explanation: Using the first equation and substituting for y and z into the second equation gives $(x)(x/2)(x/4) = x3/8 = 64$. Therefore, x is the cube root of 512 = 8.

45. Answer: 3 minutes

    Explanation: The average over the 10 days has been increased by 30 minutes, so the delay must have increased the daily average by 30 ÷ 10 = 3.

46. Answer: A

    Explanation: Using the first equation and rearranging gives $z = y/x$. Substituting into the third equation for y and z gives $(x)(4x)(y/x) = (x)(4x)(4x/x) = 16x^2 = 64$. Therefore, x is 2.

47. Answer: C

    Explanation: The total economically active = 10,000, the total employed = 6,000. The total unemployed = 4,000, so the ratio between employed and unemployed = 6,000:4,000, which simplifies to 3:2.

48. Answer: E

    Explanation: Using the first equation and rearranging gives $y = x/5$. Similarly, for the second equation, giving $z = y/4 = x/20$. Substituting into the third equation for y and z gives $(x)(x/5)/(x/20) = 4x = 64$. Therefore, x is 16.

49. Answer: 8%

    Explanation: Total receipts in 2002 = 4.5 billon receipts from banking and finance = 4.5 – 4.14 = 0.36. You must find 0.36 as a percentage of 4.5. 1% = 4.5 ÷ 100 = 0.045, 0.36 ÷ 0.045 = 8.

50. Answer: A

    Explanation: Using the first equation and rearranging gives $y = \sqrt{x}$, or $x^{0.5}$. $z = \sqrt{y} = \sqrt{(\sqrt{x})}$, or $x^{0.25}$. Substituting into the third equation for y and z gives $((x)(x^{0.5})(x^{0.25}))^4/2 = (x^{1.75})^4/2 = (x^{1.75})^4/2 = x^7/2 = 64$. $x^7 = 128$, therefore, x is 2.

51. Answer: 15%

    Explanation: All workers at Pi Corporation = 54 ÷ 3 × 100 = 1,800; the total population of knowledge workers = 270. You must find 270 as a percentage of 1,800. 1,800 ÷ 100 = 18, 270 ÷ 18 = 15, so total immigrant population = 15% of all workers at Pi.

52. Answer: E
   Explanation: Several ways of doing it. You could work out values for a and b using simultaneous equations or you could solve it as though they were fractions. Cross-multiplying gives $4b/ab + 4a/ab$. This then resolves to $(4a + 4b)/ab = 4(a + b)/ab = 4(6)/8 = 3$. Always check the answers by substituting them back into the original equations.

53. Answer: 30% profit
   Explanation: $91.20 \times 85\% = 77.52$ per unit $\times 40 = 3,100.8$ (income at 15% discount of RSP); total factory cost $= 2,170.56$, profit $= 3,100.8 - 2,170.56 = 930.24$. You must find 930.24 as a percentage of 3,100.8; $10\% = 310.8$ so $930.24 = 30\%$ profit.

54. Answer: E
   Explanation: Multiply the first equation throughout by 3 to give $1.5a + b = 9$ and add to the second equation to give $(1.5a + a) + (b - b) = 9 + 3$. Therefore, $2.5a = 12$ and $a = 12/2.5 = 4.8$ and b (from the second equation) is 1.8. $a + b = 4.8 + 1.8 = 6.6$.

55. Answer: 73:1
   Explanation: You have to express $5.84:8 cents as a ratio in its simplest form. $5.84 = 584 cents; simply, the ratio is 584:8. Divide both by $8 = 73:1$

56. Answer: C
   Explanation: Double the first equation to give $12a + 2b = 24$. Subtract the second equation from this to give $8a = 24$, $a = 3$. b is then equal to –6. $b/a = -6/3 = -2$.

57. Answer: D
   Explanation: You can tell from the graph that the current account balance is a deficit (–) and you are informed that the balance is relative to the % size of the country's GDP.

58. Answer: E
   Explanation: Rearrange the first equation to give $a = 5b$. Substitute this into the second equation to give $(5b)b = 5$, so $b^2 = 1$ and $b = 1$ or –1 and $a = 5$ or –5. The sum is then 6 or –6.

59. Answer: 24 minutes
   Explanation: $28 = 6x$ walking + 1x cycling, $28 \div 7 = 4$, $1 \times 4 = 4$ minutes cycling, 24 minutes walking.

60. Answer: A
   Explanation: When factorized, the equation becomes $(x - 1)(x - 3)$. This is negative when only one of them is negative. $x – 1$ is negative when $x < 1$, so for the expression to be negative $x – 3$ must be positive. This is the case when $x > 3$. $x – 3$ is negative when $x < 3$ and $x – 1$ is positive for $x > 1$, leading to A as the solution.

61. Answer: 2/3
   Explanation: The number of possible outcomes $= 6$, and the total number of successful outcomes $= 1, 3, 5, 6 = 4$ so the probability $= 4/6 = 2/3$

62. Answer: C

    Explanation: It is not possible to factorize with real numbers, so the answer is none. A general equation like this has the form $ax^2 + bx + c$. If $b^2 > 4ac$ it can be factorized. In this case $b^2 = 4$ and $4ac = 8$, so it cannot be factorized. C is therefore the answer.

63. Answer: 5/6

    Explanation: There are 6 possible outcomes and 5 successful outcomes = 3, 5, 2, 4, 6 = 5, so the probability is 5/6.

64. Answer: A

    Explanation: Subtracting from both sides of the inequality, this can be rewritten as $-x^2 + 4x - 3 > 0$. Factorizing gives $(-x + 1)(x - 3)$, which has solutions of $x = 1$ and 3. For values outside 1 and 3 the equation is negative, which means that for values between 1 and 3, $-x^2 + 4x - 3 > 0$ and $5x - x^2 - 3 > x$. A is the correct answer.

65. Answer: 1/6

    Explanation: There are 36 possible outcomes and 6 successful outcomes: $6 + 1$, $5 + 2$, $4 + 3$, $3 + 4$, $2 + 5$, $1 + 6$, so the probability $= 6/36 = 1/6$.

66. Answer: B

    Explanation: Since 6b is 0, b must be 0. This in turn means that a must also be 0, so $a = b$.

67. Answer: 18 m²

    Explanation: The area of the square $= x^2$. Pythagoras teaches us that $x^2 + x^2 = 6^2$, so $2x^2 = 36$, $x^2 = 18$ m².

68. Answer: A

    Explanation: From the second equation $b = 12/6 = 2$. Substituting this into the first equation gives $5a = 2(2)$; $5a = 4$ and so $a = 4/5$. a/b is then $(4/5)/2$ or $4/10$, i.e., 2/5, answer A. In C, $b = 2$, but $a = 0.8$, so it is not correct.

69. Answer: 4 m

    Explanation: The sum of the squares of the two smaller sides of the right-angled triangle = the square of the hypotenuse (the largest side), so $25^2 = 3^2 + x^2$, $25^2 = 9 + x^2$, $x^2 = 16^2$, $\sqrt{16} = 4$, $x = 4$. If you learn the Pythagoras triples (well-known triangles that have sides that are each the length of whole numbers) then you would have recognized this triangle as the triple 3, 4, 5 and not needed to undertake the calculation.

70. Answer: E

    Explanation: Subtracting the first equation from the second gives $-a + b = 6$, or $b - a = 6$. Multiplying this by 2 gives $2b - 2a = 12$, answer E.

71. Answer: 27 ft³

    Explanation: The volume of a cube is length³ so the volume $= 3 \times 3 \times 3 = 27$ ft³.

72. Answer: D

    Explanation: Cross-multiplying the first equation gives $(b/ab) + (a/ab) = 2$. Repeating the same for the second equation leads to $(2b/ab) + (3a/ab) = 5$. The new first equation is then multiplied by 2, thus $(2b/ab) + (2a/ab) = 4$. This equation can be subtracted from the new second equation giving $(a/ab) = 1$. Simplifying, this gives $1/b = 1$ and hence $b = 1$.

73. Answer: 5 m

    Explanation: This question relies on another Pythagorean triple. The $\sqrt{169} = 13$ so the hypotenuse of the right-angled triangle is 13 m long. Using Pythagoras we know $169 = 12^2 + x^2$, $169 = 144 + x^2$, $25 = x^2$, $\sqrt{25} = x$. $x = 5$.

74. Answer: E

    Explanation: Imagine where x is negative and y positive. A, B and C are all false. If they are both positive or both negative then D cannot be true.

75. Answer: 113 cm³

    Explanation: Volume of a sphere is found with the formula $v = {}^4/_3 \pi\, r^3$, ${}^4/_3 \times 3.14 \times 27 = {}^4/_3 \times 84.78 = 113$ cm³.

76. Answer: C

    Explanation: A, B and C can be true, but they may not be. For example, if x and y are both less than 1, then A, B and C will all be true. If, however, they are greater than 1, but one of them is negative, the product will be negative and hence less than 1.

77. Answer: 6 m

    Explanation: Another Pythagorean triple. If you do not recognize it then use the Pythagoras theorem $= 100$ m² $= 8^2 + x^2$, 100 m² $= 64 + x^2$, $36 = x^2$, $x = \sqrt{36} = 6$.

78. Answer: E

    Explanation: Dividing by 5 throughout gives $2y + x < 6$, so, $x < 6 - x$. Similarly, dividing initially by 10 gives $y + x/2 < 3$, $y < 3 - x/2$. None of the proposed solutions above is equivalent to either of these.

79. Answer: 170 cm³

    Explanation: Volume of a cylinder $= \pi\, r^2 h$, $r^2 = 3 \times 3 = 9$, $3.14 \times 9 \times 6 = 3.14 \times 54 = 170$ cm³.

80. Answer: A

    Explanation: Rearranging the first equation by subtracting x from both sides gives $2y < -x$ and hence, dividing by 2 on both sides leads to $y < -x/2$. Subtracting 2x from both sides of the second equation gives $y > -2x$. Combining these results in the equation, $-2x < y < -x/2$.

81. Answer: 15 m

    Explanation: This is another Pythagorean triple, $289 = 8^2 + x^2$, $8^2 = 64$, $x^2 = 289 - 64 = 255$, $255 = 15^2$, so $x = 15$ m.

82. Answer: A

Explanation: Substituting the value given for x into the first equation results in y = 1/4 + 4 or 1/4 + 16/4 = 17/4.

83. Answer: 134 ft³.

Explanation: A hemisphere is half of a sphere, so calculate as a sphere and halve the volume. The volume of a sphere is found with the formula $^4/_3\pi$ r³ = $^4/_3$ × 3.14 × 4³ = $^4/_3$ × 3.14 × 64 = $^4/_3$ × 201 = 268, 268 ÷ 2 = 134 ft³.

84. Answer: D

Explanation: Substituting the value given for x into the first equation results in y = (2 × 3) + 2/3 = 6 and 2/3 or 20/3, answer D.

85. Answer: 15 cm³

Explanation: Volume of pyramid = (base area × perpendicular height) ÷ 3, 9 × 5 = 45, 45 ÷ 3 = 15 cm³.

86. Answer: E

Explanation: Substituting the second equation into the first equation results in y = 2/3 + 5/6. This can be rewritten as y = 4/6 + 5/6 = 9/6, i.e., none of the above.

87. Answer: 47 cm³

Explanation: The volume of a cone is found with the formula $^1/_3\pi$ r²h, $^1/_3$ × 3.14 × 9 × 7 = $^1/_3$141.3 = 47 cm³.

88. Answer: E

Explanation: Multiplying the first equation by 2 gives 2y = 4x + 2x². Comparing this with the second equation leads to 4x + 2x² = x, i.e., the quadratic equation 2x² + 3x = 0. None of the possible solutions A–D are correct, so the answer is E.

89. Answer: 150 cm³

Explanation: The volume of a prism = area of cross-section × its length; the area of the cross-section (it is a triangle) = $^1/_2$base × perpendicular height = $^1/_2$5 × 4 = $^1/_2$20 = 10. To find the volume of the prism, multiply the area of the base by the length of the prism = 10 × 15 = 150 cm³.

90. Answer: 2 liters

Explanation: The ratio of corresponding lengths = 20/10, which cancels to 2/1; the ratio of volumes therefore will equal 2²/1², which = 4/1 = 4, so the volume of the similar can will be 4 × 500 = 2,000 ml or 2 liters.

Data sufficiency questions

1. Answer: E

Explanation: We cannot establish the length of the diameter of the circle with either statement so cannot calculate its circumference.

2. Answer: B
    Explanation: The first equation is a quadratic with two solutions, 2 and –1. In the second equation, if twice y is less than 0 then y must also be less than 0 and hence negative.

3. Answer: B
    Explanation: Statement 1 is true of all triangles but it does not help us answer the question. Statement 2 alone is sufficient as it is true of all triangles that the largest angle is opposite the largest side.

4. Answer: E
    Explanation: Individually the statements are not sufficient. Neither are they sufficient together, as it would be possible to have x as 0 or a very small positive number and still not be negative but satisfy both conditions.

5. Answer: D
    Explanation: A pentagon has 5 sides so both statements contain the same information. Still, either statement is sufficient to answer the question, as it is true of any polygon that you can establish the number of triangles into which it can be divided with the formula: number of sides – 2 = number of triangles.

6. Answer: D
    Explanation: A negative times a negative times a negative will give a negative. In fact, any negative number raised to an odd number power (1, 3, 5, 7...) will give a negative result. Either statement is sufficient, as a positive x will give a positive answer and a negative x a negative answer.

7. Answer: A
    Explanation: Statement 1 alone because at each vertex of a polygon the sum of the interior and exterior angles = 1,800°, so divide the total sum of the interior and exterior angles to find the number of sides. The sum of the exterior angles of any regular polygon = 360°, so statement 2 does not help us answer the question.

8. Answer: C
    Explanation: Individually, the statements are not sufficient. Together, however, they can be combined, by substituting the second equation into the first equation, to give $x^3 = 3$. x must therefore be positive and hence it is possible to answer the original question with a no.

9. Answer: D
    Explanation: If corresponding sides of two triangles are in the same ratio then they are similar triangles. Also, you only need to prove that two pairs of angles are equal to know that the three angles are equal and the triangles are similar. For triangles, you only need to prove one of these qualities to know that they are similar, so 1 alone or 2 alone is sufficient to answer the question.

10. Answer: D

    Explanation: If statement 1 is true then (n +8)/8 is an integer, so n/8 + 8/8 is an integer, so n must be divisible as required. Similarly, statement 2 would give a similar result. Therefore, either statement 1 alone or statement 2 alone is sufficient.

11. Answer: E

    Explanation: Congruent shapes are identical so the angles in both would be equal but this would also be true if the shapes were similar but not identical, so statement 1 cannot prove or disprove the question. Statement 2 will not prove or disprove the question either because it is possible for two shapes to have the same size sides but not be identical.

12. Answer: D

    Explanation: If statement 1 is true then (n – 3)/3 is an integer, so n/3 – 3/3, n/3 – 1 is an integer. n must, therefore, be divisible as required. Statement 2 would give a similar result, n/3 – 21/3, n/3 – 7. Therefore, either statement 1 alone or statement 2 alone is sufficient.

13. Answer: B

    Explanation: The sum of the exterior angles of any polygon = 360° so 1 is insufficient. However, the sum of all the interior and exterior angles = 1,800° × n (the number of sides) so the number of sides can be calculated with 2.

14. Answer: A

    Explanation: Statement 1 is simply the original equation halved. So, if statement 1 is true, then the original statement must be true. There are plenty of numbers that satisfy statement 2, but would not satisfy the original statement, for example, 2, 4, 8, 10, 12 etc.

15. Answer: D

    Explanation: Statement 1 proves the triangle is an equilateral triangle, so is not right-angled; statement 2 can be used to test the given lengths using Pythagoras theorem. In this case, the lengths are a Pythagoras triple and multiples of any triple are also right-angled.

16. Answer: E

    Explanation: In statement 1, if m were 2 it would obviously give the remainder 2 if n were exactly divisible by 3. If, however, n were 11 say, and m were 4 (which is exactly divisible by 2 as in statement 2) this would give 11 – 4 = 7. 7/3 = 2 remainder 1 so this is not the correct information to determine whether n meets the original condition.

17. Answer: D

    Explanation: The surface area is found with the formula $\pi rL + \pi r^2$. If we know the radius and length then the calculation can be made. In the case of statement 2 the length can be found from the height and radius.

18. Answer: A

    Explanation: A parallelogram has 2 pairs of opposite sides that are parallel, so the diagonals bisect (divide into 2 equal parts). Figures with 4 sides are not always parallelograms so statement 2 is insufficient.

19. Answer: C

    Explanation: Neither statement gives information about the relative sizes of x and y, but they both give information relative to a third value, a. It takes 2 of these to generate an x and 5 to generate a y, so y must be larger.

20. Answer: A

    Explanation: The cost of the similar bar of soap can be calculated from statement 1 as a corresponding ratio; statement 2 offers no information as to any corresponding features so no comparison can be made.

21. Answer: E

    Explanation: There is not enough information. For example, x could be 8 and y could be 5 or 9.

22. Answer: E

    Explanation: Statement 1 is insufficient as the diagonals are perpendicular in a rhombus as well as all kites. Statement 2 is insufficient as a rectangle also has two pairs of equal sides.

23. Answer: E

    Explanation: Because both x and y could be negative, statement 1 is not sufficient by itself. Similarly as x, y or both could be negative, statement 2 is not sufficient either.

24. Answer: C

    Explanation: Statement 1 is true of squares and rectangles, statement 2 is true both of squares and the rhombus, but both are true only of squares.

25. Answer: B

    Explanation: Because one or both of x and y could be negative, statement 1 is not sufficient by itself. For example, with $x = -3$, $y = 2$. $(-3)^2 > (2)^2$, $9 > 4$, but -3 is less than 2. If, however, x were not negative, x would be greater than y and x^2 would be greater than y^2. Cubing, however, retains the sign of the original. So, statement 2 only would be sufficient.

26. Answer: C

    Explanation: To complete the calculation we need to calculate the volume of the ball bearing and the area of the base of the beaker.

27. Answer: C

    Explanation: If y is very large, its reciprocal $(1/y)$ will be very small. Therefore, if $x < y$, then $1/x$ will be bigger than $1/y$. This will be true except when both are negative. This additional information is given in the second statement.

28. Answer: E

    Explanation: To complete the calculation we need either the length of the ladder or the distance from the wall to the base of the ladder.

29. Answer: C

    Explanation: Either statement will enable you to determine the value of a_2, which is 9.

30. Answer: C

    Explanation: The sum of the interior angles of a pentagon = 540°. With both statements 1 and 2, the size of all angles can be calculated.

31. Answer: C

    Explanation: Each successive number is generated by squaring the previous. $\sqrt{6}$ squared is 6, which squared is 36, which squared is 1,296. Both statements individually lead to the conclusion that 36 does appear in the sequence.

32. Answer: D

    Explanation: Because the semicircles are touching, the size of the square and semicircles can be calculated from either statement.

33. Answer: E

    Explanation: Not being 0 is insufficient to know whether there is a 2 in the sequence. Similarly, there are infinite solutions satisfying both the algorithm and the condition that no numbers fall between 17 and 31. For example, 66, 33, $16\frac{1}{2}$ etc.

34. Answer: B

    Explanation: The size of the disc is irrelevant. To complete the calculation you need the number of revolutions and the distance of the point from the center of the disc.

35. Answer: D

    Explanation: If a_{16} is a positive even number then continually subtracting 2 from it will eventually generate the number 2. Hence, together the statements lead to the conclusion that 2 *does* appear in the sequence.

36. Answer: E

    Explanation: For any shape other than a triangle, to establish if they are similar we need to demonstrate statement 1 and also prove that the angles of one shape are equal to the corresponding angles in the other.

37. Answer: E

    Explanation: Statement 1 is not sufficient as y could be a large negative number and x positive. Although statement 2 indicates that both are of the same sign it is still not sufficient. For example, if $x = -4$ and $y = -3$, then $y > x$. When they are squared, however, $x^2 > y^2$. If they are both positive, then x and x^2 will both be greater than y and y^2 respectively.

38. Answer: A
    Explanation: Statement 1 is sufficient, as cubing will preserve the sign. If x is negative then x^3 is also negative. If statement 2 is true then x and y have the same sign and this gives no additional information.

39. Answer: D
    Explanation: Because the two triangles formed by the building and gatepost are similar we can calculate the height as a corresponding ratio. If the angle of the sun and the length of the shadow are known, then we can use the tan ratio to calculate the height of the building.

40. Answer: E
    Explanation: Statement 1 gives no information about y, so is not sufficient. Statement 2 might suggest that $x^2 > y$, but, for example, squaring $\frac{1}{2}$ leads to $\frac{1}{4}$, which is smaller than $\frac{1}{3}$, whereas $\frac{1}{2}$ was larger. There are, of course, values between 0 and 1 for x that could lead to the original inequality being considered both true and false though they meet the condition in statement 2. There is not enough information.

41. Answer: E
    Explanation: A bit of a trick question. Using the sin ratio we can calculate the height of the kite but we do not know how tall the person is who is holding the string so we cannot calculate the height of the string from the ground.

42. Answer: B
    Explanation: The original statement can be transposed to give $1/x^2 > -1/y^2$. As any number squared will be positive this will always be true, with the possible exception of x or y being 0 when they are undefined.

43. Answer: A
    Explanation: Statement 1 is sufficient, as the original relation could be rewritten as $3x/24 > 2y/24$ and hence $3x > 2y$. Statement 2 is not sufficient. For example, if $y = 5$ and $x = 4$, this is valid for statement 2 and the original inequality, but $y = 4$ and $x = 2$ is valid for statement 2, but not the original inequality.

44. Answer: C
    Explanation: Statement 1 is insufficient, as x could be 0 or negative. Statement 2 only gives information about x, but together, obviously, $x/8 > y/12$.

45. Answer: D
    Explanation: Either statement is sufficient as both are simply the original inequality rearranged.

46. Answer: C

    Explanation: Statement 1 is insufficient. For example, if $y = 1$ and $x = 0$. This satisfies statement 1, but not the original equation. $x = 3$ and $y = 13$, however, satisfies both equations. In fact, a simple inspection shows that for values of $x = 2$, $4x$ will always be greater than $3x + 2$. Hence, application of both statements gives sufficient information to answer the original question.

47. Answer: C

    Explanation: Statement 1 is not sufficient as there are two unknowns in the equation. Similarly, for statement 2. However, the combination of both gives a solution solving for simultaneous equations.

48. Answer: C

    Explanation: The two equations give values for x and y respectively, which can be substituted into the original equation for a solution.

49. Answer: E

    Explanation: Statement 2 is not sufficient, as this simply gives information about one of the unknowns, but no information about the other. Statement 1 can be square-rooted to give $xy = 4$ *or* -4. Hence, there is not enough information.

50. Answer: A

    Explanation: The second statement is not sufficient to determine xy. The first statement, however, can be cube-rooted to obtain $xy = 2$ and 2 is the only solution.

51. Answer: C

    Explanation: Individually they do not contain sufficient information, having two unknowns, but, together, as simultaneous equations, they can be solved. The first equation multiplies out to $x^2 + 2xy + y^2 = 8$ and the second to $x^2 - y^2 = 6$. The difference between the two equations is thus $2xy = 2$.

52. Answer: C

    Explanation: Statement 1 is not sufficient as there are two unknowns in the equation. Similarly, for statement 2. However, the combination of both gives a solution solving for simultaneous equations.

53. Answer: E

    Explanation: Statement 1 is not sufficient as there are two solutions, positive and negative. Statement 2 introduces an additional unknown, y, and so there is not enough information to solve for x.

54. Answer: B

    Explanation: Statement 1 contains two unknowns. Statement 2 appears to contain two unknowns, but it can be simplified to $3 - 2x = 1$ and hence is sufficient for a solution.

55. Answer: A

    Explanation: The equation in statement 1 is cubic and would normally be expected to have three solutions, but in this case they are all the same, so this is sufficient to determine x. The second statement, on the other hand, contains a quadratic, which has two solutions and is not sufficient.

56. Answer: A

    Explanation: Statement 1 is sufficient as there is only one solution. Statement 2 has two solutions and is not sufficient.

57. Answer: E

    Explanation: Y is positive and, of course, y^2 is positive, but simply because y^2 is positive does not mean that y is. There is not enough information to determine if x is positive.

Warm up for the verbal sub-test

Sentence correction

Q1.   Answer: A

      Explanation: The verb to drink is irregular, the past simple form is drank and the past participle, drunk.

Q2.   Answer: D

      Explanation: We say that a past obligation that was not honored ought to have been because the sum is still outstanding. B cannot be correct.

Q3.   Answer: C

      Explanation: 'About' and 'around' can both mean 'not exactly' or 'scattered' but in the question they have different meanings. 'About' in this context means 'on the subject of', while 'around' means 'round'. American English would use 'around', whereas British English might use 'round'.

Q4.   Answer: A

      Explanation: Without the word 'that' the sense of the sentence is changed to suggest that something is surprising the President.

Q5.   Answer: D

      Explanation: 'Almost', 'nearly' and 'already' are all correct in the context of the length of time for which the company has been trading. However, 'already' means 'sooner than expected' so is wrong in the context of the amount of life left, which makes suggested answers B and C incorrect. You cannot say 'almost' or 'nearly' has plenty, so suggested answers A and E are also wrong. This leaves D and 'still has plenty of life', which is correct.

Q6.   Answer: C
      Explanation: The word 'that' is required to make the sentence sensible but it cannot immediately follows 'it's' in this instance. We usually say 'there's no question that...' or 'it's no question that...' In the contest of the sentence 'there's no good' does not make sense.

Q7.   Answer: E
      Explanation: In this context we can replace 'that' with 'which' or 'who' or 'whom'. In other contexts 'when' or 'where' can be used but we cannot replace 'that' with 'why' or 'how'.

Q8.   Answer: C
      Explanation: You can 'meet' a friend (past tense 'met'), but given that it is a *new* friend, it is better to say 'I made a new friend'.

Q9.   Answer: A
      Explanation: When a sentence is negative we use 'any' rather than 'some'.

Q10. Answer: B
      Explanation: She wanted the car so she wanted to borrow it (not lend it). Her brother owned the car so he would lend it to her. We bring something to ourselves or have something taken away.

Q11. Answer: E
      Explanation: We do say, for example, what has happened, but we tend not to start a sentence with 'why .... that'. Instead, we use a noun such as 'a reason why... that'.

Q12. Answer: C
      Explanation: 'Was', 'could' or 'might' in this context are wrong because of the prior death of the author. 'Might not' is also wrong because it means it is possible but unlikely.

Q13. Answer: C
      Explanation: One can say completely full but not completely high; 'the worst possible' is wrong because the index 'rose to' and something cannot rise to the worst possible. B and E are wrong because they imply relative quantities, which do not fit with the 'in 17 years' part of the sentence. One cannot say 'the highest possible' when dealing with a quantity that has no upper limit – such as a stock index.

Q14. Answer: C
      Explanation: We use 'this' to refer to a near singular object, 'that' for a far away singular object, 'these' for near plural objects and 'those' for far away plural objects.

Q15. Answer: A

Explanation: The question sentence is structured rather formally but it is correct, while the suggested answers are either nonsensical or in the case of E in the wrong tense.

Q16. Answer: D

Explanation: GMAT® is a US test and this question illustrates one of the many differences between US and UK English. In the United States, 'sure' is correctly used to mean 'no doubt' or 'yes', and 'different than' is often acceptable, although this is being debated at present. 'Different from' is also correct, but those sentences containing this are incorrect in other ways.

Q17. Answer: E

Explanation: Irony aside, the word 'congratulations' implies something good has happened, so the suggested answers with a negative clause are incorrect. We say 'well enough' or 'sufficiently well'.

Q18. Answer: D

Explanation: 'Everyone' and 'everybody' mean the same and are interchangeable. 'Everything' is correctly placed before 'possible'.

Q19. Answer: B

Explanation: When we refer to an event that begins and continues we use the present continuous tense, in this case, 'beginning'. 'Starting' is wrong as this does not mean an event that continues.

Q20. Answer: A

Explanation: 'A few' means 'a small number' whereas 'few' means 'not many' in the negative sense, so would be wrong in this context.

Q21. Answer: D

Explanation: Both 'for a month' and 'a month' are correct but we do not put 'for' in front of 'all'.

Q22. Answer: C

Explanation: We do not say 'a fraction as', for example 'a three-quarters as', and we always say 'one and a fraction', e.g., one and a half.

Q23. Answer: A

Explanation: We use the past simple tense when referring to an action in the past. 'Only of' and 'of only' are both correct. Suggested answers D and E are both wrong because the tense is wrong.

Q24. Answer: B

Explanation: Strange as it may seem, it is correct to say 'going to go' to mean something we intend to do soon. We would not say 'may be going to go' however, but could say we 'may be going'. I have intentionally made this question harder by introducing a change of tense.

Q25. Answer: E

Explanation: The sentence can correctly start with 'if' or 'when' but the tense in each of the clauses is only correct in suggested answer E. The stock is current so 'if' or 'when' it is sold is correct. When there is a connection between the past and present or future we use the present perfect 'have been purchased', not 'has' or 'had'.

Q26. Answer: B

Explanation: In the context it is correct to say, for example, 'a good runner', 'good at running' or 'run well'. We might use the phrase 'any good' to ask a question, for example 'Is the show any good?'. E uses two correct forms but in this instance when combined they do not make sense.

Q27. Answer: C

Explanation: A and B are wrong because the question states that there is hope for a cure in the foreseeable future, which implies there is still not a cure (only optimism that one will be found). D is wrong because it implies that a cure is not possible. E is wrong because it suggests an obligation.

Q28. Answer: B

Explanation: 'Most' means more than any other. We say 'the most clever', 'the most expensive'. C is wrong because 'more' is used to draw a comparison, D is wrong because it introduces an unnecessary repetition.

Q29. Answer: D

Explanation: We use the past perfect tense when describing an event that took place before another past event. B, the present simple, would only be correct if the event described were always true.

Q30. Answer: B

Explanation: 'To' implies movement; 'at', 'on' and 'in' imply position. You could correctly say 'into' church (movement) but not 'in'.

Q31. Answer: E

Explanation: When an activity has been ongoing over a period of time up to a past point in time, we use the past perfect continuous tense: 'I had been looking'.

Q32. Answer: D

Explanation: 'No sooner had' means 'as soon as', 'no longer' means 'not after this'.

Q33. Answer: E

Explanation: When we report or state a decision we use 'I will' or its abbreviation 'I'll'. A and C are wrong because they read as if the speaker is unsure of their impending action, which is not creditable. B implies a condition that must be satisfied before the decision takes effect.

Q34. Answer: E
Explanation: We use 'ago' not 'before' to count back from now to a time in the past.

Q35. Answer: B
Explanation: We use the future continuous 'will not' or its abbreviation 'won't' to refer to an event that occurs over a period of time in the future. As written in the question the sentence is incomplete. Answer A is unlikely to be right given the negative description of the decision of the authority.

Q36. Answer: D
Explanation: All the suggested answers are linking verbs but 'remains' and 'becomes' are wrong because they are plural. As something cannot grow 'too low' only 'stay' makes good sense.

Q37. Answer: E
Explanation: After 'both' we use 'of which' not 'which', but in this case 'of which' is wrong because the subject that could take two to three years to improve is the performance of the banking system, not the reasons for that under-performance. Performance of the banking system is singular so the phrase 'both of which' is not required.

Q38. Answer: C
Explanation: The 'each' refers to each year, not each disease, so the correct answer is '$10 million in each' of the next 10 years (if the subject were the disease then A would be correct, as in for example '$10 million on each over the next 10 years').

Q39. Answer: A
Explanation: Answer D is wrong as we do not say 'have got not' but say cannot, couldn't or can't. B is wrong because 'can't not' means 'cannot not'. An exam administrator would correctly say 'must not' or more politely 'may not'. C is wrong as it implies that it is impossible to take dictionaries into the exam room rather than a matter of permission.

Q40. Answer: D
Explanation: The self pronoun must agree with the main subject, which is 'everyone', which is plural, so 'yourselves' is the correct answer.

Q41. Answer: D
Explanation: In this context, 'people' is an uncountable noun so we could say 'some' but not 'any' (we could say, for example, 'some people see price stability...'). B, however, is wrong because we cannot say 'aren't some' to mean there are none. D is correct because 'many' implies the noun is countable so 'aren't' is used correctly in this instance. E implies that there are no people at all who see price stability ... we would usually use 'no one' or 'nobody' sees price stability.

Q42. Answer: C

Explanation: A train can move along or on the track but not away from it. We jump off something and into something (the girl could, for example, swim in the river having first jumped into it).

Q43. Answer: B

Explanation: An adult female (singular) is a woman, plural women. So the plural possessive is women's. A correct sentence with a different meaning would be 'the woman doctor only treats women' (meaning the singular female doctor treats only plural women).

Q44. Answer: C

Explanation: We use the present progressive tense to describe an action over time including the present that in principal is temporary (even if it has lasted for years). Answer D is wrong because 'most' implies that the questions are plural not singular as opposed to, for example, 'An interesting question in ecology…'

Q45. Answer: D

Explanation: 'Rarely' means 'not often' while 'scarcely' means not quite. It is therefore incorrect to say that prices have not quite risen so high. 'Risen' means gone up while 'raised' means lifted up.

Q46. Answer: C

Explanation: We say 'latter' to mean the second part or item (later means more late than something else). We rely 'on' or 'upon' but not 'from' something and the price is high not the cost (in the context of what the consumer must pay for the goods).

Q47. Answer: A

Explanation: We use the possessive form even in the case of 'else', which is not a noun. We would correctly say 'in a day or so' and not add the unnecessary qualification 'time'.

Q48. Answer: D

Explanation: We agree with something while we accept that something is the case or what someone has told us. We say 'latest' when something is the most recent (the robot is unlikely to be the last) and we do not use the possessive form of 'its'. D is preferred over suggested answer B because it is nonsensical to suggest that Peter is able to agree with the population of all Japanese people.

Q49. Answer: E

Explanation: 'Individual' or 'person' is used to refer to one person. We say 'people' to refer to a group. 'Loose' means not tight. 'Lose' means you will be deprived of something.

Q50. Answer: D

Explanation: 'Hers', 'yours' and 'theirs' and 'ours' in the possessive form do not have an apostrophe. 'It's' in this sentence is an abbreviation of 'it has' and so it is correct that an apostrophe should be included.

Q51. Answer: E

Explanation: When describing the past up to the present we use the present perfect tense to say that an action happened at an unspecified time before now. The exact time is not important, e.g., 'There have been many earthquakes in California.'

Q52. Answer: D

Explanation: The boss's mind cannot be open otherwise he or she would be receptive to new ways of working. We do not describe things such as doors, or eyes or minds as shut, but correctly say closed. 'Appear' or 'seem' have very similar meanings but in the negative we say 'can't seem' and not 'can't appear'.

Q53. Answer: E

Explanation: In the question and most of the suggested answers the double negative makes the sentence nonsensical. Only suggested answers E and C avoid this fault but C is wrong because the word 'more' defines quantities and the context is one of absolute support, not the amount of support.

Q54. Answer: C

Explanation: 'Arise' means begin or occurred, 'rise' or 'rose' means gets or got higher. We use 'because' to introduce new information, 'as' and 'since' are preferred when the information is already known.

Q55. Answer: D

Explanation: We say that a machine will 'not start' and not that it will 'not begin'. The meaning is also clearer if we say we are taking something back rather than taking it somewhere again.

Q56. Answer: B

Explanation: 'Besides' makes best sense and means in this context 'as well as', suggesting that she speaks six European languages in total. 'Except' means 'leave out', but it is not sensible to suggest that she does not speak her native tongue, i.e., the language she grew up speaking. 'Accept' means 'agree to'.

Q57. Answer: B

Explanation: Many words or structures can be correctly used to draw a comparison but in this instance it is correct to say 'to [not too] ...as your father'. 'Like' and 'equal to' are comparative terms and do not necessarily indicate the same profession.

Q58. Answer: E
Explanation: To make sense, the second part of the sentence has to be connected to the first as the reason for the government's actions and only 'because many' makes this link.

Q59. Answer: D
Explanation: To indicate something of importance to ourselves or to others we say 'care about' and we would say 'I can tell' rather than 'I can know'.

Q60. Answer: A
Explanation: 'When' is used to notify that an event has occurred or to provide details of the circumstances of the event.

Q61. Answer: B
Explanation: The correct term would be my wife and I 'have not' and the correct contraction of this is 'haven't'.

Q62. Answer: D
Explanation: 'On the contrary' is to contradict something, whereas 'on the other hand' is used to put forward another part of the case.

Q63. Answer: C
Explanation: We can write these nouns in any order but we treat rice as an uncountable noun and beans as countable.

Q64. Answer: B
Explanation: Journey and location are countable nouns while travel is treated as uncountable. Journey is plural as it refers to more than one location.

Reading comprehension and critical reasoning

Q1. Answer: D
Explanation: The main theme of the passage is the failure of bright children from low-income homes to achieve the same grades as bright children from high-income families. The passage is implying that children from both backgrounds are, in fact, equally bright.

Q2. Answer: C
Explanation: Suggested answers A, B and D are consequences of the inequality in the grades realized by bright children but of the suggested answers only C is offered in support of the main claim and in addition is implied to contain empirically verifiable facts.

Q3.   Answer: A
      Explanation: There is little difference between this and the previous question;
      just two ways of asking for the same thing. The difference in answers comes
      down to the suggested answers from which you had to choose. The research
      was recent and provided further evidence. These features make suggested
      answer A the best offered.

Q4.   Answer: A
      Explanation: The passage covers both the findings of the research and the
      debate from all sides that ensued, so A best summarizes its objective.

Q5.   Answer: B
      Explanation: A careful reading of the passage will confirm that suggested
      answer B is the only point explicitly made in the passage.

Q6.   Answer: E
      Explanation: The passage reports in a journalistic manner; it is not an unre-
      liable source so is not anecdotal; it is written in the third person so cannot be
      described as dogmatic or indignant.

Q7.   Answer: C
      Explanation: The word derives from the South African system but is widely
      used to mean segregation or discrimination. B is wrong because the discrimi-
      nation is not on the grounds of educational achievements but on the grounds
      of family income. D is wrong because it suggests that there is a systematized
      discrimination in place, which is not asserted by the article.

Q8.   Answer: D
      Explanation: A and C are not inferred from the passage but explicitly stated in
      the passage. B cannot be inferred because the passage makes clear that
      parental encouragement and home resources also play a key part in realizing
      potential. The article notes that there are better chances that a bright child
      from a rich family will win a place but does not say that this is the case.

Q9.   Answer: C
      Explanation: The passage describes the findings of the research and the
      reaction to those findings. It does not address questions of why the divide
      exists or what can be done to remove it.

Q10. Answer: D
      Explanation: The passage states that bright children from high-income
      families were very likely to enjoy a high income, not most children from high-
      income families.

Q11. Answer: B
      Explanation: Answers A and D are explicitly stated in the passage and so are
      not inferred from the passage. Answer C is not stated or inferred.

Q12. Answer: D
Explanation: Be careful when the question includes a negative. The author would agree with A to C and disagree with D, so the answer is D. The author would say that location within the country is also important, not 'only' the point of history and country.

Q13. Answer: A
Explanation: A careful reading of the passage proves this.

Q14. Answer: D
Explanation: If D were true, the main claim that the quality of justice varies massively depending on where the crime occurs would fail.

Q15. Answer: C
Explanation: It is stated in the passage that 'studies that compare case outcomes of a country by area have shown that for some crimes the conviction rate can be 10 times higher in one part of a country than another'.

Q16. Answer: A
Explanation: Penultimate means last but one. The preceding sentence refers to a failed system and its denial of justice to a victim and A is a continuation of this point.

Q17. Answer: B
Explanation: B is stated in the passage as a reason for local variation in the quality of justice, D is given as a reason but for the supporting point that conviction rates for drug offences were constant across a country. A is a supposition concerning the reader's background and C is evidence of a result of regional variation not a reason for it.

Q18. Answer: A
Explanation: The preceding sentence refers to the possession of drugs and so a following sentence that begins with the link word 'and' would relate to the same and this sentence further explains why offences concerning possession of drugs would have higher conviction rates. C does not do this.

Q19. Answer: B
Explanation: A careful read of the passage establishes this. 'Guilty criminals' is a term used in previous suggested answers but does not occur in the passage.

Q20. Answer: C
Explanation: The paragraph concludes by listing features of the judicial system that can fail and only C is consistent with this in that it introduces another example.

Q21. Answer: D
Explanation: The passage states this point in support for the theme that the industrialized world may have no alternative but to return to nuclear power.

Q22. Answer: B
Explanation: Ultimate means last and B best captures the main point made in that paragraph.

Q23. Answer: C
Explanation: Only suggested answer C reflects the lack of alternatives as part of the reason commentators are reconsidering nuclear power. A and B are observations in the article and the conclusion in D is not stated in the article.

Q24. Answer: C
Explanation: This is clear from a careful reading of the passage.

Q25. Answer: C
Explanation: The passage says that 'many argue' A, but C has far more implications for the claims of the environmentalists.

Q26. Answer: B
Explanation: The only reason nuclear power is being reconsidered is because viable renewable sources do not currently exist. If they did, then the temporary case for nuclear power would be greatly weakened.

Q27. Answer: C
Explanation: In the fourth paragraph it is stated that the public have become reluctant to forgo cherished features of modern life and the example of the family car is given. Frequent air travel is another example of modern life consistent with that principle.

Q28. Answer: D
Explanation: D follows on best from the sentences comprising the third paragraph of the passage. Answer C is less suitable because it raises the issue of wind farms without introduction, suggesting that it would comprise a part of a paragraph where wind farms had already been discussed. A and B are more relevant to the second paragraph.

Q29. Answer: C

Q30. Answer: A
Explanation: The reason for the change of heart is due to both the need to reduce emissions and the lack of an alternative. If there were a viable carbon-free alternative then future energy needs could be met through that rather than through nuclear. If there were no need to reduce emissions then there would be no need to change your mind on nuclear either.

Q31. Answer: A
Explanation: D and B are wrong because it is one's own mortality not mortality in general that the passage states people find uncomfortable. Answer C is wrong as lawyers are not mentioned in this paragraph.

Q32. Answer: C
Explanation: The passage states C, that the children may need to be looked after if they are dependent because if grown up there is no need to detail in a will who should look after them.

Q33. Answer: D
Explanation: In the first paragraph the normal contents of a will are described, and it can be inferred from this that someone with no assets could use a will to state their wishes to donate organs. That they might wish to have their funeral organized in a particular way is explicitly stated as a reason someone with no assets might write a will – so it cannot be inferred. A person with no assets could not make charitable donations.

Q34. Answer: C
Explanation: This point is made in the final paragraph.

Q35. Answer: B
Explanation: The 'But' at the start of D is wrong as there is no contrast to draw. In C it is impossible for the deceased to say to whom their estate should go. Answer A is of a tone out of keeping with the passage and paragraph.

Q36. Answer: A
Explanation: The passage makes all the points offered as suggested answers but A is the primary motive of the passage.

Q37. Answer: D
Explanation: All these topics are touched upon except D. That we may state our wish to make a donation in a will is mentioned in the passage but not how we make one through a will.

Q38. Answer: B
Explanation: All four suggested answers are sentences taken from the passage but suggested answer B best sums up its conclusion, as it applies to all of the circumstances discussed throughout the passage.

Q39. Answer: C
Explanation: A B and D are reasons to write a will of any type. C sets out one of the circumstances in which professional advice would be required according to the passage.

Q40. Answer: A

Explanation: Answer A continues the theme of the paragraph most suitably; there is no will to challenge so C is wrong; if D were right then it would contradict the whole theme of the paragraph. Inheritance tax is the subject of another paragraph.

Q41. Answer: D

Explanation: This is the reason given in the first paragraph for people's distrust. Suggested answers B and C are given in the last paragraph as reasons for people to become disillusioned.

Q42. Answer: B

Explanation: The media are as guilty as government, opposition parties and pressure groups in using statistics in a misleading way.

Q43. Answer: A

Explanation: Given that statistics are used with impunity then it is reasonable to infer that there is no control how they are used in debate. C is stated in the passage so cannot be inferred from it.

Q44. Answer: C

Explanation: A cynic is someone who believes everyone is motivated by self-interest or someone distrustful of everything they hear. The term occurs in the first paragraph of the passage and is used there to mean distrust.

Q45. Answer: D

Explanation: The only suggested answer that is not at least briefly considered in the passage is D. Consensus we are told, is almost never possible, the media are as bad as everyone else and other countries are mentioned in the first paragraph.

Q46. Answer: B

Explanation: The previous sentence and the paragraph in which it occurs is concerned with the effect of changes to the balance of goods and services in the basket, and this is also the subject of suggested answer B. Suggested answers C and D are only concerned with the effect of more inflationary or deflationary goods in the basket.

Q47. Answer: D

Explanation: It can be inferred that adding an inflationary service to the basket will result in more inflationary pressure than the other suggested answers. It can be inferred from the passage that actions A (removing a service) and B (adding a deflationary hi-tech item) will most likely have a deflationary effect. The effect of removing a non-hi-tech item like bread from the basket is unlikely to have a big inflationary effect (removing a hi-tech item would be potentially more inflationary as it could mean that a negative price increase is removed, leaving a more inflationary basket overall).

Q48. Answer: C
Explanation: Nullify means to cancel out and this is what the two trends do in forming the official inflation rate.

Q49. Answer: A
Explanation: The word oxymoron refers to contradictory terms that appear in conjunction, and to describe an undertone as dramatic is a contradiction of terms.

Q50. Answer: D
Explanation: A tautology is the unnecessary repetition within a statement of the same things in different words; D is a tautology because the rate is 'annual' and therefore it is unnecessary to add the clause 'each year' to the statement.

Q51. Answer: C
Explanation: The author wants independence for the offices that produce state statistics so that those statistics are more credible in the eyes of the general public. Whether or not the author wants that independence to be invested in one or more offices is not detailed.

Q52. Answer: A
Explanation: The passage does not mention the audit of state statistics but focuses instead on the more radical proposal of independence for the offices responsible for its production. The issue of educating the general public is discussed in the first paragraph.

Q53. Answer: C
Explanation: The author's case is premised on the view that the public have very little trust in official statistics and an independent office would at least give the public a reassurance that the figures were impartial. If suggested answer C were true then this reassurance would be unnecessary.

Q54. Answer: D
Explanation: No mention of the accuracy of statistics is made in the passage.

Q55. Answer: B
Explanation: To preserve the independence of interpretations it would be logical to release them prior to any government statement. Equally, they would not be independent if government approval had to be obtained either before or after publication.

Chapter 4   Twenty mini-tests to help you get off to a flying start

GMAT® mini-test 1: quantitative

Q1.   Answer: D
Explanation: Half of 800 = 400 women graduates, 15% of 400 = 60 who set up their own business, so 400 – 60 = 340 who will not set up their own business.

Q2.   Answer: B
Explanation: It is not necessary to know the values of x and y, but simply to note that the second equation is the first divided by –2. The solution, therefore, is the original answer, 9, divided by –2, i.e., –4.5.

Q3.   Answer: C
Explanation: The diameter of the circle and the length of the hypotenuse are the same and are given. We can calculate the area of the circle using $A = \pi r^2$. Area of circle = 3.14×3^2 $3.14 \times 9 = 28.26$ m². The area of the square = x^2. Using Pythagoras we know $x^2 + x^2 = 6^2$. So, $2x^2 = 36$ and $x^2 = 18$ m². Difference = 28.26 m² – 18 m² = 10.26 m².

Q4.   Answer: B
Explanation: Statement 1 has two solutions, 3 and –3. Statement 2 has only one solution, 3. Therefore, statement 2 alone is sufficient.

Q5.   Answer: C
Explanation: Multiply the first equation by 3 to give 6x + 9y = 60. Subtract the second equation from this to give (6x – 6x) + (9y – 2y) = 60 – 46, i.e., 7y = 14, y = 2.

GMAT® mini-test 2: quantitative

Q1.   Answer: C
Explanation: The segment represents 36/360° ($^1/_{10}$) of the area of the circle, so we can find the area of the segment by calculating $^1/_{10}\pi$ r2, = $^1/_{10} \times 3.14 \times 25 =$ $^1/_{10} \times 78.5 = 7.85$.

Q2.   Answer: D
Explanation: Subtract x from both sides to give x + 1 > 2. Then subtract 1 from both sides to give x > 1.

Q3.   Answer: A
Explanation: 120 items represent 15% of the total stock. 120 ÷ 15 = 8, 1% = 8, 100% = 800.

Q4.   Answer: A
Explanation: If statement 1 is true then $2n/4$ is an integer, so, simplifying, $n/2$ is an integer. Statement 2 would be correct for values of n, which do not satisfy the original statement. For example, $n = 0.5$. This would not satisfy the original condition, but $4 \times 0.5/2 = 1$.

Q5.   Answer: D
Explanation: Multiply throughout by 6, then rearrange to give $x = y$. Therefore, $x + y = 2x$.

GMAT® mini-test 3: quantitative

Q1.   Answer: E
Explanation: Add together all the values in the ratio $1 + 2 + 3 = 6$, divide the total number of cars sold by that number, $84 \div 6 = 14$, multiply the occurrence of red cars by $14 = 2 \times 14 = 28$.

Q2.   Answer: E
Explanation: $y = 6/x$, so $3x + y = 3x + 6/x$. If this is then divided by x to obtain a fraction and consequently a percentage, it is not independent of x and cannot be determined $(3 + 6/x^2) \times 100\%$.

Q3.   Answer: C
Explanation: Find the total number of pitches then find the 15% that are single. Total pitches $= 180 + 150 + 370 + 420 + 230 + 150 = 1{,}500$; $1{,}500 \times 15\% = 225$.

Q4.   Answer: A
Explanation: There is no information about the relative values of x and y, so C, D and E are unknown. A negative multiplied by a negative gives a positive, so A is correct.

Q5.   Answer: D
Explanation: Rearranging statement 1, by adding 1 to both sides, gives $x/y > 1$. Multiplying throughout by y leads to $x > y$ and hence a solution. Similarly, for statement 2, multiplying by y gives $x < y$ and hence a (different) solution. So, either statement, in isolation would lead to a solution.

GMAT® mini-test 4: quantitative

Q1.   Answer: E
Explanation: You have to work out how much the area increases when you increase the length of the sides from 100% to 130%. Let the side $= 10$, the area will equal $10^2 = 100$. Now increase the side by $130\% = 13$ and the area will be $13^2 = 169$. The area has increased from 100 to $169 = 69\%$.

Q2. Answer: A
     Explanation: Add equations to give $2x = 100$, $x = 50$.

Q3. Answer: C
     Explanation: The ratio 5,000:4,500:2,500 simplifies to 10:9:5 = 24; 3,600 ÷ 24 = 150, so B gets $9 \times 150 = 1,350$.

Q4. Answer: A
     Explanation: Statement 2 might indicate that a_2 was not a complex number, but will not give any useful information. Statement 1 will generate the sequence 0, 2, 6, 38, which is enough to know that 35 does not appear.

Q5. Answer: C
     Explanation: *12.5 is 12 and *2.5 is 2. 12 divided by 2 is 6.

GMAT® mini-test 5: quantitative

Q1. Answer: A
     Explanation: $x + (x + 1) + (x + 2) = 57$, so $3x + 3 = 57$, $3x = 54$, $54 \div 3 = 18$, so the consecutive numbers with the sum of 57 are 18, 19, 20, the factors of 18 are 1, 2, 3, 6, 9, 18 = a total of 6 factors.

Q2. Answer: E
     Explanation: Find the volume of the sphere with the formula $v = {}^4/_3? r^3$. Find the volume of the cone with $^1/_3? r^2h$. Sphere = $^4/_3 \times 3.14 \times 27 = 113$ cm^3. Cone = $^1/_3 \times 3.14 \times 9 \times 5 = 47$ cm^3. Difference = 66 cm^3.

Q3. Answer: D
     Explanation: Using the first equation and substituting for y and z into the second equation gives $xxx = 216$, i.e., $x^3 = 216$. Therefore, x is the cube root of 216, $\sqrt[3]{216} = 6$.

Q4. Answer: B
     Explanation: Rearrange the second equation to give $b = 3a$ and substitute into the first equation to give $3a + 3a = 3$, therefore a is ½ and b must be 1½. $1/a + 3/b$ is therefore $1/(½) + 3/(1½) = 2 + 2 = 4$.

Q5. Answer: C
     Explanation: Statement 1 can be rewritten as $x > y$; because it is not known which, if either, of x and y are positive or negative, this is not sufficient. Knowing that x is negative in addition to statement 1 indicates that y is a larger negative number and hence when squared will produce a number greater than x^2.

GMAT® mini-test 6: quantitative

Q1.   Answer: C
Explanation: $x + 5x = 30$, so $6x = 30$, $x = 5$, $30 - 5 = 25$, so the two numbers are 5 and 25 and the common factor is 5.

Q2.   Answer: E
Explanation: Impose a convenient figure $r = 10$, then area $= \pi\, 10^2 = \pi\, 100$, r10 × 110% = 11, $\pi\, 11^2 = \pi\, 121$, so area increases from $\pi\, 100$ to $\pi\, 121 = 21\%$.

Q3.   Answer: A
Explanation: When factorized the equation becomes $(x - 2)(x - 2)$. This is 0 when $x = 2$ and positive at all other times. The only solution therefore is A.

Q4.   Answer: B
Explanation: Statement 1 is insufficient as, for example $1/8 > 1/16$, but it states that x should be greater than y, not simply equal. It is possible to rewrite the original inequality as $2x/16 > y/16$, or $2x > y$, which is the second statement.

Q5.   Answer: B
Explanation: Adding the two equations together gives $2a = -11^3/_4$. Multiplying this by 4 gives $8a = -47$. It is not required, but the value of b turns out to be $-6^1/_8$, which could be confused with the answer D. The correct answer is B.

GMAT® mini-test 7: quantitative

Q1.   Answer: A
Explanation: The sum of the three angles of any triangle $= 180°$, and the sum of the bottom-right angle and the angle of extended side of the triangle must also equal $180°$, so $180 - 130 = 50$; $180 - 90 - 50 = 40°$.

Q2.   Answer: D
Explanation: Because the drawn card is replaced before the next is drawn, the events are independent and the probability of each event is the same. So $4/52$ for the first king and $4/52$ for the second. $4/52$ cancels to $1/13$, $1/13 \times 1/13 = 1/169$.

Q3.   Answer: E
Explanation: Statement 1 is not sufficient as this simply reduces the equation to x^2, but with no information about x. Statement 2 is identical to statement 1.

Q4.   Answer: E
Explanation: If $x > y$ *and* both are positive or both negative then the condition is true. As this is not always the case, A, B and C are not correct. D is not correct for any positive numbers where $x < y$. So the answer is E.

Q5.   Answer: D
Explanation: The value of x is irrelevant. Multiplying throughout by x results in the elimination of x from the original equation. Thus $1/y = 2/1 + 1/2$ and consequently, $1/y = 2^1/_2$. Finally, $y = 1/2^1/_2$ or $2/5$.

GMAT® mini-test 8: quantitative

Q1.   Answer: D
Explanation: The first ship to leave will cover a distance of 3x; the second ship must cover 3x in 2 hours so the average rate of the second ship must $= 3x/2 = 1.5x$.

Q2.   Answer: E
Explanation: You must find the perimeter of a square with an area of 225 m². Find the $\sqrt{225} = 152$ ($15 \times 15 = 225$). This is the length of each side, 15×4, which gives you the distance walked.

Q3.   Answer: A
Explanation: Statement 1 is sufficient as it gives a second equation to generate a solution by simultaneous equations. If the amount the man digs is x and the boy y, the original question states that $x + y = 600$. Statement 1 says that $x - y = 200$. These two equations lead to a solution. The second statement gives no information about the relative rates of work.

Q4.   Answer: B
Explanation: π is just a number so the first equation gives a numerical value for x, which could be written as $7 - \pi$. Substituting this into the second equation and solving for y gives $y = -\pi/2$.

Q5.   Answer: A
Explanation: The equation in statement 1 has only one solution, whereas that in statement 2, being quadratic, has two solutions.

GMAT® mini-test 9: quantitative

Q1.   Answer: A
Explanation: For every $ spent on the book $1.5 was spent on the CD ROM, so the cost of the book $= 30 \div 2.5 = 12$.

Q2.   Answer: C
Explanation: Divide the isosceles triangle into two right-angled triangles, then use Pythagoras to find the height of each right-angled triangle, then calculate the area. $1/2$ of $10 = 5$ (the length of the base of each right-angled triangle), $5^2 + h^2 = 13^2$, $5^2 + h^2 = 169$, $25 + h^2 = 169$ $h^2 = 144$ ($169 - 25 = 144$), $h = 12$. Area $= 1/2$base $\times$ height $= 5 \times 12 = 60$ m².

Q3.   Answer: E
Explanation: From statement 2 the amount the man and the woman achieve in $2^1/_2$ hours could be written as M + W = 400. This equation has two unknowns and the inclusion of the first statement gives no additional information to determine either M or W.

Q4.   Answer: E
Explanation: Multiply both sides by 6 to obtain $3x < 2x$ and hence any negative number will be a valid solution.

Q5.   Answer: B
Explanation: Whether x is negative or positive, x^2 will be positive, so statement 1 gives no useful information. By dividing both sides by x^4, statement 2 becomes $x > 1$ and hence x must be positive.

GMAT® mini-test 10: quantitative

Q1.   Answer: C
Explanation: It is not necessary to work out the best combination, only to realize that information about the individual cost of the burger and the fries is required. The only way to do this is to use both statements.

Q2.   Answer: D
Explanation: $^2/_7$ of the stamps were used so the 15 remaining stamps = $^5/_7$ of the original number. $15 \div 5 = 3$, so originally there were $3 \times 7 = 21$ stamps, $^5/_7 =$ 15 that remain so $^2/_7 = \$6$ were used on the package.

Q3.   Answer: C
Explanation: To calculate the average for the year it is necessary to add up all the scores and divide by the total number of students. Knowing the group size means it is possible to determine the total score for each group, adding these together gives the total for the year. If 9 group sizes are known then it is possible to determine the tenth as there are 200 students. Both statements are, therefore, required.

Q4.   Answer: A
Explanation: For the first event there are 26 letters so the probability is $1/26$, the odds then change to $1/25$ as the card is not replaced, $1/26 \times 1/25 = 1/650$.

Q5.   Answer: D
Explanation: Rearrange to $3(x + y) = 2(x + y)$, therefore $x + y$ must be 0.

GMAT® mini-test 11: verbal

Q1.   Answer: B
Explanation: The period of time (since we lived here) is continuing and he might yet still ride his bike, so we use 'hasn't' rather than 'didn't'; we need 'we've' not just 'we' lived here.

Q2. Answer: D
Explanation: The passage addresses the theme of a hydrogen economy based on the splitting of water into oxygen and hydrogen. Answers A, B and C are concerned with challenges facing the hydrogen economy in general so do not best express the general theme of the passage. E is true but does not express the general theme of the passage.

Q3. Answer: A
Explanation: No mention of solar panels is made in the passage. Be prepared for small nuances in language to make the difference in the answers in the GMAT® reading comprehension questions.

Q4. Answer: B
Explanation: Inductive means to become acquainted with or conversant in or proceeding from particular facts to a general or wider conclusion. Deductive means a logical inference from particular facts or premises, which contain no more information than that which is contained in those premises. The passage, including its main conclusion, is informative rather than deductive.

Q5. Answer: D
Explanation: You can separate 'sort' and 'out' without losing the meaning but the meaning is lost if we separate 'get down'. Note: a workout refers to exercise not tidying.

GMAT® mini-test 12: verbal

Q1. Answer: A
Explanation: The passage does not use the term social geography but it still best expresses the key point of the passage. Suggested answer D is phrased in a similar manner to the passage and reflects its main point but lacks reference to the aspect of these cities that has not changed. B is not correct because the passage does not limit itself to the period of the last 100 years but is concerned with the lack of social change over a long period _such_ as 100 years. E is a description of an assumption that the author commences the article with, not the main point.

Q2. Answer: C
Explanation: Transformation means change and the author would hold the opposite view.

Q3. Answer: B
Explanation: Sprawl means in this context the disorganized expansion of an urban area.

Q4. Answer: E
Explanation: Comprised means formed by putting together separate elements so we use the preposition 'of' not 'from'.

Q5.   Answer: D
Explanation: We say 'by' boat and plane but 'on' foot not by foot.

GMAT® mini-test 13: verbal

Q1.   Answer: B
Explanation: When we want to stress that something is being thought about carefully, the verb 'to consider' is only used in the present continuous.

Q2.   Answer: D
Explanation: The new policy is selective in that it aims to prioritize immigrants with suitable skills. The passage neither defends one position nor makes a case for one, suggesting that answers A and C are incorrect.

Q3.   Answer: A
Explanation: The argument made in the passage that the proportion of skills held by these countries' immigrant populations has steadily fallen because of immigration policies introduced in the 1970s, relies on the unproven premise that dependents of existing immigrants, political refugees and illegal immigrants have few useful skills.

Q4.   Answer: D
Explanation: The countries are described as responding to the perceived problem of alienated immigrant communities by changing their immigration policy. C might apply if the subject of the passage was drawn from science.

Q5.   Answer: A
Explanation: We say 'full of' and 'filled with'. In the case of suggested answer B we need to say whether it is the rooms or the bottles that were filled with water.

GMAT® mini-test 14: verbal

Q1.   Answer: B
Explanation: It is new laws that are requiring the blending of traditional fuels with bio-fuels and so B better expresses the key point of the passage. C describes the effect of this. The passage makes no reference to oil prices, so A is incorrect.

Q2.   Answer: A
Explanation: The issue of global warming and the concerns of environmentalists are unlikely to be introduced for the first time in the concluding sentence. The preceding sentence refers to bio-diesel and so it is unlikely that that the passage will conclude by switching back to the subject of ethanol.

Q3.	Answer: B

Explanation: It can be inferred that the new laws that have raised the profile of bio-fuels are the result of government policy (D is stated in the passage so is not inferred).

Q4.	Answer: D

Explanation: 'Can' suggests that something is definitely going to happen. We use 'could' when it is likely but there remains some uncertainty; 'couldn't' means that something is not allowed; 'hardly' is wrong because it will either rain or not.

Q5.	Answer: B

Explanation: We say 'persisted in' or 'with' and 'insisted on'.

GMAT® mini-test 15: verbal

Q1.	Answer: A

Explanation: We sit at a table not on it; someone can be related to you or a relation of yours.

Q2.	Answer: B

Explanation: The passage makes the case for and against sending children in state care to boarding school, so suggested answers A and C are not correct, while B is correct. Although A represents the bulk of the passage, both sides of the argument are presented and the author does not draw a definitive conclusion.

Q3.	Answer: C

Explanation: The passage states that the children at boarding schools go home during the holidays but it does not consider the issue of what to do with boarders in state care who do not have a home to go to. Reference to the other suggested answers can be found in the passage (consideration for the reader who may not know what a boarding school is by providing a definition of these type of school).

Q4.	Answer: D

Explanation: Better exam results are assumed to demonstrate that this kind of intervention works. The passage does not consider the question of whether or not the children are happier at boarding school, nor does it address the issue of tax breaks. That charities are willing to pay the fees is presented in the passage as a fact, so is not an assumption.

Q5.	Answer: E

Explanation: We can introduce the noise with the phrase 'there was' or ' he heard' but to combine them changes the meaning. We can correctly question 'who's there' in many forms but to ask if anyone is from there is to change the meaning. We do not say 'whose there', which is a possessive of the word 'who', but we say 'who's there' as a contraction of 'who is'.

GMAT® mini-test 16: verbal

Q1. Answer: D
Explanation: We say 'surprised by' or 'at' but not 'for' and we say 'similar to' but not 'with'.

Q2. Answer: A
Explanation: We say translated 'into'. We should say 'printed in' rather than 'printed with'.

Q3. Answer: A
Explanation: The passage is about the many types of threat that an organization's information security system may face.

Q4. Answer: B
Explanation: This is evident from a careful reading of the passage.

Q5. Answer: D
Explanation: D can be inferred from the passage, which states that 'the threat is just as likely to come from within an organization' and is reinforced by the references to the dangers of mobile working. B is not inferred from the passage but explicitly stated in it.

GMAT® mini-test 17: verbal

Q1. Answer: E
Explanation: In the context of the question after the noun 'satisfied' we would use the preposition 'about' or 'with'; we say 'ashamed of' or 'ashamed about'.

Q2. Answer: C
Explanation: The passage is about the writings of the economist J.K. Galbraith and its primary objective is to explain the views of that thinker and not just one of the views expressed in one of his many publications.

Q3. Answer: B
Explanation: If you are familiar with the writings of Galbraith then you could be at a slight disadvantage. He did consider economic life to be bipolar, and wrote that in a perfect society, the rich would accept higher taxes (he was also acclaimed for his clarity of thought). But, these statements cannot best be inferred from the passage. Statement B can be inferred from the need for state intervention to improve the environment.

Q4.   Answer: D
Explanation: The passage is about the writings and theories of Galbraith. Statement D adds further detail to the part of the passage referring to the conflict between Galbraith's theories and monetarism. B adds nothing as it is not attributed to him. Whether or not he met Keynes does not impact much on the fact that he was a disciple of Keynes. Any disappointment or otherwise he may have felt about the collapse of communism tells us nothing about his theories and works.

Q5.   Answer: A
Explanation: In this context, 'used to' suggests actions that no longer occur. We would use 'will' for the present and 'would' for the past. D and E do not make factual sense.

GMAT® mini-test 18: verbal

Q1.   Answer: A
Explanation: Suggested statements B, C and D are all supporting statements made in the passage but the general theme is that there are many good jobs available that do not require a university degree.

Q2.   Answer: C
Explanation: If this were true then the vast majority of jobs in the future will require candidates to hold a degree.

Q3.   Answer: D
Explanation: Because it offers an answer to the question posed at the end of the passage (E is not a proper sentence).

Q4.   Answer: C
Explanation: 'Leads' is wrong because we are talking about historical events. In this context we do not use 'may' when talking about past possibilities. 'Are' is wrong because the subject is singular, 'mustn't' is an instruction so not appropriate in the context.

Q5.   Answer: D
Explanation: We say 'unable to give' and 'insisted on going'.

GMAT® mini-test 19: verbal

Q1.   Answer: B
Explanation: We say 'fond of swimming' and 'preferred to swim'.

Q2.   Answer: E
Explanation: We can introduce the reason for something with the phrase 'there being'. Alternative correct ways would be 'because', 'there were', or 'because there aren't any'.

Q3.   Answer: B
Explanation: Statement B supports the main theme by quantifying the extent of the disaster.

Q4.   Answer: C
Explanation: The passage draws an analogy between endangered species of animals and the plight of nomadic hunter-gatherer communities.

Q5.   Answer: A
Explanation: The passage fails to explore ways to reverse or slow the depletion of these people's habitat so is fatalistic in that the decline seems inevitable. It is not defeatist, however, as the people are not described as giving up but as being forced to abandon their traditional lifestyle.

GMAT® mini-test 20: verbal

Q1.   Answer: C
Explanation: Suggested answers A, B, D and E can be inferred from the passage or support the main theme of the passage, but answer C best captures the key point made.

Q2.   Answer: B
Explanation: The passages describes the popularity of the move away from the hierarchical era of mass media and the benefits that it brings in terms of making an editor of everyone, and training us to better decide what to believe.

Q3.   Answer: E
Explanation: A future where success continued to come from content created by media corporations would most weaken the case made in the passage.

Q4.   Answer: A
Explanation: When a word starts with a vowel we use 'an' and, with a consonant, 'a', but this also applies to the sound of the start of a word or phrase, so the silent 'h' in honorary means 'an' is correct, as is 'a' for university.

Q5.   Answer: E
Explanation: When we refer to unique things, we usually use the article 'the': 'the future', 'the euro'. But it is also correct to have no article when we refer to these unique things.

Chapter 5   Six timed practice sub-tests

Sub-test 1: quantitative

Q1.   Answer: A
Explanation: The angles on either side of a line crossing parallel lines are equal; 2 is true but is not relevant to the question.

Q2.   Answer: D
Explanation: There are 3 odd numbers on a dice: 1, 3, 5, so the probability = $3/6 = 1/2$.

Q3.   Answer: D
Explanation: Statement 1 is sufficient as it means the man shifted 400 kg and the boy 200 kg. Statement 2 means that the boy shifts 200 kg per hour and it is therefore possible to work out how fast the man was working and how long it would take him alone.

Q4.   Answer: E
Explanation: There are 10 numbers between 1 and 50 that end in 2 or an 8. As a percentage of 50, this = 20%.

Q5.   Answer: E
Explanation: There are two equations relating the three unknowns and so it is not possible to determine their values.

Q6.   Answer: C
Explanation: In the first 4 hours he covers $4 \times 3 = 12$ miles. Now calculate how long it will take the remaining 15 miles at 2.5 mph: $15 \div 2.5 = 6$, $3 + 6 = 9$ hours.

Q7.   Answer: D
Explanation: Subtract x from both sides to give $2x + 3 < 1$. Then subtract 3 from both sides to give $2x < -2$. Finally, divide both sides by 2 to give $x < -1$.

Q8.   Answer: E
Explanation: Individually, neither statement gives any information about y, but together they show that y is greater than or equal to 0. As y can be equal to 0 there is not sufficient information to determine whether y is less than 0, i.e., negative.

Q9.   Answer: D
Explanation: Any value of x will be valid, so x is greater than minus infinity.

Q10.   Answer: E
Explanation: The calculation is not possible. The period 18 April to 9 May is less than 1 month and analysis of the calculation of the categories All items and Industrials does not identify a consistent method to adopt. To divide one year by 12 would give you the mean change not one months change.

Q11. Answer: B
Explanation: Statement 1 will work for some values of n that are not divisible by 4, i.e., n = 2. 2^2 = 4, which is divisible by 4, condition one, but statement 2 does not satisfy the original condition. $(n^2 + 4n)/16$ is the same as $n^2/16 + 4n/16$, which in turn is equal to $(n/4)^2 + n/4$. If $(n/4)2 + (n/4)$ gives an integer result the n is divisible by 4 with no remainder and hence statement 2 alone is sufficient.

Q12. Answer: C
Explanation: Volume of cylinder = $\pi^2 h$, volume of cube = length × breadth × height; v of cylinder = 3.14 × 9 × 6 = 3.14 × 54 = 170 cm³, v of cube = 6 × 6 × 6 = 216 cm³, difference = 46 cm³.

Q13. Answer: B
Explanation: Subtract x – y from both sides to give 2y = 0. x – 2y is therefore just x. Simple inspection should lead to the same conclusion.

Q14. Answer: D
Explanation: Find the average to find the sum. There are 70 – 50 + 1 numbers = 21 numbers in the range 50–70 (if you make it 20 then you have missed out number 50). The average is 50 + 70 = 120 ÷ 2 = 60; 21 × 60 = 1,260.

Q15. Answer: E
Explanation: If B is the cost of the burger and F is the cost of the fries, then statement 1 gives 4B = 6F, or B = 1.5F. This is identical to statement 2 and hence there is not enough information to answer the question.

Q16. Answer: A
Explanation: On day 3, a total of 75 m of cloth is sold, of which 75 – 45 = 30 m is yellow, so find 30 as a percentage of 75%: 100/75 × 30 = 3,000/75 = 40%.

Q17. Answer: B
Explanation: Rearrange the equation to give y = –x/10. Substitute for y into the equation x – 10y to give x – 10 multiplied by –x/10. This, then, resolves to 2x, which is 200% of x.

Q18. Answer: C
Explanation: xy will be positive when both x and y have the same sign, but statement 1 by itself is not sufficient to determine this. Because statement 2 only gives information about y, it is obviously insufficient. When the two are combined, knowing that y is negative means that x must also be negative and hence a solution is obtained.

Q19. Answer: B
Explanation: Rearrange the first and second equations to give, respectively, x = 3y + 6 and x = 2y + 8. Subtract one from the other to give y – 2 = 0, y = 2. x, therefore, is equal to 12 and x + y = 14.

Q20. Answer: C
Explanation: There are 36 possible outcomes and two successful outcomes: 2 + 1 and 1 + 2, so the probability is $2/36 = 1/18$.

Q21. Answer: B
Explanation: Statement 1 contains two unknowns. Statement 2 appears to contain two unknowns, but it can be simplified to $3 - 2x = 1$ and hence is sufficient for a solution.

Q22. Answer: D
Explanation: A quadrant is a quarter of a circle, its arc × 4 = the circumference of a circle with × 4 the area of the arc. Given its radius, its area will equal $\pi r^2 \div 4$.

Q23. Answer: A
Explanation: Subtract $x + y$ from both sides, then divide by 3 to give $x + y = 2/3$.

Q24. Answer: C
Explanation: 4 people working for 3 hours = 12 hours' work. The same number of hours' work if completed by 3 people would take $12 \div 3 = 4$ hours.

Q25. Answer: C
Explanation: Statement 1 can be rearranged to give, by multiplying throughout by x, $16 = x^2$, which has two solutions, 4 and –4, and is not sufficient. Similarly, the equation in statement 2 has two solutions, 4 and –2. x must therefore be +4 and hence a solution has been determined.

Q26. Answer: D
Explanation: &(10 × 5) is &(50), which corresponds to 2. &(20) corresponds to 8. $2 - 8 = -6$, but starting at 0 (or 12 on the clock) and moving 6 backwards gives 6.

Q27. Answer: E
Explanation: Rearrange the equation to give $y = 10 - x$. Substitute for y into the equation $x + 10y$ to give $20 - x$. If this is then divided by x to obtain a fraction and consequently a percentage it is not independent of x and cannot be determined.

Q28. Answer: B and C
Explanation: Test 81 to see if it is a prime number, then calculate the prime factors of the appropriate number. To test if a number is prime, find its square root and then divide in turn by all the prime numbers before the value of the square root. If none divide exactly, it is a prime number. $\sqrt{81} = 9$; 2, 3, 5, 7 are prime numbers before 9; $3 \div 81 = 27$, so 81 is not a prime number. Therefore, identify the prime factors of 21 = 3 and 7.

Q29. Answer: E
Explanation: A negative divided by a negative must be a positive, but if y is very large x/y is almost 0, so A, B and C are not always true. Similarly, if x has a greater numerical value, D will not be true. E is always true.

Q30. Answer: C
Explanation: x can only be found if it is established that the shapes are similar and both statements are needed before we can do this.

Q31. Answer: C
Explanation: A little work will lead to the solutions $x = 1$ and -1 for the first equation and $x = 1$ and -2 for the second. Using both statements leads to the conclusion that $x = 1$.

Q32. Answer: E
Explanation: Multiply out to give $4x + 8y = 8y$. x is therefore 0 and y cannot be determined.

Q33. Answer: A
Explanation: (2.5) is rounded up to 3. (-4) takes the positive value, i.e., 4. $3 \times 4 = 12$.

Q34. Answer: D
Explanation: $^1/_8$ of the potatoes were used, leaving 7 lb, so $^7/_8 = 7$ lb, $^1/_8 = 1$ lb, which costs 50 cents.

Q35. Answer: C
Explanation: Rearrange the left-hand side to give $3(y + z)x < (y + z)x$. Divide both sides by $(y + z)$ to give $3x < x$ and hence any negative number will be a valid solution.

Q36. Answer: E
Explanation: It would be necessary to know the number of students in each group. Imagine the extreme case where 9 students happened to get 100% and all the rest 50%. If those 9 students were each in a group of 1, the average score of their group would, of course, be 100%. If the average score of the year were calculated as the average of the averages of the groups, this would give a much higher value than the reality, where 191 out of 200 students scored 50%.

Q37. Answer: A
Explanation: Rearranging the first equation to give $(x - 3)y = 2$ and then $y = 2/(x - 3)$. Substituting this into the second equation gives the quadratic $x^2 - 9x + 20 = 4$ or 5.

Sub-test 2: verbal

Q1. Answer: A
Explanation: We say 'always disliked' (past tense) and 'I've' finished (a contraction of 'I have'), not 'I'd' or 'I'd been'.

Q2.   Answer: E
Explanation: We say 'How was the journey?' or 'What was the journey like?'. But not 'What was the journey?' or 'How was the journey like?'

Q3.   Answer: B
Explanation: The rate of corporation tax belongs to the country so we use the possessive 'country's' not the plural 'countries'. The word 'another' in this context means 'a different one'. 'One more' or 'an additional one' suggests another, also with a high rate of tax.

Q4.   Answer: A
Explanation: The bank is the possessor of the interest rate so we use 'its'; the rate is the principal one so it is singular.

Q5.   Answer: E
Explanation: The verb refers to a countable noun so we use the plural.

Q6.   Answer: A
Explanation: We can say 'ought to' or 'should' but we use 'should' in a statement such as this that offers advice. D contains a double negative.

Q7.   Answer: C
Explanation: The key point in the context of this passage is the passing off of someone else's work as your own and only suggested answer C makes this point fully.

Q8.   Answer: E
Explanation: The sentence continues both to expound the views of the experts consistently and provide a conclusion to the passage as a whole.

Q9.   Answer: D
Explanation: In the passage, reference is made to a review and at one point the view of candidates is provided in quotation marks. This is sufficient for us to conclude that the passage relies on the findings of an investigative study. Comparative assertions are simply qualified statements.

Q10.   Answer: D
Explanation: The exact wording of the passage is 'between 20 and 60 percent of grades coming from such coursework'.

Q11.   Answer: A
Explanation: That the help of parents and siblings would result in grade inflation can be inferred from the fact that children are getting help with their home-completed coursework.

Q12.   Answer: B
Explanation: When we refer to a single item (in this case the company), even if its name ends in an 's', we use the singular. Company is a singular not a plural noun.

Q13. Answer: C

Explanation: When the subject comprises two or more items we often use a plural verb but sometimes a singular. However, when linked by 'or' we use a plural verb when the last item is plural, and singular verb when the last item is singular. In the case of 'everyone' we use the singular. The insertion of brackets to form a sub-clause could change this as in: 'The company director (or his legal representatives) is to attend the meeting and almost everyone thinks', as the subject of the sentence remains the company director only.

Q14. Answer: D

Explanation: We can choose to use or leave out the link words 'to be' in many situations, but not in this case.

Q15. Answer: B

Explanation: 'Fore' and 'aft' refer to the front and back of a ship; to look 'before' and 'back' does not make sense, as in 'to look before and back through the sediment'. We can use 'forwards' or 'forward' and 'backwards' instead of 'back', but 'backward' has a different meaning and in this instance it cannot be used.

Q16. Answer: E

Explanation: The passage states that every person at risk can gain considerable benefits from the treatment and this sentiment is best stated in E. B is wrong because it says NOT every person.

Q17. Answer: E

Explanation: While the passage states a family of cholesterol-lowering drugs is used in the treatment, it is stated that the treatment itself is administered daily.

Q18. Answer: D

Explanation: Suggested answer D best summarizes the conclusion because it states who can benefit from the treatment given the evidence now available.

Q19. Answer: E

Explanation: The statement asserts that the benefits are directly proportional to the size of reduction in cholesterol levels and therefore it can be inferred that when deciding who should benefit, doctors should consider the size of drop in cholesterol that can be achieved rather than giving the treatment to those with the highest initial levels.

Q20. Answer: C

Explanation: The claim is about the risk of a vascular event and not about the risk of cancer. So the correct answer must weaken the link between a lower risk of a heart attack and the treatment of people with less than the highest levels of cholesterol. Only C does this by suggesting that the reduced risk is relatively small, rather than much lower as claimed in the passage.

Q21. Answer: D

Explanation: With nouns such as these, the first noun identifies the type of thing, the second noun, the class of thing. Usually the type is singular, as in shoe shop, but clothes shop is an exception. We say boy's (possessive) school for one boy or boys' school for many boys.

Q22. Answer: C

Explanation: When reporting what was said or using indirect speech we still write 'said goodbye' because there is no other form for that phrase. For example, we can say congratulations and report that we were congratulated. E is wrong because in indirect speech we would not write or say 'hello to them' but just hello.

Q23. Answer: E

Explanation: We use the plural when we can expect more than one of something (in this case answers). 'Were' is plural, so goes with answers.

Q24. Answer: A

Explanation: We use 'many' for units such as minutes or hours, while 'much' and 'a large amount of' when referring to more relative quantities.

Q25. Answer: A

Explanation: We use 'every' in this context because we are emphasizing the period of one month. In many other contexts 'every' and 'each' are interchangeable.

Q26. Answer: A

Explanation: The passage states that the stable job market and increases in income and wages would give rise to growth in the medium term. Pay deal inflation is another way of referring to wage growth.

Q27. Answer: D

Explanation: The passage states that most economists agreed with the monetary policy of ignoring the first-round impact of this rise in the price of oil and waiting for any domestic second effect – higher prices in the shops – before taking action. Only statement D is consistent with this view.

Q28. Answer: B

Explanation: The report is referred to in relation to growth and for its forecast to be realized, the author believed household expenditure (spending) and domestic consumption would need to increase noticeably. E is wrong because the forecast rate of 2.8 percent and the reference to historic performance against the long-term trend are unconnected points. We do not know at what point in the financial year the 2.8 percent refers (there may not be a half year to outgrow).

Q29.   Answer: E
Explanation: 64 million dollar question means the key question. To identify the key question from the author's perspective, first identify the main theme of the passage. While the passage is wide-ranging in its scope it returns repeatedly to the issue of domestic growth and only suggested answer E refers to this subject. The other answers are factors considered in dealing with this subject.

Q30.   Answer: C
Explanation: 'didn't need to go' is incorrect because it is clear from the sentence that the person did go to the trouble ('didn't need to go' suggests that they may not have done so). 'You needn't have gone' implies that the person took the trouble and so is the better choice in this instance.

Q31.   Answer: C
Explanation: 'Fewer' is used when the noun is countable and plural, 'less' is used when the noun is uncountable.

Q32.   Answer: A
Explanation: If referring to a point in time we use 'when'. E refers to continuing events.

Q33.   Answer: B
Explanation: A reflective verb such as to familiarize requires the same reflective pronoun 'ourselves' and possessive adjective 'our'.

Q34.   Answer: C
Explanation: Instead of repeating the noun 'shops' we replace it with the pronoun 'ones' (we say ones rather than one because the noun is plural).

Q35.   Answer: B
Explanation: The meeting was cancelled at the last minute so we can assume that the preparation for the presentation was completed. We would use 'mustn't' if something was not allowed, we use 'didn't need to' when something was not done and was not necessary to do. If something was done and it was not necessary we say 'need not' or 'needn't'. In this case, it was necessary to do it to prepare, but ultimately not necessary when the meeting was cancelled.

Q36.   Answer: A
Explanation: The passage states that people are switching from private cars to public transport, and trains are one form of public transport. D is explicitly stated in the passage so cannot be inferred. C and E fail because the increase in congestion has already occurred, while the increase in train journey miles is forecasted. B can, in part, be inferred from the lack of funding, i.e., one could infer that the rail service would deteriorate as more people switched to rail from cars, but whether the cost of journeys will increase cannot be inferred.

Q37. Answer: B

Explanation: The passage does not mention journey times or higher fares.

Q38. Answer: D

Explanation: E is a general definition of the meaning of paucity, but in the context of the passage, the answer is D (B fails because it is limited to the railway).

Q39. Answer: C

Explanation: A careful reading of the passage shows that the problems are already chronic in these areas, but the investment is required so that future demand can be met.

Q40. Answer: E

Explanation: The passage makes it clear that governments were investing little in any form of transport and so, in practical terms, were doing little to encourage people to switch. We cannot infer if government was in favor of people switching or not.

Q41. Answer: E

Explanation: Instead of repeating the clause 'that the legal advice was wrong' we can use 'so' as a substitute.

Sub-test 3: quantitative

Q1.   Answer: B

Explanation: An equilateral triangle has 3 equal sides and 3 equal angles so the statement can be inferred from statement 2. Statement 1 may be true but the question cannot be determined from it.

Q2.   Answer: A

Explanation: $7 + 3 + 9 = 19$; $399,000 \div 19 = 21,000$; lowest payout $= 3 \times 21,000 = 63,000$; highest $= 9 \times 21,000 = 189,000$; difference $= 126,000$.

Q3.   Answer: C

Explanation: Individually, neither statement gives any information about x, but together they show that x is greater than 0.

Q4.   Answer: C

Explanation: When factorized, the equation becomes $(x - 1) x$. When $x = 0$ or $x = 1$ it has the value 0. Between these values it is negative and outside these it is positive, so C is the correct answer.

Q5.   Answer: B

Explanation: You should note that the second equation is 2.5 times the first and therefore the answer is $2.5 \times 20 = 50$.

Q6.   Answer: E
      Explanation: The circle = 360°, so public services sector employment as a proportion of total employment in all sectors = $900/4{,}500 \times 360 = 1/5 \times 360 = 72°$.

Q7.   Answer: B
      Explanation: (-2.5) is rounded up to -2, the positive value of which is then 2. (2.5) is rounded up to 3. 2 divided by 3 is $2/3$.

Q8.   Answer: A
      Explanation: $x + (x + 1) + (x + 2) = 93$, so $3x + 3 = 93$, $3x = 90$. x, the first number in the series = 30, the series = 30, 31, 32 (sum = 93). Sum of two largest = $31 + 32 = 63$.

Q9.   Answer: C
      Explanation: If n is divisible by m and m itself is divisible by 5.5, then n must be divisible by 5.5 and hence also by 11.

Q10. Answer: E
      Explanation: The probability of getting tails once is $1/2$, and 6 consecutive times the probability is $1/2^6 = 1/64$.

Q11. Answer: C
      Explanation: Adding x to both sides of the inequality gives $2y < x$, or $x > 2y$.

Q12. Answer: B
      Explanation: The total journey = $25 + 55 = 80$ miles. To complete this at 50 mph he would take 1.6 hours or 96 minutes. He has already taken 36 minutes, so he must complete the remaining 25 miles in 60 minutes = 25 mph.

Q13. Answer: A
      Explanation: Simply add both equations to get $9a + 9b = 50$.

Q14. Answer: C
      Explanation: If x divided by 3 is still larger than y, x must be much larger than y. Once we know that x and y are positive (from statement 2) we can use statement 1 to answer the question, but statement 2 obviously gives no further useful information.

Q15. Answer: E
      Explanation: From the first equation $a = b - 3$. Substituting this into the second equation gives $(b - 3) + b = 11$; $2b - 3 = 11$; $2b = 14$; $b = 7$. $ab = 4 \times 7 = 28$ and all the other answers are incorrect.

Q16. Answer: D
      Explanation: When factorized, the equation becomes $(-x + 1)(x - 3)$. This is 0 when $x = 1$ and 3. Between the two it is positive, for example when $x = 2$, the solution is $-2^2 + 4(2) - 3 = 1$. Below 1 and above 3, the answer is negative.

Q17. Answer: C

Explanation: 63 young people are most interested in looking good and what others think, 54 in doing well in school and finding a job, so the ratio = 63:54, which simplifies to 7:6 (divide both by 9).

Q18. Answer: A

Explanation: Statement 1 is sufficient, as any number when squared will produce a positive number (unless we include imaginary numbers). There are, however, two solutions to the second equation.

Q19. Answer: C

Explanation: Rearranging by subtracting x from both sides gives $3y < -x$ and hence, dividing by 3 on both sides leads to $y < -x/3$. This is answer A, but this can also be written as $-y > x/3$, answer B. As both of these are correct, the preferred answer is C.

Q20. Answer: C

Explanation: From the first equation $a = -3b$. Substituting this into the second equation gives $-3b^2 = -12$, $b^2 = 4$, $b = \pm 2$. Therefore, $a = \pm 6$. If $a = 2$, $b = -6$ and if $a = -2$, $b = 6$. $a - b$ has two solutions, 8 or -8.

Q21. Answer: E

Explanation: The volume of the hemisphere = $\frac{1}{2}(\frac{4}{3}\pi\ r3)$; the volume of the prism = area of cross-section × height (in the case of the prism, this means that the cross-section is a triangle, so find the area of the cross-section with the formula $\frac{1}{2}$base × height). V of hemisphere = $\frac{4}{3} \times 3.14 \times 64 = \frac{4}{3} \times 201 = 804/3 = 268$; $268 \div 2 = 134$; v of prism = $\frac{1}{2}$ of $5 \times 4 = 10$; $10 \times 15 = 150$; difference = $150 - 134 = 16$.

Q22. Answer: C

Explanation: Using the first equation and rearranging gives $y = \sqrt{x}$ and so, from the second equation, $y = \sqrt{x} = 4z$, therefore $z = \sqrt{x} / 4$. Substituting the third equation into the second equation gives $(x)(\sqrt{x})(\sqrt{x}/4) = x^2/4 = 16$. Therefore, x is 8.

Q23. Answer: A

Explanation: There are 36 possible outcomes and 4 successful outcomes (i.e., 4 combinations that have a sum of 5): $4 + 1$, $3 + 2$, $2 + 3$, $1 + 4$, so the probability is $4/36 = 1/9$.

Q24. Answer: C

Explanation: If 1 appears in the sequence, the sequence will consist only of 1s. In this case, either statement indicates that it is not the correct sequence.

Q25. Answer: B

Explanation: Substituting $x = 10$ into the first equation gives $1/y = (1/10) + (2/10)$, $1/y = 3/10$. Inverting both sides then gives $y = 10/3$.

Q26. Answer: C
Explanation: Rearranging the second equation gives x = 1/3. Substituting this into the first equation results in y = (1/3)/3 + 3/(1/3), y = 1/9 + 9 = 1/9 + 81/9 = 82/9.

Q27. Answer: A
Explanation: Find the average to find the sum. There are 48 – 20 = 28 + 1 numbers in the range (you have to add the 1 otherwise you miscount the numbers). The average is 20 + 48 = 68 ÷ 2 = 34; sum = 29 × 34 = 986.

Q28. Answer: D
Explanation: The original equality can be rearranged to give y > x, squaring both sides then transposing. Both statements 1 and 2 can be written as x > y, giving a solution to the original question.

Q29. Answer: A
Explanation: Subtract 2x from both sides to give x + y = –y.

Q30. Answer: E
Explanation: This is the same as $x^2 - 2x$ greater than 0. This then factorizes to x(x – 2). This is 0 when x = 0 or 2, and between these values it is less than 0. The answer is therefore E.

Q31. Answer: A
Explanation: We can only find x and y if we prove that the two triangles are similar (that the 3 angles of one triangle match the 3 angles of the other). The minimum we need to prove they are similar is to know that 2 pairs of angles match (once we know this then the 3 pairs must match, as the sum of the angles = 180°) so statement 1 is sufficient. Statement 2 does not allow us to calculate y.

Q32. Answer: C
Explanation: If y = x, the original inequality can be rewritten as $x^2 > x$. This is true everywhere except for x between 0 and 1, as specified in statement 2. Both are therefore required.

Q33. Answer: C
Explanation: The equation is (x/2)/(y/4) = 10. Rearrange to give, 4x/2y = 10 and eventually y = x/5. – y is therefore x – x/5. This is 80% of x.

Q34. Answer: E
Explanation: At first inspection it seems that the two statements could be used as two simultaneous equations to solve two unknowns. The two equations are, however, identical, the latter being 2.5 times the former and hence there is not enough information to solve the question.

Q35. Answer: E
Explanation: If y is negative and x positive, then A is not true, neither is B or D. If y > x then C is not true. E is true.

Q36. Answer: B

Explanation: Rearrange the first equation to give $7a + 4b = 40$. The second equation becomes $a + 3b = 30$, so $a = 30 - 3b$. Substituting this into the first equation gives $7(30 - 3b) + 4b = 40$. Simplifying gives $17b = 170$, $b = 10$. If $b = 10$, $a = 0$ and the product must be 0.

Q37. Answer: E

Explanation: The cubic equation in statement 1 has 3 solutions: 1, 2 and 3. Statement 2 allows one of these to be eliminated, but there are still two possible solutions and hence it is not possible to determine x.

Sub-test 4: verbal

Q1. Answer: A

Explanation: The prepositions 'about' and 'of' follow the verb 'to know'.

Q2. Answer: A

Explanation: Either by or at 12 noon makes good sense; in the case of a large city such as New York we properly say 'we arrived at'.

Q3. Answer: A

Explanation: After the noun 'likelihood' we use the preposition in the -ing form and not the to- infinitive form.

Q4. Answer: E

Explanation: The correct prepositions are absorbed 'in' and accustomed 'to'.

Q5. Answer: B

Explanation: The passage is primarily concerned with the crisis and then possible solutions. The tone of the passage supports a description of the challenge as a crisis rather than a problem or catastrophe.

Q6. Answer: D

Explanation: Only D is mentioned explicitly as a solution to fuel shortages; the others are factors or alternatives that may not eventuate.

Q7. Answer: E

Explanation: Fiscal policy is how governments spend and tax in order to achieve goals, and this topic is covered in the passage in terms of the Chinese policy of keeping the price of oil products artificially low. International relations between Russia and China are touched upon in the passage, as are the topics of fuel exports and retail price of diesel at the pump. But rationing is not discussed.

Q8. Answer: C

Explanation: In the last paragraph, the author describes his alternative solution as more viable, which implies that he would not expect Russia to hold the solution to China's supply problems.

Q9.   Answer: A

Explanation: The passage gives reasons for keeping the price of diesel artificially low, not the price of gasoline.

Q10. Answer: A

Explanation: We say or write that we are angry 'with' a person or thing only. We are angry 'at' events, newscasts etc.

Q11. Answer: E

Explanation: The verb 'to care' is followed by the prepositions 'about' and 'for', but in the question sentence good sense is only made with the preposition to care 'for'.

Q12. Answer: B

Explanation: Both 'has she not' and 'hasn't she' are correct but in the case of an indirect question the usual order is subject then verb: 'the languages I speak'.

Q13. Answer: D

Explanation: Particular prepositions tend to follow particular verbs and others we tend to avoid. The verb 'to learn' is usually followed by 'about' or 'of'.

Q14. Answer: D

Explanation: Sequencing is only mentioned in the passage in relation to the work of the Human Genome Project.

Q15. Answer: D

Explanation: New treatments and diagnostic tests are mentioned in the passage but this issue of preventative therapies is not touched upon.

Q16. Answer: A

Explanation: It is stated that the mapping of human genetic differences will hasten the identitification of new ways to treat common ailments. It can be inferred that this will be possible because the map will accelerate the search for genes involved in common diseases. B and C are explicitly stated in the passage.

Q17. Answer: B

Explanation: It is the claim that some of our genetic differences explain our propensity for particular diseases, which supports the conclusion that some of us enjoy good health while others are more susceptible to many common diseases.

Q18. Answer: E

Explanation: We are told that the mapping will afford new treatments but not how the sequencing of genetic differences will make these new treatments possible.

Q19.   Answer: D
Explanation: We say thousands, hundreds and so on, but three thousand or nine hundred. We say people, not persons, when referring to a group.

Q20.   Answer: E
Explanation: All the suggested answers serve to introduce exceptions, but only 'aside from' is correct given the structure of the question.

Q21.   Answer: B
Explanation: In this context 'while' means although; to indicate a continuous length of time we would use 'since'. We could say 'the time when' or 'it was 5am when' the shift started.

Q22.   Answer: A
Explanation: We say 'during' 'in' or 'over' a period of time in which an activity takes place.

Q23.   Answer: D
Explanation: An adverse association is one in which harm results, an inverse association brings benefits, no adverse association means no harm, and while the author would not agree that an inverse association exists, he would agree that a diet of fiber does not bring an increase in risk.

Q24.   Answer: B
Explanation: The fact that any link is coincidental can be inferred from the passage. D is a valid summary of one of the points made in the passage but is not inferred from it. No reference is made in the passage to a study. The passage states that it used to be thought that a link existed, but it cannot be inferred that there may appear to be a link between fiber and the risk of the cancer.

Q25.   Answer: C
Explanation: The passage states that the majority of cases occur in the over-50s, and given that there are said to be a total of 9,000 cases a year, more than 4,500 of these would be aged 50 or more. Statement A is not disproved by the passage, because although the disease may be more common among men, this does not necessarily imply that it would be a more common form of cancer for men than women when compared with other cancers. Equally, statement D refers to the number of people treated and more women may be treated even though more men contract the illness.

Q26.   Answer: A
Explanation: A is correct because the context is a contractual one where obligations are detailed.

Q27. Answer: C

Explanation: We use 'among' when referring to three or more people or things, but we use 'between' when referring to connections, and say 'relationship between' and not 'relationship among'.

Q28. Answer: E

Explanation: To add 'so', 'that' or 'it' to the statement introduces an unnecessary repetition of the act of making an offer.

Q29. Answer: D

Explanation: When an object is directly over or under another, we use 'over' and 'under', but when something is not literally over or under, then we use 'above' or 'below'.

Q30. Answer: C

Explanation: The main claim of the passage is that our criminal system is failing to prevent re-offending. This claim is premised on the assumption that the prevention of re-offending is the principal objective of the criminal system.

Q31. Answer: E

Explanation: The reason given is overcrowding, making staff unable to spare the time or resources. C is wrong because it states that staff must forgo the provision, but it is the prisoners who must forgo it, not the staff. The answers that best capture the reason are answers E and A, but E is preferable, as A introduces the issue of security, which is not raised in the passage.

Q32. Answer: A

Explanation: D refers only to young offenders and the passage is not so limited. C's reference to rehabilitation programs is inconsistent with the position taken in the passage. Sentence A has the same urgent tone adopted in the passage and is consistent with the passage's main theme. Recidivism means to go back to crime, and crime would remain, not decline, as long as our punishments fail to deter further offences.

Q33. Answer: B

Explanation: We say 'almost all' or 'every', not 'almost each'; we use 'finish' not 'end' when followed by an -ing word; 'further' means additional, 'farther' means greater distance.

Q34. Answer: C

Explanation: All the suggestions connect ideas. To make proper sense of the two ideas in this sentence we need a connector between actions and their results and C is the only one.

Q35. Answer: D
Explanation: The sentence does not make sense as it is written in the question. It needs 'unless' to make sense of the condition under which you can open a bank account.

Q36. Answer: A
Explanation: The prediction turns out to be correct, which gives rise to the surprise, not the other way around. So B is incorrect, as is 'as if' and 'as though', because they imply the second clause is conditional on the first rather than the other way round. D could be correct but the word 'as' is missing.

Q37. Answer: B
Explanation: It is stated in the passage that giant squid have been found in the stomach of sperm whales.

Q38. Answer: D
Explanation: The only suggested answer supported by the passage is D. No other indication of how or from which direction the squid approached is given, other than that its tentacles were outstretched and its beak was snapping. The approach was vigorous, as the squid is described as 'shooting out' (so C cannot be conjectured) but from the passage, we cannot infer that it is a predator as it could equally be a scavenger.

Q39. Answer: E

Q40. Answer: C
Explanation: The main clause is about a choice in the past, so the verb must be in the past tense and is required to refer back to the past.

Q41. Answer: E
Explanation: The second clause does more than qualify the first but also introduces new and contrasting information. For this reason 'while' and 'whereas' are insufficient while the phrase 'despite the fact' correctly emphasizes the contrast. C is wrong because the speaker would know if he or she tends to get stressed or not and 'whether or not' implies he or she does not definitely know.

Sub-test 5: quantitative

Q1. Answer: B
Explanation: Using Pythagoras we know that $62 + CD^2 = 10^2$, $36 + CD^2 = 100$, so $CD = \sqrt{64} = 8^2$. So, the area of the rectangle = $6 \times 8 = 48^2$ (you should have recognized the right-angled triangle ACD as the Pythagoras triple 6, 8, 10).

Q2. Answer: E
Explanation: The two equations are identical, the second being 3 times the first, so you are left with one equation for two unknowns and it cannot be solved.

Q3.   Answer: E
      Explanation: The two equations are the same and are quadratics, with the solution $x = 0$ or 1. This is not sufficient to answer the question.

Q4.   Answer: D
      Explanation: They are 345, 354, 435, 453, 543, 534.

Q5.   Answer: A
      Explanation: Subtract 1 from both sides, divide by x, then divide by 2 to give: $x < 1/2$. This is not the whole story, as inspection shows that because of the squaring on the left-hand side, x less than 0 will not be valid.

Q6.   Answer: D
      Explanation: If $n - 1$ is divisible by 6, then n, which is 1 bigger, would result in a remainder of 1 when divided by 6. The same is true for $n - 7$.

Q7.   Answer: E
      Explanation: For the first event, the probability is 4/52, but, because the first card is not replaced, for the second event the probability is 3/51. So, the probability for the two events $= 4/52 \times 3/51 = 1/221$.

Q8.   Answer: D
      Explanation: Rearrange the equation to give $y = 2.5 - x/2$. $5 - 2y$ is therefore $5 - (5 - x) = x$. This is 100% of x.

Q9.   Answer: E
      Explanation: Both statements are true if either x or y is negative, but neither statement gives any information on which it might be.

Q10. Answer: A and E
      Explanation: 79 is a prime number. You can prove this by taking the prime numbers up to the $\sqrt{79}$ (just below 9) and seeing if any divide exactly into 79. The prime numbers in the range are 2, 3, 5 and 7. None divide exactly, so 79 is a prime number. So, you must identify the prime factors of 44, which are 2 and 11.

Q11. Answer: D
      Explanation: A positive divided by a negative must be a negative, so A and E are not true, but B and C are, but B is not always so. D is always true.

Q12. Answer: E
      Explanation: This algorithm simply generates a repeating sequence that oscillates between a positive and negative value. For example, 3, –3, 3, –3, 3. Simply knowing that one of these is negative is not sufficient to determine whether the number 1 appears.

Q13. Answer: C
Explanation: The volume of the cone = $^1/_3\pi$ r²h; the volume of the cylinder = π r2h; cone = $^1/_3$ × 3.14 × 9 × 5 = $^1/_3$ × 3.14 × 45 = 47 cm³; cylinder = 3.14 × 9 × 3 = 3.14 × 27 = 85 cm³; difference = 85 – 47 = 38.

Q14. Answer: D
Explanation: Multiply the first equation by 5 to give 25x + 20y = 110 and the second by 4 to give 12x + 20y = 84. Subtract the second from the first, giving 13x = 26; x = 2.

Q15. Answer: E
Explanation: The original question can be rewritten as: 'Is x² > y²?'. Statement 1 can be rewritten as x > y, by dividing both sides by x. This is not sufficient, as y could be a large negative number and x a smaller positive number. Knowing that they have the same sign, as in statement 2, gives no information about their relative sizes. Even together there is not enough information, as it would be necessary to know if they are both positive or both negative.

Q16. Answer: A
Explanation: Multiply the first equation throughout by 4 to give 20a + 16b = 80 and the second equation by 5 to give 20a + 25b = 150. Subtract the new first equation from the new second equation, giving: 9b = 70, b = 70/9. a = –20/9, a + b = 50/9.

Q17. Answer: C
Explanation: The first two equations are identical, but there is still sufficient information to solve the problem. If x = z/y, then 1/x is y/z. Substituting this into third equation gives x/(1/x) = 64, i.e., x² = 64; x = 8.

Q18. Answer: B
Explanation: Rearranging leads to the following: 2x/5 > 3y/4, then 8x/20 > 15y/20, and then 8x > 15y, and finally, x > 1⁷/₈y, which is statement 2. If this is sufficient, then, by inspection, statement 1 cannot be sufficient.

Q19. Answer: C and D.
Explanation: A is false because France was ranked 20 – 3 = 17th in 2004, B because Canada was ranked 4th, while Mexico was ranked 6th in 2004, and E because no information is given to tell whether or not Singapore has returned to the top of the index.

Q20. Answer: B
Explanation: Double the second equation to give 6b – 6a = 18. Add this new equation to the first equation to obtain –4a = 20, a = –5. b is then –2 and ab = 10.

Q21. Answer: C
Explanation: Statement 1 is not sufficient, as this simply reduces the equation to $3y^2$, but with no information about y. Statement 2 can then be substituted into this new equation to obtain a solution.

Q22. Answer: E
Explanation: There are 26 letters in the alphabet, so 26 possible outcomes. As each card is replaced before the next event, the probability remains the same for each. So the odds are $1/26 \times 1/26 \times 1/26 \times 1/26$ or $1/26^4$.

Q23. Answer: B
Explanation: Subtracting x from both sides of the inequality, this can be rewritten as $2x^2 - 4x > 0$. Factorizing gives $2x(x - 2)$, which has solutions of x = 0 and 2. For values outside 0 and 2 the equation is positive, therefore B is the correct answer.

Q24. Answer: E
Explanation: In general, two equations for two unknowns would lead to a solution using simultaneous equations. In this case, however, dividing by 0 (substituting the second equation into the first) would result in dividing by 0 and hence no solution.

Q25. Answer: C
Explanation: $x + (x + 1) + (x + 2) = 117$, so $3x + 3 = 117$, $3x = 174$, $174 \div 3 = x = 58$, the first number in the series. The consecutive numbers are 58, 59, 60 (sum of 177). Sum of two with lowest value $= 58 + 59 = 117$.

Q26. Answer: B
Explanation: If $3/6 = 2/4$ then $6/3 = 4/2$. Using this rule we can invert both sides of the two equations to obtain $a + b = 1/6$ and $a - b = 1/12$. Adding these equations together leads to $2a = 3/12$. Inverting once again gives $1/2a = 12/3 = 4$.

Q27. Answer: A
Explanation: Statement 1 has two solutions, both of which are positive (3 and 2), so is positive. Statement 2 can be rewritten as $4 = x^2$ and because this has two solutions it is not sufficient.

Q28. Answer: D
Explanation: House costs 75% of land, so for every $1 spent on land, 75 cents was spent on building the house. Land $= 105,000 \div 1.75 = 60,000$ (check the answer: 75% of $60,000 = 45,000$, $60,000 + 45,000 = 105,000$).

Q29. Answer: E
Explanation: Dividing by 5 throughout gives $2y + x < 6$, so, $x < 6 - x$. Similarly, dividing initially by 10 gives $y + x/2 < 3$, $y < 3 - x/2$. None of the proposed solutions above is equivalent to either of these.

Q30. Answer: D
Explanation: The first statement gives relative speeds and hence it is possible to determine the woman's work rate. Similarly, knowing how much the man and girl together have achieved, it is possible to determine how much the woman has achieved. Either statement gives a solution.

Q31. Answer: A
Explanation: Rearrange the first equation to give $2x + 2y = x - y$, then $x + 3y = 0$. Rearrange the second equation to give $x + y = 2x + 2$, then $x - y = 2$. Subtract the second from the first, giving $4y = -2$ and hence $y = -1/2$.

Q32. Answer: A
Explanation: Dividing both sides of the first equation gives $y = (1 + 2x)/x$, which is equal to $1/x + 2$. Rearranging the second equation gives $x = 1/2$. This then can be substituted into the first to produce $y = 1/(1/2) + 2 = 4$.

Q33. Answer: E
Explanation: If x is negative, x^3 will also be negative and hence less than x^2, which will always be positive. Statement 1, therefore, is not sufficient. Statement 2 is not sufficient, either. Whereas $2^3 > 2^2$, $(1/2)^3$ is not greater than $(1/2)^2$. For any x between 0 and 1, $x^3 < x^2$, so statements 1 and 2 together are not sufficient.

Q34. Answer: C
Explanation: Multiply both sides by 6 to obtain $3x + 18 < 2x + 12$ and rearrange to give $x < -6$.

Q35. Answer: B
Explanation: Statement 1 is self-evidently insufficient. Statement 2 is more interesting. If this is combined with the original algorithm, it gives two simultaneous equations: $a_5 - a_4 = 2$ and $a_5 = 3a_4$. Substituting the second into the first gives $3a_4 - a_4 = 2$ and hence $a_4 = 1$, so it does appear in the sequence.

Q36. Answer: C
Explanation: Rearranging the first equation to give x in terms of y results in: $x = (105 - 29y)/57$. Substituting this into the second equation gives $x = 1$ and $y = 48/29$, which is nearest 1.655.

Q37. Answer: C
Explanation: The original statement can be transposed to give, first, $x^2 - y^2 > 0$, then $x^2 > y^2$. Knowing that both are positive gives no information about their relative sizes. And, as has been shown previously, knowing something about the relative values of x and y is not enough to know about the relative values of x^2 and y^2. Together, however, it is possible to establish that $x^2 > y^2$.

Sub-test 6: verbal

Q1.   Answer: C
Explanation: The passage covers many issues. However, C best describes its primary objective.

Q2.   Answer: A
Explanation: The term is used in the context of stamps as investments, and in this context the term means a collection of various investments held by an individual or institution.

Q3.   Answer: E
Explanation: The passage mentions dealers and their customers all over the world and the fact that you need a magnifying glass to realize the detail that can make stamps very valuable. Their size is not mentioned.

Q4.   Answer: C
Explanation: We are told that the majority of collectors collect new issued commemorative stamps and these are often discovered to be worth less than their original posting value. Answer C offers an explanation of this phenomenon, which will apply to all stamps including commemorative stamps.

Q5.   Answer: E
Explanation: A careful reading of the passage will show that the motive of simply collecting stamps is not mentioned in the passage while the market-maker is described as fanatical, which can mean obsessive enthusiasm.

Q6.   Answer: E
Explanation: Emphasis and humor aside, in the case of a quantity such as 'the low rate' we use an adverb that makes clear the amount. Totality, excessively and perfectly do not do this. We would not say 'a bit low'.

Q7.   Answer: A
Explanation: Formally, A is correct, but informally, B would also be acceptable but not in a test of grammar. C and E involve unnecessary repetition, while D does not make sense.

Q8.   Answer: D
Explanation: Normally, 'reason' and 'change' are treated as countable nouns (abstract) but when they follow little and much they can be used in the uncountable form.

Q9.   Answer: A
Explanation: 'Interested' is like many past participles that can occur before or after the noun, but 'well' in 'well behaved' is one of a number of exceptions that only correctly occur before the noun.

Q10. Answer: D

Explanation: It is clear that a positive image is achieved through publicity, both as advertisements and news and public interest pieces.

Q11. Answer: D

Explanation: The fact that the abbreviation PR is spelled out and the term is defined means that the audience is new to the subject.

Q12. Answer: E

Explanation: In the case of the candy manufacturer, it tampered with tradition, but this was not the reason its campaign went wrong; its mistake was that it failed to judge correctly the attachment its customers placed on the product.

Q13. Answer: A

Explanation: We are told that the object of PR is positive image building and the effect when things go wrong is negative image building – the exact opposite.

Q14. Answer: B

Explanation: The logic of the market place makes B the only viable reaction and means that suggested answer A is highly improbable. C is a good summary of the passage but not a suitable follow-on sentence. Expedite means speed up, making E nonsensical.

Q15. Answer: D

Explanation: In this instance, 'professional' cannot take an adverb, but 'technical' and 'academic' can. We say 'highly' or 'intensely technical', we cannot say 'nearly technical' and while 'extremely', 'fairly' and 'largely' academic are acceptable, 'practically' academic is not.

Q16. Answer: E

Explanation: Strictly speaking we do not say that something is 'fairly impossible' (it is either impossible or it is not). For the same reason we do not say it is 'very impossible'. But we can say it is 'quite impossible' for emphasis, because in this context 'quite' means 'completely'.

Q17. Answer: D

Explanation: Answers B and C do not make sense, so are wrong. We use many adjectives before the noun, but 'applying' is one of the number of exceptions that we place after the noun.

Q18. Answer: C

Explanation: We can say that we are certain or not certain 'about' or 'of' something but not that we are certain or not certain 'about/of why'. We simply say we are not certain why.

Q19. Answer: B
Explanation: The passage concludes on the subject of workers with inadequate private pension schemes and therefore the follow-on sentence is most likely to be on that subject. Suggested answers B and D are the only sentences that continue that theme, but D can be rejected because no reference is made in the passage to long-awaited proposals on how to resolve the crisis.

Q20. Answer: A
Explanation: Had the government been putting these contributions aside for the benefit of the pension holders, then (assuming that the pensions are self-funding) there is no reason why the contributions should not be available to meet the commitments.

Q21. Answer: C
Explanation: The passage states that it is estimated that future pensions will have to be cut by 30 percent of the current rate if the government is to make ends meet. A is wrong because the figures given refer to the relative numbers of pensioners and workers, B is incorrect because no estimate is given beyond the next 20 years, so the question of how far the ratio might ultimately fall is not answered.

Q22. Answer: D
Explanation: 'Slowly', 'elderly' and 'supposedly' are all examples of adverbs formed by adding 'ly' to the adjectives 'slow', 'elder' and 'supposed'.

Q23. Answer: E
Explanation: We use 'as much as' and 'as many as' to indicate something is greater than expected, or 'as little as' or 'as few as' to indicate that something is less than expected. 'Many' and 'few' are used in the case of numbers and for quantities such as currency, percentages and weights.

Q24. Answer: D
Explanation: A definitive date or time is usually in the front or end position of a phrase, so September should occur as in C or E. However, C is wrong because it reads as though they consulted someone called 'extensively'. We would avoid the confusing form 'begin immediately implementing' in E.

Q25. Answer: E
Explanation: Sentences are often constructed so that adverbs (such as 'nearly') are placed in the middle part of the sentence. However, when an adverb indicates the timing of something, it would normally be placed at the end, or if emphasis was required, at the start of the sentence.

Q26. Answer: E
Explanation: Answer E embraces the widest number of design aspects and so provides the best summary.

Q27. Answer: D
Explanation: The term used in the passage is 'cambered', which means slightly arched or convex.

Q28. Answer: B
Explanation: Answer A sums up the opening statement of the passage but does not weaken the case made within the passage. A plane built using these items might fly further but this is not the subject of the passage. A paper plane made only from a single sheet of paper that has a pointed nose or non-delta wings would weaken the case only if it was an indoor test in still air. B is the only statement that complies with all these requirements.

Q29. Answer: B
Explanation: When we detail the extent of something we say 'very much' before some verbs, including 'agree', rather than 'much agree'.

Q30. Answer: A
Explanation: The adverbs in these sentences are passing comment on our intentions. Usually we place these at the start or end of sentences when they are separated by a comma. But in this case, when the adverb applies to the whole clause it can occur in other positions in the sentence. A makes best sense in that it is clear that the speaker is talking from a personal perspective. E fails because the adverb is far from the personal content of the statement.

Q31. Answer: C
Explanation: The terms 'owing to', 'because of' and 'due to' serve to introduce a reason for something. We avoid the phrases 'is owing to' but do write 'is mainly owing to' and 'is largely owing to' etc. B is wrong because 'of' is missing.

Q32. Answer: A
Explanation: The passage describes features of the recruitment process of popular courses and responses B, C and E are not qualified so they relate only to popular courses. D (and also B) fail because they assume the course is an academic one, which is not stated in the passage.

Q33. Answer: D
Explanation: Suggested answers A, B, C and E are effectively a rewriting of the features attributed to the recruitment process described in the passage and so are likely to win the author's agreement. Statement D however, reflects a sentiment not attributable to the passage and therefore is the most likely to be the point with which the author disagrees. It is wrong to assume that the applications would finish before the courses started filling up.

Q34. Answer: E
Explanation: The term originated in the context of the liberal interpretation of religious doctrine but has come to mean any wide group of views or people. In the context of the passage it refers to a class of students able to draw on a wide range of experiences in discussions and seminars.

Q35. Answer: E
Explanation: The sentence needs to link the system with its purpose and the suggested phrases all do this. However, only the rather academic 'such that' completes the sentence properly.

Q36. Answer: A
Explanation: In D it is not clear to which fact we are referring. We say 'even though' (not 'even although') but in this case we correctly end the sentence with though (and not although) to emphasize the contrast between the two sentences.

Q37. Answer: E
Explanation: We use the word 'get' a lot and mean 'obtain'. We say 'I get the train', and we say 'I got an e-mail, letter' etc. We use 'was' rather than 'got' when referring to something that took some time to complete, such as a painting.

Q38. Answer: B
Explanation: 'Fit' is properly used to refer to size or shape, 'suits' refers to taste or satisfactory arrangements. It is usual to say something 'suits very well'.

Q39. Answer: E
Explanation: The gardener cannot go home early if it were not to rain or if we suppose it was to rain so B and C are incorrect. Either 'was' or 'were' are correct in most instances but 'was' is incorrect in this case unless the statement read 'if it was to rain'.

Q40. Answer: B
Explanation: The plural of work (works) means a factory and the publications of a writer.

Q41. Answer: C
Explanation: We do not put two contractions next to each other. 'n't' is added to the end of, for example, 'have' to make 'haven't' (have not). 'Much' has a relative meaning and we can't correctly say 'too much' in this instance because we are either interested on not in the film.